Diversity
on
Campus

Diversity on Campus

David Schuman
University of Massachusetts

Dick Olufs
Pacific Lutheran University

ALLYN & BACON
Boston • London • Toronto • Sydney • Tokyo • Singapore

Library of Congress Cataloging-in-Publication Data
Schuman, David.
    Diversity on campus / David Schuman, Dick Olufs.
        p.   cm.
    Includes bibliographical references and index.
    ISBN 0-02-408142-6
    1. Multicultural education—United States.   2. Minorities—
Education (Higher)—United States.   3. Minority college students—
United States.   I. Olufs, Dick.   II. Title.
LC1099.3.S38   1995
370.19'6—dc20   94-8971
                                                                          CIP

Production Supervisor: Jeffrey H. Chen
Production Manager: Francesca Drago
ETM Manager: Kurt Scherwatzky
Text and Cover Designer: Eileen Burke

ISBN: 0-02-408142-6

As an exercise, pretend you are from another planet and you want an example of a typical human being for your photo album. Having never heard of racism, you'd probably pick someone who represents the majority of the people on the planet—an Asian person.

—Amoja Three Rivers

It is part of growing up that one gives up a simple and single view of the world; one suffers the loss of illusions. At the time, it is painful. But beyond it one discovers a richer complexity, and one has gained strength in the process. One acquires courage for the next phase of life.

—Jacqueline Smutherst

What I propose...is a reconsideration of the human condition from the vantage point of our newest experiences and our most recent fears. This, obviously, is a matter of thought, and thoughtlessness—the heedless recklessness or hopeless confusion or complacent repetition of "truths" which have become trivial and empty—seems to me among the outstanding characteristics of our time. What I propose, therefore, is very simple: it is nothing more than to think what we are doing.

—Hannah Arendt

Preface

The seeds of this book were planted when Johnstone Campbell asked one of us to join him in teaching a diversity course. Right away, it was apparent that there was just too much to cover and not enough material organized in a way that helps teachers with such courses. We have taught different versions of the course, and many of the ideas in this book come from those classes and discussions about them. In a sense, the book arose backward. Teach, think it through, then write.

Not long after the book project was underway, one of our sons, Ben, went away to school. Not far, thirty miles away, but it was overnight, and for a fourteen-year-old those thirty miles sometimes seemed like a million. His roommate was from Japan; a very nice guy who was only a twenty-four-hour flight from his home.

Shin, the roommate, rarely spoke about home or his parents. He enjoyed school, kept his half of the room neat, and worked hard.

One afternoon, during the first week of school, Ben called home. He sounded tired. When asked to explain, he said he had gotten up in the middle of the night. Shin, he said, had a nightmare. Shin was yelling, in a panicked voice, in Japanese. Poor Ben was scared to death. He was half awake and did not quite know where he was—and he was in a dark room with somebody yelling in Japanese.

That seemed just about right. It seems that just about everyone who goes to college has, at least metaphorically, the same emotional experience—of either Shin or of Ben. Higher education can give you nightmares or make you panic. We are in a new environment, asked to learn new things, and surrounded by people who are not always like us. That is one of the emotional undertones of this book.

More Than That

The book, of course, is more than that. The basic idea is that diversity is a broad and inclusive concept. Race, gender, and class are the commonly cited features of diversity. There is more to diversity than that. Color, sex, and class matter. So do religion, sexual orientation, and ethnicity. Even where we were born, where we live, and where we attend college matters. Each of us grows up with a set of beliefs about many things. Each of these things must be part of how we think about diversity.

The book is meant to be read and talked about. It is an array of ideas and facts that lead to an array of emotions. There are arguments in the book. We don't present perfectly even-handed treatments of all the issues. We do try to explain what is at stake in thinking about issues in different ways and to identify the stakes of choosing one way or another. This book was written to inform and to provoke.

Diversity, at least diversity at the end of the twentieth century in the United States, is full of ambiguities and conflicts. Trying to paper-over problems using the style of a standard textbook seems to miss the point. Feelings and positions are closely connected to reasoning. This is a place where David Hume's claim that reason is a slave to the passions seems to be true. Our feelings are in turmoil about diversity, and that is why our culture is having such a difficult time discussing it.

This Book

Begin with this fact: Human beings are complex creatures. We are made up of an enormous number of traits. Each of us is a unique collection of objective and subjective realities.

Imagine that there are twenty identical people standing in a circle. Each represents just one part of a single person's identity. Make this your identity. There are twenty of you standing in a circle. Each self is one aspect of you—one is your color, one is your height, one is your religion, and so on. There are many parts to your identity.

And what if someone were to see you, were to meet you? That person would break into the circle.

Where that person broke into the circle would matter. Maybe that person would see you as a sexual object, and would see you according to the things that add up to physical attractiveness. Maybe that person would see you as a color, or as a fellow sports fan. The point is that some of the different traits would be clear and close, while other traits would simply not matter to the other person. Some parts of you would matter to that person, and other parts would not.

Also, as the circle is broken, all of the circle would readjust itself.

And every time a person sees you—tries to know you by entering the circle that is you—nothing is quite the same as the time before. The parts rearrange and readjust themselves with each new person and each new situation.

To make things worse, who you think you are is probably not who the person entering the circle thinks you are. For example, the color of your skin may be very important to you, but at that moment the person who is defining you might be interested only in your religion.

The mosaic of the ways in which you are categorized keeps changing. If everyone who met you saw just one part of the circle—say, your color—they would know so little about you. This, in turn, would also limit what you could be with those other people.

But we are more than simply who others think we are. Certainly we have our own ideas about our identity.

Molly Mead put the idea very clearly. Molly read the rough draft of the manuscript and wrote this:

> All the categories we use . . . are imperfect categories which change their meaning depending on who is seeing me. The categories are not meaningless—in fact they are packed with mean-

ings—but those meanings shift and change. Thus we have to be more thoughtful when we use the categories in reference to ourselves and others. People have killed each other over these categories (and over less), so we can't dismiss them or wish them away. However, who I understand myself to be when I call myself a lesbian, and who you understand me to be when you call me a lesbian are two distinctly different things. In other words, this is all very complicated, so pay attention and be thoughtful.

The situation, then, is remarkably complex. First, others see what they are looking for. When they see us, they may see hair color or social class or whatever. They may look at sexual orientation. And what they see, and how they define sexual orientation, may be different from how we define it for ourselves.

Diversity, in many ways, is about all the things people see, all they ways they might define them, and all the ways we define them for ourselves.

The ideas about identity are understood through different themes and in different settings. For example, we explore the traditional American tension between individualism and group identity. This tension is one of the classic American political and social tensions, and we will return to it over and over. We will see it begin with the second-generation Puritans, and continue to the separatist politics of some contemporary groups.

The setting for much of the material is college. We believe that the examples we find on campus are a good way to begin to understand what it means to live in a diverse culture.

Finally, we explore some of the context of campus issues by taking examples from the wider culture. We give a historical perspective, both on and off campus, in order to show how the problems of diversity began and have developed. We also discuss the philosophical strands at the center of some of the controversies.

What we offer, then, is a book about how one's identity is affected by diversity. We will show that it is an ongoing issue, both on campus and in society. We will argue that diversity is a social issue, a group issue, and an individual issue. We will see that diversity affects each of us.

The book is meant to be discussed. Each of us, ultimately, must reach her or his own solutions, but those solutions will be played out in relationship with others. Living in a diverse world is not a matter of merely making up your mind about what to think and how to act, it is a matter of genuinely understanding differences.

We hope this book helps that learning. We are interested in your response.

Thank You

A great many people helped us. Special thanks are due to Johnstone Campbell, Michael Ford, Michael Fried, Larry Friedman, Marion Hoar, Beth Craig, Lisa Markowitz, Molly Mead, John Moritsugu, Alana Mueller, Dani Newland, Jacqueline Smethurst, Lee and Chris Totten, Robert Waterman, Jill Whitman, Leo Wiegman, and Pat and Steve Zwerling. Susan Rabinowitz, our editor at Macmillan, was just great from our first conversation. Paul Shang, Colorado State University; Karl Taeuber, University of Wisconsin — Madison; Donald C. Smith, University of New Haven; and Trudie O. Coker of Florida International University read the entire manuscript, made helpful suggestions, and pointed out numerous errors.

Some ideas need to be talked about. They have to go through many heads before they make sense. We are each blessed with families where that happens. We appreciate this great gift.

Contents

Contents

— 1 —

Introduction

The fathers have eaten a sour grape, and the children's teeth are set on edge.

—Jeremiah 31:29

This book is about differences and similarities. It is a collection of facts, questions, and genuine problems that need to be thought about and talked about.

This chapter introduces you to diversity on campus and asks you to consider the idea that we never know exactly what others think of us. It is a general introduction to the differences you encounter in your immediate surroundings. Who, for example, is the teacher, and who are the other students, what are their ages, colors, educational backgrounds, personal likes and dislikes, socioeconomic class, and so on?

In this chapter, we begin to see how we differ from those around us.

This chapter also asks that you think about the fact that we never know how others understand us. Although each of us has a sense of who we are, and has an opinion of those around us, we can never know exactly how others see us and judge us.

These points are introduced in the context of college life. College is as real as any other part of life. The things that happen off campus are just different versions of the things that happen on campus. Each college is a special place, with its own calendar and rhythm, but it is also subject to the problems found in the surrounding society. Chapter 1, then, is about coming to college. It is about the differences you encounter, and the problems you have understanding who you are and where you fit.

So, you're sitting there in class looking at your teacher. The Professor. A person who, for the next quarter or semester, will tell you things, read what you write, and grade what you do. Have you ever given that person much of a thought—outside of grades, work assigned, and the like? What is that person going to teach and tell you, and what does that have to do with his or her personal life? The professor's color and age, tastes and preferences, and even sexual orientation may make a difference. That is not the myth. The myth is that all professors are involved in the impartial pursuit of knowledge—which is just like the myth that the highest priority for all college students is to get the best possible education.

Who is the person in front of the class? Funny? Well-dressed? Articulate? Bisexual? Homophobic? Married with children? Would that person make a good friend? Drive a Porsche or ride a bicycle? Rather be a lawyer?

Did you know that men, on average, think about sex once every ten minutes? If the person in front of the class is a man, do you think he thinks about sex once every ten minutes?

Maybe this professor will introduce himself or herself—give a little autobiography—the first day of class. The autobiography might be witty and charming, but what will you really know about this professor?

In truth, not much.

Many underlying themes of this book—of diversity—have to do with who we think we are and who others think we are—the stuff of our identities. We define ourselves, and we define those around us, and everyone else is doing the same thing. There is a tension between our own self-definitions and how each of us gets defined by those around us. What others think about us limits what we can become.

The person you are looking at can never see what you see. Each of us has an internal life: emotions and thoughts, a particular past, and wonderful plans for the future. There are fierce loyalties and loves and maybe a rich fantasy life. All of those things are both real and invisible. There is an enormous amount of stuff that you cannot see when you look at another person. Does that person love Indiana basketball? Wear silk underpants? Go to church twice a week? Watch the soaps? Attend opera? Who can tell? And so what if they do?

One way to think about this side of identity is to take a test about who you are. It is called the truly disgusting joke test.

For one of the authors, the test might involve being told four truly insulting and disgusting jokes about divorced people, bald people, Jews, stepfathers, and anything else that might apply. The jokes that offended us most would suggest which of those traits were most important to our identity. Make your own test. Does it have to do with religion, weight, color, sex, height, pimples?

What a way to begin to sort out who you are.

The point that is important to remember is this: The who we are can only be judged by others. It is impossible to know how others see and judge us. No matter how hard we try to control what we do, we still are powerless over what people see. We do our best, but others are our judges.

As we are judged, so too do we make judgments about others. We have our own reasons to decide as we do.

The bottom line is that each of you comes into a class, or a dorm, or anywhere else with a sense of who you are. You identify yourself by all of the things that you learned at home, or at school, or in Sunday school, or on the corner. Other people may be looking at those things, but it is entirely possible that they are looking at entirely different things. They may well be judging you and acting in ways toward you that make no sense to you.

You might think you're too thin; they might think you're too loud. You might worry that you're gay; they might not like people your color.

And, of course, you look around and make all kinds of decisions about others.

This book and the class discussions will begin to sort out what you think about yourself and others, and why. They will begin to get at why some of the things you do seem natural but are, in fact, deeply rooted in how you see yourself and others, and how others see you. The book has to do with how each of us has an identity based on things that may be offensive to someone else. We believe that attention to these ideas is important because of changes going on in this country and the world, changes that are going on right now: The nation is moving toward an ethic of greater access to employment and public places for groups that formerly were not fully welcome. Whether it is the Americans with Disabilities Act of 1990, setting standards for employment of handicapped people; state or local government sexual orientation antidiscrimination ordinances; affirmative action programs for women and minorities; or the fact that in most states most of the labor force growth will come from groups other than white males, or even white females; or the idea that English is not the only language spoken in the United States, it is clear that changes are a part of our lives. More of you will have to know about diversity because it is a growing fact in the workplace and where you might live.

This book is about who we are in the context of genuine and difficult changes. It is about how we define ourselves and others during a time in which our culture gives us too few—or maybe too many—clues.

Coming to College

Imagine that you are the traditional college student—young, living on campus, and new to this.

Think about that first day at college. It was all about leaving home and coming to college. Serious nervous-time for most. Many of you lived through the agreed-upon American rhythm: First there was high school, a time that seemed would never end but finally did, and then you put your family through the post-high school/pre-college summer that was full of anxiety and tension. During that transition summer, the idea of no parental authority was exciting. Also, admit it or not, there were the vestiges of childhood terror about leaving home. You got to college and, at least metaphorically, unloaded the old family station wagon. All that stuff went right to your room. What went? It was much more than your stereo, clothes, and toothbrush; *what really went was your identity.*

All of the family biases were carried directly to your dorm room. You brought in your whole past, you brought up what you believed as well as what your parents believed. Up went your religion, social class, parents' prejudices, and personal prejudices about sexual orientation and color and which baseball team to follow.

But the traditional world has shattered. Maybe you are in your mid-twenties, live at home, and come to college in the subway; maybe you are in your mid-thirties, divorced, and drop the kids off at day care on your way to class. Whoever you are, identity is still in play.

The other side of the identity equation is there too. Others have seen you, and judged you, and you have learned to live with that. You may not think of yourself as Protestant first, a baseball player second, and a pianist third, but others may have told you, in subtle ways, that is who you are.

All of that baggage you brought was your self-definition. Those biases and beliefs formed the basis of how you looked at and judged the world. Don't be put off by this; it is not intended to make you feel guilty or silly. The simple truth of the matter is that, more often than not, when we get to school, we are a collection of the things we have been taught. The world of home and neighborhood high school are the places in which we begin to define ourselves and others.

The world of home and high school makes an effort to solidify certain parts of your life. If you grow up black, in a black family, then it seems obvious that, in no small measure, you understand yourself as black. And that goes for Catholics and Japanese Americans and Mormons. During those years you are being taught something much more than how to take tests, program the VCR, and do your own laundry.

But it is very hard to know all of the things that get solidified these days. There are those of us with different sets of parents, and different sets of siblings. Your parents may be remarrying, so you are in the position of going to different weddings and giving away your mom or your dad or both. You may live in one of those families that have four grandmothers, three religions, two houses, and no peace. A surprisingly large number of people come from homes with a parent or parents who are alcoholic. Or Dad beats Mom. Or Aunt Mary did too much dope. Or a big brother molested a little sister.

The point is that from the station wagon to the dorm room, from the subway to your first-year English course, the first thing you bring in is your identity, with its ways of seeing, with its biases and prejudices.

And then you are left alone. The traditional first-year student (the innocent metaphor of this section) is left with a roommate whom you might know, and a whole floor of people you don't know. There are others who seem to be everything you are not. Islamic, rural, brown, lesbian, smart. They like different music, clothes, teams, food. Where everybody was the same in your old house, everybody is different now. What to do? How to judge? Who are they? Who are you?

Diversity, indeed.

High School

There are about 13,000,000 students in college. That's counting undergraduates in four-year schools and community colleges, professional-school students, and graduate students. The majority of them lived at home, went to high school, and then to college. Most of them went to a public high school, fewer to a parochial school, fewer still to a private boarding school. Many of us live at home, get restless by our junior year, and are more than ready for college by the time we're 18. Many of us graduate from high school and wait before we begin college. Whether you're 18 or 28, college is new and scary.

We know that in the United States, local districts, with the help of the states, finance public high schools. We are, in no small way, at the will of where we live. When we unload the metaphoric station wagon, we unload just what our towns and cities think about education. To be more specific, we reflect what our neighbors were willing to pay for our education.

Now here is the part that should come as no surprise: Public education has nothing to do with justice or equality. It might not even have much to do with education. All too often, public education is a reflection of how much money your part of town is willing to spend on schooling. The rich have better public schools than the poor.

Of course, private education is an entirely different enterprise. The first difference is money. If you lived in Los Angeles and attended Catholic schools, the cost of your kindergarten through high school education was one third what it cost to send the average child through the same grades in the public schools. And you probably did much better on the tests you took to get into college. Of course, someone, probably your parents, paid the private school costs plus the taxes to support the public schools. It cost less to educate you, but your family paid more. If you went to a good private boarding school, money mattered. It costs more to send one student to a good boarding school than it does to support a family of four living just above the poverty level. If you get to college with a boarding school degree, you are often way ahead.

Inner-city students from low-income backgrounds get schooling that is very different from that of middle- and upper-middle-class people in moneyed suburbs. Students from families that can and choose to afford private schools generally get different schooling than students from families that can't or don't.[1]

The fact is that lower-class schools have more to do with rigid, external discipline than with figuring out which courses will best help get a person ready for college. The thrust of the school seems to be to make the student learn to take orders and respond to authority. The students need written passes to go to the bathroom. If they break rules, they get kicked out of school.

People from these high schools go to college, but they are the few, the special, and the very very bright or talented.

—— 7 ——

Mostly, home and high school prepare them for a life in blue collars. Upper-middle-class public schools naturally steer students toward college. There are not as many rules, and everybody knows that it is hard to get suspended. Rules are made to be plea-bargained. Counselors take care to track their students through the right academic program and on to the right college. In most upper-middle-class high schools, it is not unusual for students to be treated like human beings.

And we have known about the differences for years. A classic study, published in 1949, found this: Sixty-four percent of the upper-middle-class and upper-class high school students were being tracked for college, while 4 percent of the lower-class students were in that track.[2] In a more recent study, the inequality was still clear. For the upper-class students, 80 percent of those who qualified for the top academic track in high school were in that track. For the students from lower-class backgrounds, only 47 percent of those who qualified for the top track were enrolled in that track.[3]

Numbers reveal. In 1978, 22 percent of the people from lower-class families went to college, while 58 percent of the middle class went.[4] Of course, the differences are more striking in private, powerful, fancy colleges. There, 7 percent come from low-income families and 56 percent come from high-income families.[5]

Diversity (and here we only mean color) depends on where you live. In the suburbs, it's very white; in the inner city, it's very black. There are whole states that are not very diverse: Almost 92 percent of school-aged people in Idaho are white, which pales compared to Vermont, where 99 percent are white. Ninety-nine percent.

If you are from Vermont, and you go to Berkeley, or Hawaii, or Chico State, imagine your surprise. There you are, unloading your station wagon. You take your first load of almost all white background to your room, and you notice something unusual. What could it be? Then it comes clear: More than half of the people on your floor, more than half of the undergraduates you see, are not white.

Suppose you are unpacking New England WASP, or Rocky Mountain Catholic, or Central Pennsylvania Methodist, while your Asian roommate is unpacking a Buddha. A fat, smiling Buddha. And the person next door is a Mexican-American. How will those good college boards scores help you now?

Then there are the people who are unpacking their private schools. Theirs was a $20,000 a year upbringing in the best surroundings. They come from well-educated families, and the better of the boarding schools have a high percentage of black and foreign students. A good college is assumed. They have been worked hard. Academics is only a part of the well-controlled environment of these schools. The other activities—work and play—teach the lessons of cooperation and competition. Most of them are well-traveled. They have made powerful friends for life.

Although they work hard, they are not necessarily used to good grades. About 2.5 percent of the students at boarding school are able to maintain an A-minus average or better.[6] That compares to 14 percent at suburban high schools. At one private school, 46 percent of the graduating students had a C average or less.[7]

But watch out for those private school students, no matter what their grades were. Over the years, they have been taught how to study, how to write, how to do homework. They have been in classes of 15 or fewer and have learned how to "do" school. They have friends who will be in high places. They might not be as bright as you are, but they do have skills. When they unpack their high school degree, it has nothing to do with bathroom passes.

Now we're back to you, our model undergraduate.

So there you are, all unpacked. Family is gone. You're on your own. You read somewhere that there are people on campus to help you, but it doesn't feel like it that first night. It was great to graduate from high school, you and your family were so proud, but now you are beginning to wonder just how good the education was. Some hotshot down the hall took a test and was placed in second-year Chinese—and she's blonde and from Florida. Great, you took two years of French. There wasn't even a Chinese person in your high school, much less a Chinese language class.

Well, at least you were in a social club in high school and there are fraternities and sororities here. Maybe you'll go through rush after all.

Age and Other Differences

What if you are not the typical undergraduate? If you are not, one of the ways you are likely to be different is that you are not as young as college students used to be.

Ten years ago, there was almost no need to talk about age. After all, college-aged people went to college. Ages 18 to 21. Normal. Everybody else was either too young or too old. The too-young part still seems true, but the too-old part is dead wrong.

After World War II, veterans came home and were given benefits in order to go to college. It was a genuinely extraordinary time. Higher education was accessible to people who would never have been able to afford it; education was opened to a group of adults who were rarely seen on campus. Middle and lower-middle classes came to college in large numbers for the first time. After the war in Vietnam, vets again came to college.

But the students over 18 years old are now not necessarily war veterans who are getting their education paid for by the government. As the number of 18-year-olds drops, colleges and universities actively recruit older students. To avoid calling them older, which is sometimes seen as a pejorative word in this society, the colleges call them returning students. Community colleges offer a variety of programs for people who have been out of school for years. Colleges and universities sometimes have powerful programs designed for people over 25. The percentage of these students has increased dramatically over the last decade. The number of older students has increased from 4.8 million in 1981 to 5.8 million in 1991. About 43 percent of all college students are at least 25 years old, compared with 39 percent in 1981. Most of these are white, female, aged 25 to 34, married, and working full-time.[8]

What if you aren't the typical young college student? Instead, you are the typical older college student.

It makes sense to assume that someone who lives at home with two kids knows things that an 18-year-old doesn't necessarily know, but it is foolish to generalize. When it comes to being in school, when it comes to sitting in class, you are no more academically secure than the 18-year-old. Indeed, if you were out of school for 15 years, weren't you more than a little scared to write that first paper or take that first test? Nursing a baby at four in the morning might be easier than having to write a five-page paper about nursing.

It is important to remember something about people like you. As an older person, you are still a person. And the older person brings in as much baggage as the younger one, but the older person's baggage is older. A high school education is different today from what it was in 1979. It doesn't matter whether it was better or worse; what we know for sure is that it was different. If you have been out of school since 1979, coming back is a shock. You are out of the loop. Everything from favorite television shows to presidents to AIDS is different. *The Brady Bunch* has not prepared you for *Beavis and Butthead.* When you come back to school at 35, it is easy to feel terror.

A Vietnam vet described what it was like coming to the university. He said he learned to kill. He did kill, and he was tough. But, he said, as tough as he was, he wasn't ready for the advertisements for the Gay/Lesbian/Bisexual Dance, or for the first time he saw two men kissing.

It took him some time to sort through his reactions—two years, he said—but he's OK with it now. The culture of even a decade ago is not the culture of now.

So part of diversity on campus is age. Professors are not the only people on campus who are older than the typical college student. Chances are there are people sitting in class who are older. People like you, with your own problems, who also share many of the same anxieties as the younger students. There is personal stuff, and growing-up stuff, and academic stuff that seems to cross age lines.

But you have some other things to think about. If you are 30-something, and especially if you are 40-something or more, your body sometimes fails you. Your children need you, and friends often wonder what you are doing. Many of you have doubts about your ability to compete with "kids" who are well into the routine of school. Maybe you wonder if your mental processes have slowed down as your body has. The coming of age on campus comes with its own set of problems. There are enough of these problems that we return to the subject in Chapter 8.

Add age to diversity.

We have to add more to our idea of diversity. A quick list was offered in the table of contents of this book. Here are some numbers that suggest what to expect on the average college campus.[9] Of the approximately 13 million college students in the United States, the vast majority—around 10 million—are white. In 15 states (Illinois and states in the West, South, and East), minorities (people of black, American Indian, Asian, and Hispanic heritage) make up more than 20 percent of the college population, and another 18 states have minority enrollments between 10 and 20 percent. More than half of all college students are women. There are other ways to classify students. In the Northeast states, students average more than seven alcoholic drinks per week, compared to less than three in the West, a little over five in the Midwest, and less than four in the South. A majority of Northeast students go on binges (five or more drinks at a sitting) from time to time, but less than 30 percent do so in the West, about 35 percent in the South, and 46 percent in the Midwest. Among NCAA Division I schools, 56 percent of white students graduate (55 percent of the men and 58 percent of the women), compared to 33 percent of black students (30 percent of the men and 36 percent of the women), 41 percent of Hispanic students (39 percent of the men and 44 percent of the women), 61 percent of the Asian students (58 percent of the men and 64 percent of the women), and 31 percent of the American Indian students (28 percent of the men and 33 percent of the women). You can see from the numbers that women graduate at significantly higher rates than do men. To serve these diverse students, there are about 700 programs in African-American studies, Asian and Pacific-American studies,

Native American studies, and Hispanic studies, and about 620 women's studies programs.

These kinds of comparisons can go further. Diversity is as complicated as you care to imagine.

Making a World

We are defined, in part, by the generation we grow up with and the company we keep. In this section, we will begin to discuss cultures and subcultures.

College culture is something the students make, subject to some limits the faculty and administrators impose.[10] Administrators want the routines on campus to happen, so that a certain basic order exists in spending money and paying bills. They want students to keep paying tuition and enrolling in classes, and they want university objectives about teaching and research to be met. But within that context, and sometimes beyond it, students create where they live.

In some decades, it's fairly obvious that students help make their social world. In the period spanning World War I through much of the twenties, students on many campuses protested, in some cases effectively, the exclusion of Jews from the clubs and organizations that conferred status on undergraduates. During the 1930s, politically active students were taking over student governments and newspapers, and criticizing college administrators. During the 1960s, there were movements to stop racism and the war; there was an in-your-face attitude about government, college administrators, and people over 30. Accompanying the activism was a pushing of the boundaries on sex, drugs, and rock and roll. For most of the in-between times, and for most of the students during the times of change, the core of college culture was the GPA.

Then, as now, every campus has many subcultures to choose from. Students form groups, each with its own rules and values. Your choice of activities helps define you.

What if you don't participate much in college social or political life and pursue, mainly, the GPA? College will not be

the same for you as for someone in the black student organization, or the Christian student organization, or the social science grad students working on dissertations, or the gay and
lesbian student organization, or the students who play college
sports, or the organized environmentalists, or the College
Republicans, or the serious beer drinkers, or the serious drug
takers, or the serious computer hackers, and on and on.

To repeat: The choices of college subcultures are choices
about identity—how you define yourself and how others
define you.

Identity questions have a lot to do with what you get out
of college. Consider this summary of a study of undergraduate
life.

> [T]his is a difficult time to be a college student. The pressures
> are great; the life, often grim. Although undergraduates enjoy
> partying on weekends that can begin on Wednesday night, they
> confine their friendships to the narrow social groups from which
> they spring. For some, extracurricular activities form part of
> their work or recreation, but the college no longer inspires any
> sense of community or service. Few college students ask existen-
> tial questions about the meaning of life. As they compete for the
> grades that will get them into professional schools, they allow
> themselves little room to grow and become. College moves them
> along to a job or a career, but for most it no longer serves to lib-
> erate their souls.[11]

How much are those questions about diversity connected
to the meaning of life? Should college help you prepare for a
profession *and* give you chances for serious introspection—
should it help you change the way you define yourself and the
way others define you? Do you have a soul, and if you do, is
liberty a good thing for souls? And should college help you
ask, and maybe suggest answers to, those questions?

Who are you?

College may be the first time you have encountered this
diversity business. On many campuses, a diversity course is
required. Maybe you have heard that diversity is a fact of life
you will have to live with, so you need to understand it. If one
of the points of college is to be thoughtful, then everyday life
is certainly one of the things that needs to be thought about.

Take those examples a few paragraphs before. How do you deal with the facts of GPA, the black student organization, the Christian student organization, the social science grad students working on dissertations, the gay and lesbian student organization, the students who play college sports, the organized environmentalists, the College Republicans, the serious beer drinkers, the serious drug takers, or the serious computer hackers? Have you joined any of these? Do you hang out with one group more than the others? It might be an interesting exercise to construct a web of the connections you have to people and groups at your college and to compare it to the webs of other students in a class. What do the connections say about the differences between us and the similarities among us?

We know that black students, particularly academically successful black students, do hang out in the places white students hang out, and join similar clubs, in addition to starting many of their own clubs. White students tend not to reciprocate.[12] There seems to be a strong tendency for students to hang out with and participate in activities with students much like themselves.

Simply put, you make choices about how you live. The first obvious question, of course, is why you make the choices you do. The sum of all those choices, the way people see you and the way you see yourself, in a particular place, equals a subculture. What does yours look like? How diverse is it?

Is that what you want out of college?

What's It Like

To close this introduction, imagine again that you are that typical 18-year-old college student.

We assume many if not most of you have read *The Lord of the Flies*, by William Golding.[13] To remember that book is one way to begin to think about entering college.

A group of English schoolboys (perfect little darlings) are in a plane crash. The survivors end up on a small, warm island. No adults survive. Our band of choirboys find themselves in a state of nature, but it seems to be friendly nature. Fruit to eat, fish, fresh water. Questions arise: how to live, what to do.

They organize. We meet the key people, see how they decide to be democratic, hear some of their panic, listen to them figure out that they need to eat and start a signal fire so that they can be seen and rescued.

The youngest ones go along with anything. A couple of the older boys seem destined to fight for power, the chubby one (Piggy) acts as a kind of whiny voice of reason and civilization. The island is explored, groups are formed, and the elements of society begin to emerge in a crude but real way.

The hunters, led by one of the older boys, begin to play rough. They hunt for pigs; they begin primitive rituals that involve painting themselves and having feasts. An imaginary monster is conjured up and the hunters become warriors. The group splits. Piggy and the other older boy become isolated.

The signal fire goes out.

One boy is killed by accident, but it makes no impact on the warriors. They paint themselves and dance around and generally enjoy their sense of power. When things slow down, and tensions get tightly wound again, they sharpen their sticks, grab their rocks, and go after their enemies. They kill Piggy.

Just as they are about to kill the other older boy, the last of their enemies, as they chase him out of the forest and onto the beach, he stumbles and falls at the feet of an adult, a member of the landing party come to rescue them.

That's it. The end.

In all too many ways, coming to college is our version of *The Lord of the Flies*. You land on campus, seemingly abandoned by the controls of home (certainly left by your parents), with a whole group of people as innocent about what to do as you are. Students may wander the halls trying to discover friends, figuring out how to act, where classes are, what to eat.

Your hall sorts itself out, and generally not in the most friendly and democratic of ways. There are informal fights for who can be whose friend, for which room will be the social center, for who will be leader of the pack. There is macho stuff, and bitchy stuff, and an effort to become ritualized and routinized. Pretty soon, there will be competition over who can drink the most, get the best grades, go to bed with the most people.

The veneer of home civilization remains—students tend to associate with students like themselves—but you find that you are in what seems to be a state of nature, where new, wild opportunities and challenges present themselves. Like the English lads, you seem to have enough to eat and a comfortable place to sleep, but beyond that things get dicey.

Although nature might be friendly, there are all of the people around you who seem to be different. For some perverse reason, what people have been saying are the best years of your life seem to be starting out like some strange version of *The Lord of the Flies*. What a bad trick.

The rest of the book is about many of the things that make college (and, in truth, much of life in the United States) a sometimes very difficult time. The book is about the strains and tensions of landing in a place where everybody brings something different, seems to expect something different, and often reacts in different ways.

If you decide not to read *The Lord of the Flies*, maybe you should see the movie. Like many things in life, there are two versions: The most recent is American, and is very pretty and in living color. We suggest you see the other one, the English version. It is older and has a gritty, grainy quality.

It's in black and white.

— 2 —

Location, Location, Location

Although Midaq Alley lives in almost complete isolation from all surrounding activity, it clamors with a distinctive and personal life of its own. Fundamentally and basically, its roots connect with life as a whole and yet, at the same time, it retains a number of the secrets of a world now past.

—Naguib Mahfouz

Wanted: an ex'd person for ADMISSIONS OFFICE. Must have good speaking voice, telephone skills and ability to close.

—*New York Times* classified advertisement

One of the differences we want to consider is geography. There are regional differences to consider, as well as rural and urban differences. These matter in terms of where you were raised and where you have decided to go to school.

Each of us is made up of a variety of things, and one of those things is the particular culture in which we have lived. We are not asking you to believe that everyone from the South

or the Midwest is somehow the same, but we would like you to consider regional differences, as well as urban, suburban, and rural differences.

We use geography to begin to explore the idea of stereotypes. How accurate is it to generalize, what do we gain when we do it, and what do we lose when we do it?

In this chapter, we also introduce the ideas of individualism and community. They are at the core of much of our political thinking, and will continue as themes in later chapters. The Puritans came to America to establish a religious community, yet individualism propels us. There is an ongoing tension between individualism and community.

The cooperation and conflicts between town and gown are also explored in this chapter. All of these divisions feed into life on campus, and should be understood as a part of the diverse society in which we live.

Location—where we come from and where we end up—is laced with meaning and is mixed up with our identity.[1] *Others define us, in part, by our location.* Location is something that needs to be understood on several different levels. It is, of course, connected to other things. If you are in a town with a "right" and "wrong" side of the tracks, the dividing line probably has a lot to do with class and color. The different sides of the tracks may celebrate different festivals, attend different churches, and speak different languages.

Location, by itself, is an important part of identity. To begin to explore this claim, we start with this question: How can address be identity?

It is simple to start at the grossest level of generalization. For quite a while during the early nineties, there were almost daily reports out of the Persian Gulf countries that we Americans were "White Satans." It is rare that I feel like a devil, so there was no real reason to give it much thought. But with the war and the ongoing hostage problems, it became almost impossible to avoid. Someone defined us that way. There was no way to get around considering the idea that, indeed, we in the United States were White Satans.

One of the first conclusions that seemed reasonable but a little surprising was this: It did make some sense to think of Americans as White Devils. If one begins with very strong beliefs about a god, and about what is right and what is wrong, then it is easy to make the judgment that Americans are quite high up on the corruption scale. Given my political beliefs and my bad habits, an Islamic fundamentalist could certainly confuse me with the White Satan.

The case can be made, and made surprisingly well, that we Americans have few ideals and often are not prepared to die for what we believe in, and that each generation appears to be more vile and corrupt than the last. We seem to pass on our moral weaknesses as farmers once passed on the family farm to their children. In traditional religious terms, we are sinners.

But it seemed there was more to the White Satan business than that. If we really were White Devils, then what sense did it make that there were many American people of color who fought in Vietnam and in the Persian Gulf? We know that in the eyes of the militant fundamentalist Muslim world, the blacks are as much White Satans as are whites. In the United States, bad habits cross color lines with ease.

We know that a large percentage of American troops in the front line of the Gulf War were people of one color or another—and they were considered White Devils. It seemed clear that in some global sense, skin color is not as important as home address.

We can put it in another way: For a militant Islamic fundamentalist in Iran or Iraq, the shades of difference that we seem so concerned about here in the United States are sheer foolishness. We are all the devil and the color of the packaging simply does not matter—all because someone else defines us this way.

Environment is destiny. Home town is identity.

Although that might be right, it still does not seem to be the complete answer. There is much more to everyday language and everyday ideas about identity.

What about our friends, whom we like a great deal, and the people we just can't stand? It has nothing to do with where they were born or with where they grew up. We all know brothers and sisters who are about as dissimilar as they can be—we might like one and dislike the other. But the question lingers: If they had the same parents and grew up in the same house, why aren't they more alike?

One of the authors of this book is an academic who lives in an academic valley. He is Jewish and was born and raised in Oklahoma. Short, white, and bald. When it comes to understanding the world, he has the most in common with a friend who also lives in this valley. That friend is tall and black, was born and raised in New Jersey, is a Muslim, and makes his living as a tennis coach.

That seems to suggest that address is not destiny.

At least two levels of understanding the world are going on at the same time. The first level is the easy and sloppy way of sorting out the world, such as "All Americans are White Satans." The second level is the careful individual decisions we make about who our friends will be.

The first way is too crude and the second way is too little understood. Just why are those people our friends?

These levels of sorting out the world revolve around different visions of who we think we are. Are we violent or passive, nasty or sweet, cheap or giving, corrupt or moral, and on and on? Do we have a basic nature that is the core of each of us, or are we all products of our teaching and conditioning? Are all people from New York City pushy? Are all people from Los Angeles laid-back? Even if we know those characterizations are not true, are these our first thoughts when we meet someone from New York or Los Angeles?

If we have a human nature, *what is it?* If we do not have a human nature, *what does that mean?*

It is altogether possible that we cannot even begin to think about diversity until we figure out where we want to start. Your actions stem exactly from how you think and what you believe. To put it a different way: If you decide that you want to be a bigot, where do you want to begin?

Most of the readers of this book will be spending much of their time on a college campus. In the next sections, we take these issues about place and bring them to campus.

Location: The Academic/American Community

In our everyday language, we talk about an *academic community* and the *campus community*. But it is important to be careful about language. *Community* is a high-powered concept and it means more than people merely living in the same place.

Community has to do with the people who are in a place, how they act together and apart, who stays and who goes. In academic settings, some of the people are relatively permanent residents, and some are relatively temporary.

In the United States, all this takes place in the land of individualism, where there may be less of doing things together. With the background noise of individualism, it is tough to define community. It might be easier to do where other forces lend some common values, like in the East, where the land has been settled longer than in the West, or in Salt Lake City, which is mostly Mormon. Our point here is that the surrounding community helps to confer identity on people in a college.

Let's start with an example from the Northeast.

White folks came here and formed a community.

The university where one of the authors teaches is in New England. Being in New England means something for our politics, education, and language. The campus is in the Pioneer Valley (people who left Boston came west to this valley), and the town was named after Lord Jeffrey Amherst. Lord Jeffrey was for a time the commander of all British troops in North America, and his victories against the French in 1758–1759 were a major turn in the course of those wars. He is remembered for refusing to lead the English army in New England during the Revolutionary War, but was also accused of poisoning Indians through a gift of diseased blankets. Pioneer lore runs strong in the valley.

We have to see the valley as the frontier for second- and third-generation Puritans. The first-generation Puritans came to Boston in order to worship God the way they wanted to.[2] These were not humble people. They were so sure of themselves and of their righteousness that they believed Boston would become a beacon on the hill. They believed that their mission was so just and their goodness so bright that their example would shine all the way back to wrong-doing and evil-acting Europe.

The Puritans believed that they could begin to clean up corrupt Europe by being a moral light.

And what of their community, their legacy and this New England? Was it bright, did it shine?

As we think about the Puritans—and the famous definition is that a Puritan is a person who is afraid that someone somewhere might be having fun—we think about a group of cranky, uptight, rigid, religious fanatics. That is not entirely wrong.

But the Puritans were more than that. They also formed a community that we can learn from. The Puritans all believed the same thing—they believed in the same God and the same religious laws—and they all subordinated their individual wills to the common will.

They were same-thinking people who shared a powerful vision of right and wrong and who lived together under a distinct moral code.

That is, traditionally, the definition of community. That singleness of shared purpose is what gives life and meaning to its participants. It is different from everyone working at the same company or everyone having the same major. The idea of community has always been centered on shared moral purpose.

Community is exactly what we, as twentieth-century Americans, seem totally unable to do. Our lives are laced with a powerful form of individualism. We make it on our own. We are brought up with an ethic of each person for himself or herself. At best, we draw up a set of rules so that individual competition doesn't get too out of hand. Even in this Pioneer Valley, individual wills were never subordinated to a common will. They weren't 300 years ago, and they certainly are not now.

So, what happened to the Puritans? What happened with their covenant with God? Interestingly, what happened was to become the prototypical American relationship between generations—the first-generation Puritans decided that they did not quite trust their children.

What to do? They told their kids that until they proved themselves as virtuous citizens and religiously correct people, they could only have a halfway covenant with God. Mom and Pop Puritan were full members; the kids were only partial members.

The children were rightfully insulted. Unlike Europe, this New World was far from being fully settled. It didn't take the kids long to realize that all they had to do was pack up and leave. They could settle their own land and build their own villages. And they did. For all practical purposes, that was the end of white community in America.[3]

The people who left their Puritan ancestors, and others like them who wanted out of the confines of their eastern Massachusetts communities, came to this valley in New England. As we will see in the next chapter, religious choice is one of the ways people define themselves and define others.

New England is a tough place. The soil is full of rocks and the winters are cold enough to freeze people to death. People stay inside a lot, and when the summer comes, they are busy building fences in order to be good neighbors.

One of the more positive things New England seems to have is town meetings. The image of these meetings is wonderful; it is the essence of democracy. The ideal is that in all of these old and quaint New England towns, people meet together at the town hall to discuss and vote on the important issues. In some instances, that is exactly what goes on.

But you have to remember that town meetings have to do with politics, not with community. They are a way to make decisions, not a way of life. New England town meetings are the local politics of liberalism, and American liberalism is generally two parts individualism and one part capitalism. It is individualism and capitalism that Americans have in common, not community.

Individualism is one kind of identity. Community is another kind of identity. If you belong to a community, you get a lot of your identity from it. Alone, you are at the mercy of the masses.

That is the story behind one academic community, in one place in New England. Its history gives us something to hang onto and distinguishes this place from, say, Duke University or Oregon State. Location is a part of what this university means, but it allows us only a murky view. Somehow, the things going on in this century right now define us more than the events that gave the place its name.

You can look at the story of your own place and what that has to do with your college. Some traces of identity probably remain.

Location: College

Colleges can be seen as communities, and the making of those communities can be very independent of their histories.

What about your college? Do you live in a community? We can begin with those of you who live in a building put up to make a college community—the dormitory. Think about who you know, who you have relationships with, and who you hang out with. As an exercise, make a chart with lines connecting yourself with the people you know, spend time with, and like. What you will see is that each of us has a web of relationships that, for the moment, defines our social world.

Each of us is in the middle of our very own web. That is an accurate definition and description of our individualism. There is no centering moral or spiritual force that everyone agrees to. Each of us puts together a web, a world.

And the web, we know, is fragile.

What we have is not a web of common belief but one of convenience. We end up being with some of the people on the floor, with people who share majors, with other Italians, cokeheads, Deadheads, jocks, or Jews.

If you have been at school long enough, you know that the karma of individualism comes out in strange ways. For whatever reasons, friendships change, relationships change, good halls become bad ones, and bad ones become good ones. There seems to be no rhyme or reason to what goes on. You are probably offered all sorts of entertainment to keep you and your friends busy.[4] Nothing is strong enough to guarantee relationships in the "community" of college.

How different is it for those of you who live outside the dorms? Where is the college community if you live off campus?

The very structure of college does much to reinforce our individualism. Is this the way it is at your school? We each take four or five classes. The classes are not particularly tied together by any common vision of truth. What we know, in fact, is that classes are often less a pursuit of the truth than pursuit of the vision of the professor. Each professor gets to think for himself or herself, and each student gets to learn what the professor is thinking. Certainly it's a good deal for teachers.

It is your job to go to classes and learn different visions. There is little or no intellectual overlap when it comes to papers or exams, and when it comes to papers and exams, you are in direct competition with those around you. In almost all institutions of higher learning, there are few group projects. You write your papers and take your tests. To do differently is to risk getting caught for cheating and being kicked out of school.

You learn, by the very structure of the place, just how to act when you leave.

Ah, you want to argue, *you are making it sound awful. Don't you know,* you want to say, *that we do have friends here? College is a wonderful place to meet new people. These people will be our friends for the rest of our lives. You can't deny that.*

True, true. We could not agree more. Friends for life if you are lucky. But the point is that friends are not community. They are necessary and important and often make life worth living, but friends will end up as a kind of personalized support group, or an old-girls' or old-boys' network. Friendship in America is important, but friendship in America is not community.

It turns out that we in the United States are perfect subjects for group studies and impossible subjects for community studies. Groups are generally collections of individuals who are continually sorting out their individualism. Communities are people who have common beliefs and try to live out a collective vision. While you and your friends might have common goals, you probably don't have a collective vision. We are no longer spiritual descendants of the community of Puritans; the closest we can find are descendants of liberal/capitalist Puritans. We are all second generation.

Would you even dare to try to live in a community? Would you give up your individualism for the security of a shared belief? *Hare Krishna, hare hare?* We suspect not.

Is it possible to find community in the United States? The campus community seems unlikely. Sports teams come to mind. The good ones—good meaning winning and successful—talk about being a family. But let's get serious. The very best athletes—the heroes and heroines of our time—negotiate their own contracts and are elected to their Halls of Fame individually.

"I'd like to thank my teammates," they all say, but the truth is that our society is set up to honor individuals. It is an unusual program that runs on a different ethic.

We have weaned our language of words like *community* and have substituted the words of individualism and of the social sciences. Let me tell you an awful story. It is a lawyer/Native American story. You can already get the idea that the two don't go together.

The Native Americans in this story are from the Pacific Northwest. Historically, they had a very strong tribal sense. What they lack in the twentieth century is power, so lawyers came in to help them.

One of the things the lawyers did was to organize the tribe into a corporation. Each tribe member was given stock and became a shareholder in the newly formed corporation. The attorneys we talked with did not see the difference between the traditional tribal values of community and merely being a stockholder with a voting interest.

It is, one must honestly admit, not an unusual mistake for an American to make.

And our language has changed. It has gone from moral to mechanical. The priest who once gave forgiveness now offers feedback. The organic ties of community have long since been betrayed by our very choice of words. Just what information loop are you in? One? Many? And who are your sources, connections, ties?

So, here we are, settled down in a college community. But it isn't a community at all.

One response, a seemingly normal one, does give us some insight into location, if not community. We go to our rooms, close the door, turn up the stereo about as loud as we can stand it and lie down on the bed. It is, says a friend, the closest we can come to crawling back into the womb. Leave me alone. Let whatever is playing surround me, completely envelop me. Block out the world. To misuse language, create a community of me and my music. American liberalism driven to its logical conclusion.

Yo, crank up the sounds.

Location: Town/Gown

Universities do have a past, as well as a history. To get a sense of town/gown relations, consider the example of the University of Padua, U of P, located just west of Venice, Italy. It began in 1222 when teachers and students migrated from Bologna, which was the first European university.[5]

All went well for Padua until 1405, when there was a drop in enrollment. To help fix things, the Venetian Senate passed two laws. The first said that the two new schools that were competing with Padua should be closed, and the second said that any Venetian subjects who wanted to attend a university must attend the University of Padua. If they went somewhere else, they would be fined 500 ducats. Over the next 200 years, they repeated the second law several times. Town supports gown.

Over the next decades, the Senate was busy with the university. In 1463, it approved a plan to announce courses months before a new semester so the students could know what was to be taught. The Senate also fined professors who were absent from their classes without permission. A little later, the Senate decided to offer more courses by hiring what we know today as junior faculty. It also made laws to prohibit the prominent local families from monopolizing the faculty. That was unusual for the times. In Bologna, for example, ordinary professorships were restricted to Bolognese citizens by birth. Town owns gown. The University of Padua prospered with the help of the Senate. It grew famous and it grew in size. The school developed outstanding programs in law and philosophy and, especially, medicine.

The government helped with all of the programs. For example, in medicine, anatomical research depended on the dissecting of numerous bodies. Civil authorities went out of their way to help the university by scheduling executions to coincide with the research needs. One professor remarked how pleased he was to get bodies "scarcely dead."[6]

If there were not enough bodies from the executioners, students were encouraged to grab bodies from funerals (they had to be "lowborn and unknown" so their families' protests could be ignored) or simply to rob graves. The officials would let the students do what they needed to do. While a little dramatic, the town/gown relationship in Padua was very close. The question is Why? What did the citizens get out of it?

The most noble answer is that there was a love of learning fostered by the Renaissance, and the citizens of Padua wanted its elite to be well educated. Education was understood as an important thing.

The university was also a source of pride for the citizens of Padua. It had an international reputation for excellence, and the people of Padua had every reason to be pleased.

Finally, it was a source of income for the city. In the middle of the sixteenth century, there were approximately 1,000 students at the school. These students spent more than 100,000 ducats annually for food, dress, lodging (there were no dorms on campus), and other expenses. It cost only about 10 percent of that to run the university. In other words, the city of Padua made a bundle from being a college town.

Although some of the details are different, the basic story remains about the same today. Colleges are good businesses. The students and faculty and staff, as well as the institution, spend a lot of money. People in college towns treat students in a special way. Most towns no longer plan executions around research schedules, and grave robbing is frowned on, but there are college towns that do special things for special students. Merchants seem to want to please outstanding athletes, for example. State and federal tax codes generally do not tax college land and real estate. Some towns schedule events around the college calendar.

And why?

For the love of learning? Maybe. For pride? Maybe. For 100,000 ducats annually? Not a bad guess.

But there is more to town/gown than that.

Location: Dorms and Pastures

We have a vision of college here in the United States. You see it in movies: a cultural icon of what college is like. The vision, more or less, includes a beautiful, quiet, rural setting, and in that setting is a small college with perfect buildings and a kind of idyllic peaceful environment for the pursuit of higher learning. The dorms are comfortable, each has its own dining room, laundry service, and sensitive and caring counselors. Professors, all of whom seem to like each other as well as the students, live in gingerbread houses near the gingerbread village.

What could be better?

Because very few of you live that version of college, the question becomes this: Where did we get the myth?

We know that dorm life in the rural setting is part of our myth. That dormitories are part of our history is no mistake. Colonists chose dorm life for two reasons. First, it was the English way of housing students, so naturally the colonists brought it with them. Second, there were no big cities in the new world. Without dormitories, there would have been no place for students to live.

And when there were cities, they were looked on with some skepticism. When Bowdoin College was looking for a home, North Yarmouth, Maine, argued that it was the best location because it was "not so exposed to many Temptations to Dissipation, Extravagance, Vanity and Various Vices as great seaport towns frequently are."[7] Dissipation indeed. Those in rural settings know little of Various Vices.

There also seemed something special about a rural setting. Henry Ward Beecher said that it was a liberal education merely to be in the presence of the scenery of Amherst.

That myth continues today.

—— 31 ——

There were cynics and others who liked the action of a city. In 1830, friends of the school that was to become New York University argued that "Seclusion may be the nurse of poetry and the parent of romance, but not so of literature and true philosophy."[8] And on the West Coast, it was argued that "country towns are less religious . . . and are steeped in a coarser, baser depravity." More to the point, "There is a certain vulgarity . . . in provincial vices, which makes them more brutalizing."[9]

When you were trying to figure out which school to go to, one of the factors you probably thought about was whether you wanted a big city or a small town. But does it really make a difference? Are there Various Vices in small midwestern schools? Is there no poetry at the University of Southern California?

The location of your school might make a difference. Is a political science course that is taught in Troy, Alabama, the same as one taught in Newark, New Jersey? Even if the same books are used, the professors are about the same, and the students are equally bright, would the course be the same in such different environments? Life isn't the same, so why would learning be the same?

Where the family station wagon stops is important. This book reads differently in the hills of Colorado than it does in the canyons of New York City. Place counts. Perhaps it is because all the subjects discussed in this book—religion, class, sex, race, sexual orientation, cultural heritage, and so on—do tend to have locations. Troy, Alabama, is really different from Newark, New Jersey.

And there are the dorms. So many people living together like one big happy family. What fun.

Dorms, in the beginning, were a way for colleges to help control students. While they form a part of our fantasies of what college life is like, there have always been critics. In the early 1800s, it was argued that dormitories were an invitation to trouble. Get a lot of different people together, put them under the pressure of school and everyday life, the argument went, and you could expect the worst.

In 1833, two students at South Carolina College sat down to eat. They reached for the plate of trout at the same time.

Trouble. One killed the other in the duel that followed.[10] The fact is that the past is littered with stabbings, stonings, and killings that have grown out of dorm life. In 1800, Manasseh Cutler said that "Chambers in colleges are too often made the nurseries of every vice and cages of unclean birds."[11]

Are dorms on your campus the cages of unclean birds?

Dormitories are a part of college life. When people did try to live off campus in the early 1800s, the "better people" in the community would not take them in. It seemed tacky to take in boarders.

So colleges have learned to do their best to keep people on campus—if not in dorms, at least in houses of some kind. By keeping you on campus, they make you special. Colleges often try to segregate students from the general population. Students have a certain status. You are literally set apart. The townies might like you or resent you, but they all know you as students.

And the townies think that you live in a community. They really believe that there is a campus community, that you all share something, and that you are all doing the same things. Maybe they have fantasies that those dorms really are "nurseries of every vice" and resent you for it. Or envy you for it.

The townies who believe we are a community are wrong. How much do they understand about being thrown together with a bunch of people you don't know and forced to live under rules you didn't make? What do they know about needing to study chemistry when somebody next door needs to listen to Pearl Jam?

What do they know about individualism on campus, being assaulted by love groups and hate groups and sensitivity mongers? While college might look like a community from the outside, it rarely feels like one on the inside.

Location

Being in college is a special status. To be in college is a signal that you aspire. Right or wrong, it means that you have the ambition to be a something and/or a somebody. You want a career, you want status, you want to know the right people and use the right fork.

And college can do that for you. No doubt about it, college is the single best institution to help you be middle-class or better. Being born rich is the best way, but there doesn't seem to be an application to fill out for that. For most of us, going to college is the statement we make about how we want our future to be.

Part of the American myth is that we are all pretty much middle-class, and all of us can make it. Whether we are in college or not, we are equal. It is wrong to think in terms of superior and inferior; we Americans are the same.

In fact, the myth implies that there is something better about the honest, hardworking townie than the rich, spoiled college student. If everything has been given to you, including college, it is hard to appear anything but precious and unlikable. Snotty. There is a wonderful movie that makes the point. The title of the movie is *Breaking Away*.

It is a town/gown movie about the tensions between the two. Near the end, the honest, likable, hardworking townies (real Americans) win a bike race. They beat the spoiled fraternity men. Everyone cheers. At the very end, one of the townies and his dad enroll in college. Myth is heaped on myth. The virtuous townies not only win, but they have the opportunity to go to college too. The movie was filmed at Indiana University. The year it came out, applications to Indiana went through the roof.

The other town/gown story comes out of the Pacific Northwest. It has to do with a small religious school set in a medium-sized town. Not rural but certainly not big city. The story is about a party in a house very close to the campus.

The party was going on and some people from town came by. The party looked like fun, so they asked if they could join it. No, the students said.

Words, as they say, were exchanged. The townies left and came back with their guns and shot at the students. Hit and wounded some of them. Drove away but got caught a little later. The students got medical care and counseling.

Black townies and white students at a religious college. Town/gown.

The place where the college is located counts. The kind of community the college members try to make counts. Where you live counts. That you are even in college counts. But this counts most of all: The wheels of American life turn on individualism. No matter how clubby and cozy college seems—or is viewed from the outside—we are all on our own. We will see that there are various ways in which we identify ourselves, but those ways rarely provide us with much security.

— 3 —

Different Gods

*It's uh known fact, Pheoby, you got tuh go there tuh
know there. Yo' papa and yo' mama and nobody else
can't tell yuh and show yuh. Two things everybody's got
tuh do fuh themselves. They got tuh go tuh God, and
they got tuh find out about livin' fuh theyselves.*

—Zora Neale Hurston

*At the last minute the Lord stayed Abraham's hand and
said, "How could thou doest such a thing?"*

And Abraham said, "But thou said—"

*"Never mind what I said," the Lord spake. "Doth
thou listen to every crazy idea that comes thy way?"*

And Abraham grew ashamed. "Er—not really . . . no."

*"I jokingly suggest thou sacrifice Isaac and thou
immediately runs out to do it."*

*And Abraham fell to his knees, "See, I never know
when you're kidding."*

*And the Lord thundered, "No sense of humor. I can't
believe it."*

—Woody Allen

I n this chapter, we look at religion as a part of diversity. At
the heart of religion is belief, including belief about who we
are and who others are.

Religion, we will find, has played a central role in higher education in the United States. We will briefly review that history.

Higher education in this country by and large began as an extension of religious groups, but a difference developed: the difference between religious belief and scientific belief. The strain between the two resulted in a very diminished role for religion on campus. With the diminished role of religion came an important question: Where, if anywhere, will values be taught? We take up this question in the final part of the chapter.

Religion is something we get at home. Life on the college campus, with some notable exceptions, is not centered around religion. But it comes to campus along with the other things brought in from the outside.

On the outside lives a religious population. Among the industrialized nations of the world, U.S. citizens are the most religious.[1] Compared to German, Dutch, British, Japanese, Italian, Canadian, and other citizens of the rich world, we more often believe in God, worship in organized settings, pray, and so on. The culture is infused with religion, and many of the core values come from it. As a nation, we have fairly strong ideas about mission, work, and spreading our values to other places. Many of these ideas come from religious accounts of good and evil, sin and salvation, and witnessing.

College students share these religious values. A 1984 survey found that three out of four college students said they believed in a God who judges people, and 78 percent of students said they were moderately or deeply religious. Among faculty, 59 percent reported similar beliefs.[2] Religion and religious belief are a fact of life in our society and on campus.

Even for nonbelievers, religion is part of the background of the surrounding culture, the white noise that drowns out other noises. It is part of identity.

For most of us, religion looms. Our parents urge us to date a nice Catholic or marry within the faith. While growing up, we are told to go to youth group meetings or services or prayer meetings, or even parochial schools.

Yes, one of our best friends might be Jewish, Protestant, Catholic, Lutheran, Episcopalian, Baptist, or whatever. But, in our hearts, we know that—for some obscure reason—those friends might just be different from us. Who can really trust someone who routinely drinks the blood of Christ, goes door to door handing out little magazines, won't call a doctor but has somebody read to them when they get sick, hopes in the next life they will come back a cow, carries around a little rug and bows to the East periodically, or mumbles Hebrew and doesn't understand a word of it?

What seems clear enough is that our parents and our religions do a pretty good job on us as we grow up. At some basic level we learn to categorize the world—at least in part—according to ideas about what God really wants.

Is it important that no one can really prove that there is a God? Belief in God is an enduring fact in our behavior. We have prayer books, and places to pray, and in some cases huge hierarchies and great amounts of money built on two points of faith: There is a God, and God is listening to us and is happy about the way we worship.

In our society, there is a tension between the impossibility of proving God by our prevailing ways of knowing and a strong desire to believe that there is a God. Our agreed-upon ways of knowing come from science, from experiments and repeatable results. Our belief in God comes from a leap of faith. There is a constant strain to resolve the contrasting ways of knowing. In an important sense, the tension is a minor one. People who believe Elvis is alive are more numerous than people who believe there is no God. Belief, and the will to believe, is powerful.

The numbers don't matter, and the proofs or lack of proofs don't matter. What you believe does matter. Religion, in matters of diversity, is about belief and identity.

Remember that wars have been and are fought over religion, not over science. This is true for the entire world and for all of recorded human history. Religion has mattered.

Religion is part of identity because our beliefs make us part of some groups and set us apart from other groups. Does God tell you to witness and spread the good news? Jehovah's Witnesses who act on that belief have been a persecuted minority, having to go to the Supreme Court several times to defend their right to practice their religion. Does your God offer a cure for the loneliness of individualism? Is God a kind of magic that can make you feel happy? Is God a judge, a cosmic conscience that watches and guides your behavior? Is God the maker of a natural order, a knowable order, that we humans should follow? Is God about being grateful for every little piece of creation? Will you see God someday? These questions may sound innocuous, but they separate people.

College and Religion

How does college fit into all of this? In truth, religion is a major theme in higher education. It has to do with more than self-identity and diversity, but that is where we can begin.

College can be a time-out from Mom and Dad's religion. This is true not only at the godless big state universities or the progressive liberal arts colleges. There are Catholics at Catholic colleges who wonder about why women aren't priests and what is so wrong with birth control; some people at Oral Roberts University wonder about Oral's constant conversations with God; some students at Southern Methodist University party and break rules and just don't act the way Southern Methodists are supposed to act.

The fact is that you are away from home and are free to get a little distance on Sunday mornings, Friday nights, or whenever. You can date people who believe anything or nothing. It's kind of interesting, and can even be exciting. You discover that people might be nice, handsome, pretty, very appealing regardless of their religious beliefs.

And fantasy comes into full play. Mom, Dad, you say in your fantasy, this is Sally Catholic (or Abe Jewish or Fuad Muslim or whoever) and we are in love and we are going to get married. Mom faints. Dad walks out of the room. And you marry and love each other and live happily ever after.

And you have children and they are raised. Raised what? And here come the holidays. Whose holidays? What's a wake? What's a bris? What's going on here? This fantasy isn't fun at all.

Wake up Mom. Get Dad. Tell them you're kidding. You're just messing around for a few years. Taking a little time out. "Believe me," you say, "my fantasy mate really does believe in Christmas, Passover, (fill in your favorite holiday here)."

If religion is not alive and dominant on campus, it certainly lurks. Many sororities and fraternities are predominately one religion or another. Do we really think that is just a gigantic coincidence, or are there some very obvious reasons that there are not a lot of Muslim Kappas or a lot of Christian Science ZBTs? Certainly there might be one here, or one way over there, but that's about it.

There are religious groups on campus. There are places to pray. There are Newman Clubs and Hillels; there are priests and rabbis and the like. And these formal religious groups are becoming more active.

Without a doubt, religion is here on campus. Even when we do not think that others believe, people continue to believe. Even if we do not join a religious organization, a large majority accept the idea that there is a God and that God is judging. As we suggest in the next section, this is a part of a deep and continuing tradition of religion in American higher education.

Old Time Religion

The very same Puritans who gave us community and our first taste of a generation gap also gave us a lasting sense of sin. Part of our religious heritage in the United States is a profound sense of being morally dirty and needing to be spiritually cleansed. You might get more of that heritage if you are a congregational Protestant, a little less of it if you are a Vatican II Catholic; more of it if you are a Criswellian Southern Baptist, less of it as an African Episcopal Methodist. But it is there. To the amusement of Europe (the very people whom the Puritans wanted to show up), sex was close to the dirtiest thing the Puritans could think of. Faith was central to forgiveness and for eternal life.

The Puritans offer a lesson about community in America. Although they were officially separatists, who believed that religious and civil authorities should not be mixed, in practice their ministers were very influential in their politics. They exiled Roger Williams from their colony for upbraiding them on this cozy relationship and for calling into question their right to the land they used and the legitimacy of their ministry. No such dissent in our community, said the Puritans.

Williams's answer to the problem, in his new colony of Rhode Island, was to allow religious freedom in civil matters but to continue to confront those with heretical beliefs in his capacity as a citizen. The reason the state had to stay out of religion was that the state always got religion wrong. Religion needed protection, but not direction from civil authority. Religious community (for the Puritans, the only real basis for community) was not something anyone could make rules about. Each individual had to find his or her own. Williams thought it his duty as a citizen to argue with his neighbors over religious questions, but never to bring the arguments before the state.

In our common understanding of the separation of church and state, we get it the other way. James Madison's wall of separation is offered as a protection against religious zealots using the powers of the state to enforce community standards on unbelievers. In this sense, community might have something to do with religion, but it was no business of the state to make it so.

Both sides of the separation of church and state are behind that simple statement at the beginning of the first amendment to the constitution:

> Congress shall make no law respecting an establishment of religion, or prohibiting the free exercise thereof.

The particularly American approach to the balance between state and religion means that if you want religion and community, you do it on your own. One of the ways people tried to make their own communities was by founding colleges. The religious background of college in America helped set the tone for people trying to make communities in today's colleges.

College, in the colonies, began as male, white, religious, and elitist. No surprise there. After the initial disappointment of utterly failing to have any influence on Europe, the Puritans changed their focus. They focused on the New World. They joined other denominations in seeking a way to create a better world through religion. Those in charge needed a way to make certain that the people had proper religious and political leadership. They needed "a learned clergy, and a lettered people."[3]

Harvard College was founded for just those purposes. The early colonial schools were not narrowly religious, but they aimed at producing an educated clergy. They were religious, but not evangelically religious. Those colleges came later.

Colleges followed religions. For example, as debates about orthodoxy at Harvard seemed to be leading to a spirit of toleration, Yale was started. No toleration there; Yale began as Puritan, as religiously correct.

Then the Presbyterians wanted a school, so they started Princeton. And the Congregationalists in New England started Dartmouth, and the Baptists founded the College of Rhode Island, and the Dutch Reformed created Queens. All of that was by 1766.

The roots of our higher education were the belief in a higher being. For God's sake.

By the nineteenth century, we had entered what one person called "the regime of petty sectarian colleges."[4] Religions, both big denominations and narrow sects, founded and dominated higher education. For the want of students and money, they went almost as fast as they came. The history of higher education is cluttered with failed religious colleges.

During that time, many of the grand fights were about religion and about morality. For example, when the Calvinists attacked Harvard as being corrupt, enrollment at Harvard fell.

In the American tradition of individualism, there were constant revivals on campus. In a nation that would not have an official religion or support a specific church, it is not surprising that there was a tendency for people to take religion (and their own souls) personally. It was not unusual for everyone on campus to get involved in a revival. There were times when classes would stop so the important work of soul saving could be carried on.

Religion is central to much of our history. The natural place for religion to be carried on was in school. Religion is still all around us today, but there are those who choose not to look. Although most colleges do not admit people on the basis of religion, there are certainly religious schools. And they are good, credible schools where some religious parents feel best about sending their children. Do Mormons stay in Utah? Do Muslims stay away from Notre Dame? Does Brandeis attract lots of Jews?

Let's skip forward for a moment. Until very recently, there were religious quotas at many schools. The elite eastern schools commonly accepted only a few Jews. (If this were the chapter on race, the sentence would have ended ". . . only a few minorities.") After the formal religious ties were broken— or at least the more compulsory parts of religion were no longer a part of college life—religious quotas were still a fact. Many colleges continued to be white and Christian.

Ezra Cornell said that his university's aim would be "to make true Christian men."[5] But, liberal that he was, he said that his students did not have to fit into "the narrow gauge of any sect." In addition, Cornell University's charter specified that people of any religious denomination—or no religious denomination—would be eligible for any appointment. There was a reaction. Students were warned that they would be "raw recruits for Satan" if they went to Cornell.

Back to mainstream nineteenth-century colleges. Revivals periodically saved souls, and religions conspicuously dominated higher education. But what was it like? Would you have fit in? Would it have been good for you?

At Oberlin College in Ohio, a young man wrote what was considered an indiscreet letter to a young woman. Heaven forbid. His fellow Christian students gave him 25 lashes on the back of his hand. There were, in other words, standards.

One important standard was imported from the English colleges. They had a tradition of having single, celibate faculty members. It wasn't so much that sex couldn't mix with learning (it might not) as it was a question of how to afford a faculty at all. Celibate resident faculty were inexpensive to feed compared to nonresident heads of households who wanted a middle-class life. The single, celibate faculty tradition was a rare phenomenon by the turn of this century.

Until almost the end of the nineteenth century, there was compulsory chapel at most colleges. There were morning and evening prayers. And there were problems. The brother of the president of Illinois College was suspended for "repeated disorders tending to disturb the worship of God in chapel." A student got in trouble for dancing in the aisle during chapel at the University of Georgia. At Williams, compulsory prayer sessions were marked by indifference, disrespect, absenteeism, writing dirty things in the prayer books, and "ogling" female visitors.[6]

Near the end of the century, many schools began to put religion on a volunteer basis. No wonder. Ogling.

Colleges also had an annual day of prayer. Classes were called off and everyone was expected to pay serious attention to the saving of his (most students were male) soul. It was a time for religious experiences.

But religion was more than chapel. Religion helped form the basis for what was studied and discussed. Colleges considered theological questions in serious ways. At Harvard they asked if "any Sin is Unpardonable," if there was "any Standard of Truth," and "Whether it be Fornication to lye with ones Sweetheart (after Contraction) before marriage."[7]

At Williams College in Massachusetts, they tried to get to the heart of the matter and asked whether Christians should take one another to courts of law.

Put in a little different way, context often dictates substance. In a religious United States, it is not much of a surprise to see that religion dominated education. In the nineteenth century, we were nowhere near the time when the Supreme Court would rule that there could not be prayers in public schools. The people in power gave lip service, if nothing else, to religion. Our history, in no small part, is dominated by Protestants fighting each other and then getting together and fighting everybody else.

A current example might help. The person involved is William F. Buckley. He is a conservative. Getting older. He publishes an influential magazine and is seen on his own Sunday television talk show. He sails, writes spy novels, and always seems very pleased with himself. How did he first come into public view? With a book.

The book was written by the then young Yale graduate who understood that his beloved Yale was filled with liberal professors. He also understood that under the guise of academic freedom, those very liberals were teaching godless humanism. Buckley was not a happy alumnus. *God and Man at Yale* was the result.[8]

His solution to the situation was straightforward enough: Establish a religious orthodoxy at Yale. Because it was a private school, Buckley saw nothing wrong with making religion a requirement. He wanted a Christian Yale. The sentiment was not strong enough to make a Christian Yale, but it was more than enough to make him famous.

For most of you, there is probably nothing so surprising about that. Indeed, it may well be just another idea, and not even a very interesting or original one. And right you are on all counts, unless, of course, you don't happen to be a Christian. If you are not a Christian, the idea might make you a little nervous.

Identity tells us who we are, and who we are not.

Different Gods

Some of you might be going to a religious school and have chapel and prayer meetings and repeated opportunities to have religious experiences. But for most American college students, those things just don't happen.

But one thing that affects everyone is the notion of Truth. Your pursuit of it is probably mentioned somewhere in your college's mission statement. The notion of Truth was accepted much more easily a thousand years ago than it is now. Indeed, Truth with a capital "T" stayed around for a long time. It was only when the gods of science matched—then began to overpower—the gods of religion did the Truth become the truth, and we had to learn about statistical probabilities instead of absolutes.

In the United States, statistics and absolutes, science and religion, fought for domination in the university. Our one nation, under God, has had a fascination with things that require more than faith. We like fast cars, giant metal tubes that take people to the moon and bring them back, powerful computers, rockets that shoot down other rockets. Do you know how a microwave oven works? We spend more time collecting and using things than in practicing religion. We have learned that merely believing in a god does not produce nearly as many things as math and technology do.

The movement from those religious beginnings of colleges to the scientific powerhouses of today was a struggle, in part, about the role of God in finding truth.

One side of the argument is summed up by Daniel Coit Gilman. He wrote that the university should recognize "every where the religious nature of man, considered individually, and the religious basis of the society into which every American is born."[9] The graduate would understand the Truth of life, and be educated in the Bible and the classics. Ideally, a religious spirituality should form the core of college.

As we know, the compulsory and rigid practice of religion found fewer and fewer supporters among students. While the idea of religion remained important, organized religion was never fully accepted. And more than that, the new curriculum of science came into being.

Basically, the biblical God of the New Testament must be accepted on faith. One must believe in God for God to be successful. The Bible is full of information—a full-blown moral code as well as wonderful myths—that is meant to order whole societies. The biblical God does not have to prove His or Her existence. Indeed, those who do not believe in God argue that there is no proof. But believers have faith and through that faith seem to affirm their God.

Should a religious college be built around discovering God's true message? Denominations could differ on the content or how to find the message, but is that how religion and truth merge? In the Presbyterian catalogue it would read: "We want to discover God's true words and in doing so, we will know the Truth." The Baptist catalogue would read: "We want believers to discover how God wants them to live their lives."

The message varies with denominations, but there it is. What could compete with that, especially since doing God's business is what it takes to get to heaven?

Or should colleges with a religious tradition seek to blend it with the world of science? Do standards of scholarly objectivity mesh with the religious dimension of human experience? Most schools with a religious heritage say yes, of course they do.

The actual mixing is often difficult. Because religion matters so much to us, it can be at the core of identity. That can make the search for Truth into a spiritual and godly hunt. How many professors and students have seen this: When we talk in class about subjects such as homosexuality and women's rights, some people will quote the Bible. Right here in a state university, in a very progressive valley, in a state that is noted for being much more liberal than most—right in class, someone will say that the Bible clearly states that being gay is wrong.

Two thoughts are mixed together in the example. One is the general notion that truth is knowable and is perhaps fixed and constant. If that is so, shall we follow science or religion to learn it? A second thought is the notion of right and wrong. Science has its domain of explanation, and religion has its domain—in setting standards for living. You don't have to reject science to follow a biblical injunction.

But what is the relationship between science and religion? Throughout the history of colleges in the United States, it has been more a matter of politics than epistemology. The politics grew heated toward the end of the nineteenth century, when there was a move to include science in a typical course of study. Darwin had written *The Origin of Species*, the English philosopher Herbert Spencer had brought Darwinism to the study of how humans act, and the Bible was in retreat.

People began to practice science without God and they had the optimistic idea that if we studied everything rigorously enough, we would not only understand the world but we could also begin to reshape it. If you believed that the biblical God had already spoken the Truth, then this scientific talk was at once foolish and dangerous.

One of the tricks of science is that its aim is not Truth, or even truth, but predictability. Good science measures things very carefully, counts things very thoroughly, and then gives us the odds that something will happen. And then happen again. It is the most reasonable and rational way to discover what this material world is about.

In the last century, good science was at war with good religion.

In 1870, the National Liberal Reform League was formed. It was established for "the dissemination of liberal sentiment; the opposition to all forms of superstition; the exposition of all fallacious moral and religious doctrines." The League found great fault with "the leading doctrinal teachings of the so-called Catholic and Evangelical Protestant Churches" and encouraged "the mental emancipation of mankind from the trammels of superstition." The League wanted "the triumph of reason and science over faith and theology."[10]

What could be more clear and straightforward than that? It was a fight for what was to be taught in college. More than that, of course, it was a fight about how we were to think and how we were to find meaning in our lives.

We know science won. "Science after Darwin's time was seized with a fever of world conquest; its language must dominate. In correct circles it became bad form to use any word that was tinged with theology. New words were invented; modern psychology was developed. . . . The word 'God' was, of course, taboo, unfair, incorrect, a boorish survival."[11]

The old religion that so dominated our early colleges has been beaten up pretty badly. Science is Lord of the Campus.

We have come to the rational and reasonable college to study the odds. In truth, some people find little comfort in the predictability of science. But if we get no comfort from science, we at least get things. Lots of things. One of the great advantages of science is that it works even if you do not believe in it. Who cares if you believe in electricity? The light goes on when you flip the switch.

But we know that underneath our study of science seems to lurk our willingness to believe in God. Underneath our willingness to befriend many people in college, we continue to define ourselves with our religion—the religion of our parents. One of the ways we live is by associating with "our kind" and not letting too many of the others get too close. By having the category "our kind," we are making a powerful statement about who we are and who others are. "Our kind" is a "them and us" way of thinking about the world. It is a way we define ourselves.

Not Just College

It is not just college that has a religious history. The schools that get people ready for college, primary and secondary schools, have their own religious histories. The search for a balance between religion and science led to big changes in the conduct of schools.

In the 1700s, religion and moral education were straightforward enough. The population was still relatively stable, so it was no problem for a child to learn these things at school, at home, and from others in the community. There was no great rush to make certain the lessons were learned because not much changed and the village had a lifetime to teach moral values. These were stable communities that took many of their values for granted.

Common schools—which are what public schools are—taught common values. It was the Bible. It was Christianity.

By the 1800s, things began to change. The world speeded up and people began to move. Communities were no longer stable. There was the West, and with it came free land, and endless hope, and few rules on the perimeter of village life. There was the sheer adventure of it all. There was running away. Communities broke down and individuals went in search of their own private gods.[12]

Parents and schoolmasters needed to refigure how to make certain this new, wandering generation would Know God and would Understand Moral Goodness.

The job of teaching morality no longer had the luxury of a lifetime project. The new plan was that a rigid right and wrong had to be instilled in a child at a very early age. The task fell first to the mother. "By the plan of creation and the providence of God it is the peculiar duty of the mother, to watch over her child for many of the first years of its life; and on her more than the father rests the responsibility."[13]

The other part of the education was to be done by the common schools. Again, "the business of instruction in schools must be performed by females." The school boards were even willing to forgive a woman "her ignorance of syntax and low level of scholarship" if she had "common sense and a good heart."[14]

Just what were the women of nineteenth-century America to teach? Not surprisingly, they taught a combination of the Protestant ethic and a sense of good citizenship. Students were rewarded for punctuality, regularity, self-restraint, industry, and respect for others. They were punished for sloppiness, inattention, and disorderly behavior.

As in the colleges of that time, religion and morality had a particularly rigid quality. The goal was to somehow implant absolute, inflexible rules in the children that would act as guides to behavior. The thinking was that no matter where these people wandered, this internalized set of rules would guarantee individual virtue and good citizenship.

Children learned that worthwhile achievements came only from "a good conscience, a proper use of opportunities, and a firm belief that God will help those who bravely strive to do their duty."[15] Who knows, you might believe exactly the same thing. Does it have a familiar ring to it? Women as moral agents, rules of behavior to help us do the right thing, and God on our side. Much of our culture seems laced with these beliefs.

By the twentieth century, however, the United States had changed again. Not only were people still moving around, but the very nature of work and organized life was different. Technological sophistication and social change meant people had to act in a different way. To keep up, schools once again had to rethink morality.

One of the first things to go was the rigid set of moral rules. Flexibility replaced inflexibility. All of a sudden, life was divided into different parts. People were expected to act one way at home and another way at work. Even at work, a person might have several roles. In the emerging world, people were judged by their efficiency rather than their reputation, and they were rewarded for their competence and not for their character.[16]

The job of schooling was to help an individual gain the "ability to know what is right in any given situation."[17] It is important to understand just how far this was from the slow-paced moral training of the 1700s. This kind of situational ethics came along about the time that science was conquering colleges. The changing intellectual climate, along with the changing technological and social worlds, meant that there was going to be a fight for who controlled morality and ethics. It was a struggle, in no small part, over how people were to be defined.

Not everyone accepted the changes. Religious fundamentalists have never accepted them, and certainly the old virtues that were once taught are still taught today. But it seems to be a losing proposition. Also, during the middle of the last century, Roman Catholics began their own schools. They were angry that the King James version of the Bible was required reading in common schools.[18] There was even a court case that legalized the reading of the King James version. So the Catholics started their own schools and read their own Bible.

There were Protestants who did not like Catholic schools, or even Catholics, very much. Catholics were newcomers from Ireland, were "foreigners" who came here and flooded the labor markets with their cheap labor. They looked different and had accents. They lived in slums and had what seemed to be a great affinity for their own saloons. And they had their own private schools. They were un-American.

As the common schools strained to accept the various religious groups, the Catholic schools kept their faith. As public schools pressed for situational ethics, Catholic schools pinned their hopes on faith, hope, and charity. Right now, almost 15 percent of the elementary and secondary school population is enrolled in Catholic schools.

Slowly, God has been forced out of our public schools. Beginning in the 1960s, the courts have seriously tried to sort out what religion is and what belongs in the public schools. For example, the courts decided it was illegal to read the

Bible in school (unless it was for literary purposes). They decided that it was illegal to teach transcendental meditation—unless it was part of a comparative religion class. The Court has tried to take religion out of public school.

It makes sense for the Court to act this way. The First Amendment does prohibit the state from establishing a religion. The Court adopted a test to see whether a state action does establish a religion.[19] It comes in three parts:

1. Does the action pursue a secular purpose?
2. Does the action primarily have a secular effect?
3. Does the action avoid excessive entanglement between government and religion?

If the Court can answer "yes" to all three questions, then the action is permitted. Under this test, praying in schools is against the law. Teaching the Ten Commandments is against the law.

So where does that leave us? Do schools no longer teach about right and wrong? Many parents want the schools to contribute to their children's moral development, but it has to take place within the law. The long history of teaching morality in schools is not likely to dry up because of the Supreme Court.

One example of the compromise found in the public schools comes from Lawrence Kohlberg's ideas about moral development. According to his theory, children go through developmental stages of moral development. Educators are supposed to teach the appropriate level of virtue for each age group. Kohlberg is a behavioral scientist who believes specific rules are nothing but "a bag of virtues."[20]

We now learn things like values clarification. The logic is something like this: Real values are supposed to be taught by the family and organized religion. It then becomes the role of the school to teach the student to clarify his or her own values. One of the amazing things about values clarification is that those who endorse it claim that it is value-free. It is as if a method carries no values. It is as if the "skill" of "making choices on one's own, without depending on others" does not rest firmly on a value choice.[21] This "skill," to take it one small step, has nothing to do with community and everything to do with individualism. Is that a value? Maybe it is a very, very big value. In terms of community, it is the original sin.

In one form or another, we get moral development and values clarification from our public schools. We get God and morality from home and religion. And we get to college and figure out pretty quickly that they don't quite fit.

Old Slick down the hall "processes" life really well. He can talk you into almost anything. He has passed through all of the levels of development and has the skills of a clarifier. But can you trust Old Slick? Deep down, do we believe that we can process morals?

When the world of college opens up opportunities that you rarely imagined when you lived at home, how long does it take you to think about religion? What happens when all of a sudden nothing seems clear and just about everything (including yourself) seems out of control? The priests on campus say that business picks up by the middle of October. The people at the counseling center say the same thing.

For all of those who are lost and alone, there are those who seem to seek their identity by picking on people who are different. Anti-Semitism is up, for example. Some people burned a cross on the campus of Amherst College a few years ago. Now that's a religious statement. Did someone find comfort in it?

In the Pacific Northwest, there is a white Christian group that calls itself the Aryan Nation. No values clarification for them. They understand all about blacks, Jews, Catholics, and the rest of the unchosen. There are no Buddhas on their mantels. Believe it.

So here you are at college. You want to like everybody. You want everyone to like you. You want everybody to believe whatever they want to believe. You would like to be able to make no judgments about other religions. But it seems harder than you imagined. After much thinking, you figure out that before you can be comfortable with others, you have to be comfortable with yourself.

A sense of what is right and what is wrong helps you to be comfortable in your own skin. As you sort out right from wrong, what should enter into your ideas but religion. Religion, with God serving as the background. And if you keep at the idea, you begin to see that religion really does form a sense of who you are.

And for some strange reason, you sometimes feel much more comfortable with people who think like you do.

And the world slowly transforms itself back into an "us and them" place.

My God.

— 4 —

Class

U.S. education is by no means an inept, disordered mis-construction. It is an ice-cold and superb machine. It does the job: not mine, not yours perhaps, but that for which it was originally conceived.

—Jonathan Kozol

To suppose, as we all suppose, that we could be rich and not behave the way the rich behave, is like saying that we could drink all day and stay sober.

—L. P. Smith

There are ways in which others judge us—and we judge others—according to socioeconomic class. Although judging according to class is common, it is surprisingly difficult to discuss. It is difficult because the concept of class is not a popular one in the United States. In a nation that is devoted to individualism, the notion of class is unwelcome.

In this chapter, we will suggest that there are several ways to understand socioeconomic classes. We will see that there are class differences throughout our education system. Public education does not mean equal education. The rich and the poor are educated differently, and we will speculate about what that means.

We will look at the differences between colleges as well as differences on campuses. Class differences often take root on campus. The college we attend and the major we choose may have lasting effects.

There are two underlying issues in this chapter. First, what is the relationship between socioeconomic classes, equality, and excellence? Each of these is an important element in American life, and each takes on a particular meaning in education. The second issue revolves around how a person's identity is tied to money and social status. When we think about diversity and identity, we must think about the role that money and social status play. It is one of the most important factors in understanding what we, as a people, are about.

Why class? It's always safe to answer a question with another question, so the next question is this: If you are a Hispanic, are married, take two night courses a semester at a community college, and work full-time during the day, do you have more in common with (1) a Hispanic who went to a prep school and goes to Harvard, (2) a native Mexican who is graduating from the University of Mexico and going to do doctoral work at Stanford next year, or (3) the white person sitting next to you who works full-time, is married, and takes two night classes a semester?

That is not a trick question.

If you have taken a sociology course, you know that there are all kinds of formal proofs that tell us about class. But you don't have to take a sociology course to know about classes. If you simply read the newspapers, it is easy enough to find examples of how class is played out in the United States.

For example, not long ago management at the Copley Plaza Hotel in Boston told their maids not to use mops to clean the bathroom floors. No, the maids were told to get on their hands and knees and scrub those floors.[1]

The union filed a grievance. The management, seemingly very unimpressed, issued this statement: "A maid is a maid and this is what she has to do." That certainly seems clear enough.

Is it just possible that the message here is that one class has to do painful and unpleasant work so that another class can have a sparkling bathroom? Maybe so.

Or, what do you make of a rich couple that could not have a baby? They found a truck driver's wife, who was having financial problems, and paid her $10,000 for the services of her womb. Do you honestly believe that if the rich Sterns and the poor Whiteheads had similar incomes, Mary Beth Whitehead would have sold the use of her womb for nine months? Is this a sign that there are classes in America?[2]

Or, finally, we can talk about incomes. Here we have a chance to see anything we want to see. It is easy to see that there are classes.[3] If we agree that it takes about $40,000 a year to live a relatively comfortable middle-class life (comfortable, but certainly not the Copley), then we are appalled to find that more than 65 percent of the households make less than $40,000. This means that 65 percent of the people are in economic trouble.

On the other hand, it is easy to see how middle-class we all are. If we define economic want for a family of four at $20,000 or less a year, then it will be satisfying to know that almost 60 percent of households make between $20,000 and $100,000 a year. That makes most of us middle-class. Lucky us.

The figures do not lie: Either two-thirds of us are in trouble or two-thirds of us are in good shape.

One of the central lessons of the chapter is this: Class is part of identity. How you think of yourself—whether it is working class, middle class, a cut above middle class, or as part of an elite—class forms our view of ourselves and other people.

When I was growing up, I knew a nice younger kid who was just a little boring and didn't get into the right social club. Kind of a nerd. This kid has grown up. He still looks pudgy in the pictures I've seen. And he bought RJR Nabisco for more than $24 billion. Is he now above me in social class, or does he just have more money than I do, and, deep in my heart, do I still feel that he is kind of a nerd?

We think about class, and it is part of our identity. Others think about class, and use it to identify us.

In Chapter 3 and here, on the curious topics of class and religion, we see this interplay between facts and belief—much of our diversity revolves around belief, and that belief revolves around what is most advantageous. One of the very difficult things about accepting diversity is admitting the possibility that some of our most dearly held beliefs may make us narrow-minded and socially dangerous.

Seeing Class

You might read about or study class during college, but you should know that in America, there is a big division on how to study class. There are two strains of class studies. One comes from Karl Marx, and the other comes from Max Weber.

Marx wrote that class has to do with the organization of production in a society. The people who own property and capital get to decide what to do with the surplus (the surplus being the wealth over and above what it takes to feed and house people at some basic level). In late twentieth-century America, for example, the owners of property and capital build themselves big houses and big glass-and-steel office buildings. They own planes, summer and winter homes, expensive cars, and the like. People who believe in capitalism believe the rich deserve what they have. In the last decade, the richest 1 percent of households saw their income grow by more than 90 percent, and the lowest 90 percent of households saw their income grow by 4 percent (both figures adjusted for inflation).

For Marx and his followers, the roots of these inequalities are not in individualism. The conflict is one class versus another, and at stake is social power—control of the economy (that question of who gets to spend the surplus), status, law, and ideological spoils.

Modern followers of Marx often focus on objective class interests. That means an upper class wants to control something, and a lower class wants to control it too. They fight over it. One of the things they can fight over is access to a good education. Both want it, and both will struggle to see that they get more of it. Here is a question that tests your class position: How would you like it if admission into all colleges were based solely on test scores and grades, regardless of which colleges your parents attended, how much money they had, and so on? It is a question that brings issues of justice and advantage to the surface.

Max Weber gave us a different way to see class, partly in response to the Marxist view. For Weber, the class picture wasn't about large social classes fighting one another but individuals looking for status. True, status takes place in a context of institutions (it is higher status to work at Harvard than at Green River Community College), but your status rests in you as a person.

For Weber, status can be conveyed by family, occupation, region of the country, and other things. The higher-status people will be those who are able to find careers and social standing closest to the centers of power in a society. In late twentieth-century America, those centers of power are the institutions that make and interpret the rule of law and that operate the larger or faster-growing corporations. In medieval Europe, they were the church and the royal court.

Modern followers of Weber like the relative simplicity of measuring class his way. You can count how much money a person makes, and that is a way of seeing class which can be compared to other people. This approach also deemphasizes the larger Marxist picture of social conflict surrounding our institutions. Followers of Weber don't deny that this larger pattern of conflict happens; they just don't think it matters very much.

Since the breakup of the Soviet Union, Marxism has lost much of its power. We in the United States, being firmly committed to individualism, have always been more Weberian. But who was really right?

This is neither a Marxian nor a Weberian chapter. Sometimes you are asked to think about yourself in comparison to other people. Sometimes you are asked to look at the larger trends surrounding the individuals and how those individuals fall into classes.

You might find that part of your idea of class is tied up with identity. If you believe in equality and think we have a lot of it, it is hard to take Marx seriously. If you believe that the rich put up barriers that keep you from important things, it is hard to take Weber seriously.

Classes in School

One of the things that makes the idea of social class so distasteful is that we do not like the thought that some people are more equal than others. Our individualism demands that we believe we are all equal. The maid who is using a toothbrush to clean the hotel bathroom is every bit as equal as the $24 billion guy who just flew into Boston in his private plane, was picked up at the airport in his stretch limo, and was taken to a suite that had a really clean bathroom. Equal as they can be. Peas in a pod.

Our individualism, if it doesn't quite go that far, at least says that we all should have an equal chance. The maid probably did not go to college but the billionaire did. Was education the difference? Don't be silly. Probably the biggest difference was that the billionaire began his life as a multimillionaire. An aunt of his once told me that it would have been hard for him not to get richer. She said he would not have enough time in his life to spend all of the money that he inherited.

Well, our individualism says, some people do start off better than others, but at least each of us can get an education and be a member of the middle class. That may or may not be true. But even if it is, it would be foolish to buy into the myth that all education is equal. It is not equal on any single campus and it certainly is not equal between campuses.

When you choose a major, you are making an interesting choice. In order to understand a little about that choice, I would like for you to do a fairly simple exercise. The exercise is to conduct an unscientific, very casual survey.[4] Go out and find people who you don't know and ask them to rank different majors: what major is hard, what is easy, what is impressive, what is foolish. You will find that all majors were not created equal.

At the top are the pre-meds, the math majors, and sometimes the business majors. At the bottom are the communications majors, the education majors, and the sports management majors. Each campus is a little different depending on certain professors, but basically that is the way the biases sort themselves out. People who are training to teach the next generation of children are near the bottom in status. People who are training to earn money are near the top. Does that turn out to be true at your campus?

Now that the unscientific results are in, do some casual empiricism. Just look around. Do the biology majors hang around with the communications majors? Do the math majors talk to the people majoring in elementary ed? No and no.[5] Some majors just seem better than other majors, and people are already sorting themselves out by what they are studying and what job they are training to do.

Are these socioeconomic classes in the making? Do the classes you take have an effect on the class you will enter? Are different social groupings really social classes? If they walk like a class and talk like a class, do we really have to call them a class?

If there is a hierarchy on campus, just think what it is like between campuses. We all know that some schools are "better" than other schools. Graduates from top colleges and universities are given preferential treatment. That is no surprise to anyone.

What do you think about that? Is it fair? The American way? Would you like to invent something different? Fantasy time: Imagine a system in which every university, college, and community college had exactly the same entrance requirements. To get accepted, every student would send his or her application to a central office. The student would be either accepted or rejected. In or out.

The next step would be to put the names of all those students who were accepted into a huge bowl. Then you would have the drawing.[6]

The drawing could be held in any number of ways. Maybe the first three names drawn would go to the University of Alabama, the next three to Dade County Community College, the next three to St. Mary's College, and so on. The benefits are obvious. In the long run, the sheer randomness of the process would give each school diversity in every imaginable way. Race, gender, religion, interests, intelligence, geographical origin, and so on. Genuine diversity.

Randomness would break the lock that alums have on the upper-level schools. It would be true equal opportunity. The daughter of the factory worker would have as much chance to go to Pomona as the daughter of the owner of the factory.

What do you say? Do you like the idea, or is it offensive? Aren't we equal?

But there you are, thinking about genuine equality and a thought occurs to you. What about, you think, the whole idea of excellence? Isn't education, at least in principle, supposed to be about excellence? Would anything ever be thought of, built, discovered, or accomplished if we had some screwy system that sent a lot of jocks and lit majors to the Massachusetts Institute of Technology and people who wanted to be electrical engineers to St. John's to study the classics? Get serious.

Of course, you would have a point. Equality and excellence seem to be every bit as compatible as oil and water. But what if we, as a nation, want to believe in both? Can we have it both ways?

Schooling

We now have these three things on the table: socioeconomic classes, equality, and excellence. Equality seems to be at war with the other two. Also, socioeconomic classes do not necessarily have anything in common with excellence. Wealth and excellence are not the same thing. To understand something about schooling (and here I mean school up to college) will help us see these three themes more clearly.

In the quote that opened this chapter, Jonathan Kozol wrote that school was "an ice-cold and superb machine. It does the job."[7] Does that sound right? Just what job does Kozol mean? After all, it doesn't seem like public schools are turning out very well-educated people. While we know that people in rich school districts get the best public school education, the general impression is that very few public schools are first-rate.

What's going on?

The answer seems to be that schools may not be in the business of providing the kind of education you might think. Sam Bowles argues that (1) schools in the United States evolved to meet the needs of a disciplined and skilled work force, (2) inequalities in school systems have become more important in order to reproduce the class structure from one generation to another, and (3) the school system is pervaded by class inequalities that have shown little sign of diminishing over the last half-century.[8]

Could that be true? In 1987, the U.S. Department of Education published the following figures. In terms of social class, 56 percent of the people in the richest quarter of the population go to college; 32 percent of the people in the bottom quarter go to college. The richest people go to "better" colleges. So the Department of Education seems to add some weight to Bowles's argument.

In a recent survey, John Goodlad talked to students, parents, and teachers about how they understood school and college. He concluded that there were four different goals in schooling: vocational, social, intellectual, and personal.[9] Goodlad found that, by the time students got to high school, parents wanted their kids to learn academic skills, while the school was set up to help prepare the students for jobs. A genuine split in private desires and public goals.

That split is taken up by Joel Spring, who modifies the argument and concludes that there are three major goals of schooling: political, social, and economic gain. He writes that "the most important political goals of public schooling are educating citizens, selecting future political leaders, creating political consensus, maintaining political power, and socializing individuals for political citizens."[10] This should come as no great surprise. It is difficult to think of any group that does not try to educate its young in the things it believes are right and good. Politics may well be the center of all public education.

Spring also argues that there are social purposes of schooling. "The major social purposes of education are social control, improving social conditions, and reducing social tensions caused by economic inequalities."[11] Education, in this sense, is the way the country tries to teach people to live together. The logic is that if we can provide an education for everyone—from Head Start through high school or even college—then we will be able to break the cycle of poverty so many Americans are in.

That is easy enough to understand. The young person who drops out of school an illiterate doesn't have much of a chance of making it in America. What can such a person do? Selling drugs is one job opportunity. Robbing stores is another. For the unskilled and uneducated, a large number of minimum-wage jobs are waiting. But the point is that a good education can socialize the person into the system and teach him or her certain civic and economic skills.

It seems that we all either believe that or want to believe that. We also know that so far it hasn't seemed to work. Although some break the circle of poverty through education, most do not. Why not? We agree that it is a good idea to change people through education. Probably the easiest and best answer is that we have yet to fund education well enough. That sounds simple, but is it true? Do we spend less on education than, for example, other rich democratic countries? That's fairly easy to check.

There is another problem, one that we don't have a clue about solving. It does not matter what kind of education you have if there are no jobs. In an economic recession, a high school degree is not a sure bet to get you out of poverty. Neither is a college degree.

Tied closely to socialization are the economic purposes of schooling. School "increases national wealth and advances technological development."[12] Public schools are able to teach students how to fit into our complex modern organizations, and help sort and train the labor force. To show how this economic dynamic works, Spring used George Bush's 1990 State of the Union address. Candidate George (prep school and Yale) Bush campaigned to be our "education President."

Bush outlined plans for schools. These are the goals he wanted to achieve by the year 2000: (1) All students would start school ready to learn, (2) the high school graduation rate would be 90 percent, (3) all students had to demonstrate competence in critical subjects, (4) U.S. students would be first in the world in math and science achievement, (5) every adult would be literate and have skills to compete in the economy, and (6) schools would be free from drugs and violence.

Spring wants us to look closely at that list while keeping this in mind: International economic competition is getting stronger, and our entering workforce is getting smaller. Spring argues that what Bush really wanted was for education to produce good economic citizens. He wanted people who can compete in the modern workplace. Spring tells us that the whole list is about economics, except the part dealing with drugs and violence. Because drugs and violence make it tough to learn, they should be eliminated.

In the mid-eighties, the Carnegie Foundation funded studies on schooling and college.[13] Its findings are in line with what we have seen. In the category of "reasons for going to college," 90 percent of the college-bound high school students said they were going in order "to have a more satisfying career." Eighty-eight percent of the parents agreed. A satisfying career was the top choice for both students and parents. Twenty-seven percent of the students wanted to go to college to "become a more thoughtful, more responsible citizen." Twenty-eight percent of their parents thought that was important. And the very best way to judge a college? Students and parents agree: "If a college has a good reputation, its graduates usually get better jobs." Better jobs were at the top of the list. All of this seems to suggest that when you were in high school there was a not-too-subtle focus on training you for work in our modern economy. And how did you choose the college you are in? Was it pure economics—are you at the school that you can afford? Or is it the best school you can afford that will help you get into a good career? Or is it the school that will teach you the most? Do you really want to graduate well-educated but unable to do anything?

Are you in a school where the parents of most students have about the same amount of money? Is it a solid, middle-class state school or a full-range community college or an elite school that has a ton of economic aid as well as some very rich students? Is it a private "finishing" school for people who will go into the family business?

And what about your professors? Were they hired to be good teachers, or were they hired to publish and be major players in their academic fields, or are they just putting in time before they retire? Does it matter what they teach and why you are there? Is it a class difference?

When you unpacked the metaphoric station wagon that first day, you unpacked your high school education. You also unpacked the not-so-subtle messages that your high school taught you. In order to understand those messages better, it is important to study high school a little more closely.

High School

We aspired to high school. It was the freedom we dreamed about. Finally a car (or at least someone who you knew had a car) and serious dates and sports and parties and what to do about birth control. It was the beginning of the final showdown with your parents. Whether they liked it or not, they had to start treating you more like an adult.

From grade school—when you had high school people as baby-sitters—it seemed like high school was Very Big Time.

And it certainly was . . . at least for a while.

Depending on the group you ran around with, and how you were tracked in classes, and how much pressure you got from home, and how much trouble (or awards) you got, high school was marginally good or terrible. It was the time of cliques and being awkward and trying to grow up. Hormones were racing through students' bodies at uneven rates. Some ninth-graders were women and some seniors still didn't have to shave. High school was unfair in just about every way you could think of.

In Chapter 1 we noted that the structure of high schools differs from neighborhood to neighborhood.[14] These differences have everything to do with money and social class. The poor neighborhoods run crack-down, in-your-face, military-tough schools. Bathroom passes and weapons searches at the door. Not the kind of school that sends many students to college.

The teaching in these schools is generally very mechanical. It involves "rote behavior and very little decision making or choice." There are few explanations, not much effort to make connections between different assignments or attempts to explain the ideas or significance behind what is being taught. They are the classes from hell.

The suburbs offer a mixed education. The top-level students take college prep classes, get good counseling, and have their silly childhood mistakes forgotten. College is taken for granted. Students in the other levels are urged to continue their education somewhere. The whole focus of school is to produce good, hard-working, solid citizens. And that is what happens, unless you get strung out on drugs, or get pregnant, or run away.

Middle-class schools are about getting the right answer. Enough right answers equals a good grade. If you follow directions, and do some figuring and make the right choices, then you will succeed. In the more affluent schools, work "is a creative activity carried out independently. Students are constantly asked their opinions and are made to apply ideas and concepts to different situations. If a right answer is called for, and the student doesn't get it, the teachers' response is: 'Think about it some more.'"[15]

Private schools offer an entirely different kind of structure. It is about preparing people for college and, if successful, for leadership positions. In their way, these schools are tougher than the schools at the bottom of the scale. People have to work, but the payoffs are big. The reward for most of the students in the poor schools is that they do not have to go to school anymore. And why would they want to? The reward for the private school graduates is a network of powerful friends, a good college, and a head start in life.

In the executive elite school, work is developing one's analytical intellectual powers. Children are continually asked to reason through a problem, to produce intellectual products that are both logically sound and of top academic quality. A primary goal of thought is to conceptualize rules by which elements may fit together in systems, and then to apply these rules in solving a problem. School work helps one to achieve, to excel, to prepare for life.[16]

There is, then, a structure of school and a structure of how each class operates. People are organized in a certain way, and so too is learning. Did you come out of high school smarter or dumber than when you went in? If you were asked to recruit people for your college, how impressed would you be with people who spent four years learning to do things in a mechanical way, learning things by the numbers? Not very? Not at all?

What does this mean? Does it mean that although we have public education in the United States, we do not have equal education? Does it mean that we really are stuck? Is it all so one-sided?

Not really. We know that things in the United States are more complicated and even better than that. We see examples of people from the poorest backgrounds make it to the top. People from all different kinds of high schools go to all different kinds of colleges and then go out and do well. From the outhouse to the penthouse, as the trite old saying goes.

And some rich people lose their money. And the fool from prep school down the hall is a dunce and will never amount to anything. And the 32-year-old divorced mother of two may turn out to be a great lawyer or doctor or nurse—all because she went back to school, worked hard, and got the degree.

All of those things are true. Very true. Ours is a society in which elites circulate; the elite strata are permeable. It is possible (at least in principle) for some to break into the very highest levels of power, money, and social life. Individuals do it all of the time, or so it seems. The California Institute of Technology wants math brains, and it doesn't care where they come from. Hollywood wants beautiful and handsome flesh, and it doesn't care where it comes from. General Motors wants a CEO who knows how to make money, and it doesn't care what kind of family that person comes from.

So there! High school be damned. Even college be damned. You can make it in America.

That may be true, but is it the whole truth? Do you think that it's just random chance that almost everyone who goes to prep school then goes to college? Random chance that most inner-city kids are lucky to get a high school degree and then do not do well on their college boards—well, those few who actually take college boards? And how surprised are you that children of college-educated parents are more likely to go to college than children of parents who did not go to college?

There are overwhelming statistics on the one hand and our strong and equally overwhelming belief system on the other hand.

The richer we are, the better our chances of succeeding. The poorer we are, the greater our chances of staying poor. Don't we already know this?

There we are, lugging what we know and what we feel up the stairs of our college buildings. Are you going to take over your family business when you graduate? Can your parent, the doctor, help you get into medical school when the time comes? Are you going to spend years paying back the loans you are taking out for college?

What was your high school education like? Did you learn to sit in your seat for 50 minutes? Learn how to take standardized tests? Learn to memorize? Learn shortcuts to learning? Learn about sex, drugs, and drinking? Learn to conceptualize and make connections between the different ideas you were learning? Learn about friendships and the agony of rejection? Learn that your parents were human, your siblings were people, and your goals in life would be easier to reach if you were born rich?

It might be helpful to ask yourself, right now, what you believe about education and class and fairness in America. On balance, is life fair? Does education give people the opportunity to improve themselves? Do enough people have access to that opportunity? While you are answering those, try these as well. Is your identity tied to money and social status? Do you judge those around you by their wealth or position?

All of these questions, all of this frantic contradiction between fact and belief, is central to identity. Education seems to sit in the middle, sits right there between what we know are facts and what we want to be true. Education is a way out. A good education at a good school can be a ticket to escape a lower social class. That is simply the truth. It might even be a ticket to a more thoughtful and interesting life.

There are two examples that might be helpful. The first is about our faith in schooling. At its nub, it is about having faith in what good schooling can do.

There is a program named A Better Chance, Inc. that was started in 1963.[17] It was founded by a group of Ivy League administrators and prep-school headmasters in order to send lower-middle-class and lower-class minorities to prep schools. In order for the Ivy League schools to recruit more minorities, they needed a kind of farm system from which to pick.

ABC, as the program is called, was to find bright minorities, send them to prep schools, give them aid and comfort during those years, and prepare them for an elite college. It was a wonderful way to give people a chance to succeed.

Over the years, more than 7,000 students have graduated from ABC. It has been a remarkable program and it stands as a tribute to how we feel about the power of education.

It is important to understand that ABC needed to do more than merely find the right students and pay their way through a private high school. These students were sent away from home and into a very white and very elite setting. Being black at some of those schools can be a remarkably difficult experience—and that is over and above the tough enough job of just staying in school. ABC had to provide support so that those students could cope and adjust.

Many of the ABC students went to elite colleges and have done very well. These are bright and talented people who were given a chance and who made good. They were able to jump social classes because they were given an educational opportunity.

School worked just the way we visualize it working: bright students bettering themselves by first doing well in school. Education as a proving ground, school as a place where skills are tested and rewarded.

Consider the huge flip side of this particular coin: the more than 7,000 students in about 30 years who were chosen to be given a chance, and the tens of millions who were sentenced to hard time in a ghetto school. The fact is that school really can work, at least for the few.

On the other hand, we have the Bohemian Club.[18] Now that's a bunch.

It is a club that has 600 members. You are nominated for membership at birth, and if you are very lucky you are accepted by the time you are in your mid-forties. The high-light of the year is a three-week summer get-together when each member (all men, of course) brings a guest to their little place in the California woods—Bohemian Grove.

There they are, the elite. The power. The Who's Who of American business and commerce. A gathering place of lim-ousines and private jets. Tucked away in the woods, these men of means are free to be themselves, to talk business or talk dirty or gamble, or visit the open-only-once-a-year broth-els. The guests might include a former or current president of the United States. While presidents come and go, the Bohemian Club stays selective and elite.

They have all kinds of entertainment. Swimming and boating and talks and even plays. The plays cost up to $30,000 per production. That is a one-time, one-night stand. They bring in people for informal chats and briefings: Nixon while he was President, Bobby Kennedy while he was Attorney General, Neil Armstrong after he returned from the moon. They hear about art and literature and science and politics. Just the powerful old boys, bonding. Not a bad way to spend time.

To read about this self-conscious meeting of the rich and powerful is to again begin to acknowledge that there are social classes in America. My dad did many things for me, but I don't think it crossed his mind to nominate me for membership in the Bohemian Club. I don't know if Dad even knew about it.

But it is there. As active as ABC and certainly more potent.

And would you even want to be a member of the Bohemian Club? Why would you? Why not?

And how do you feel about it if you are a woman? Does it make you feel good to think that the Giants of American Com-merce can just be boys once a year? Does it endear them to you? Or does it reconfirm your suspicion that men never really mature; they just age?

Classes and Education

If we really believe that education can solve class problems, what would it take to eradicate poverty by using education?

To answer that, we have to understand how much poverty there is in the United States.

First of all, there is persistent poverty in the United States. The more important way to put it is probably this: We thought there would be less poverty by now.

People have studied poverty a great deal, and there is some consensus about it.[19] The poor are very diverse—many colors, many different kinds of households and families, poor for many different lengths of time. It is true that some situations make it much more likely for someone to be poor. If you are black, a child under the age of 18 living in a female-headed family, an unwed mother of very young children, or all of the above, you have a much greater chance of being poor than do other people. A lot of poverty is temporary. The best predictor of staying in poverty is whether you came from a poor family. More poor people live together in smaller geographic areas, and for these people, who have fewer contacts with middle-class people, getting out of poverty is unlikely.

Since the 1960s, when many antipoverty programs were invented or grew, income poverty (a measure of poverty that does not take account of payments received from government) has declined only slightly. Relative poverty has grown by some measures. For example, the top 4 percent earned as much as the poorest 35 percent of the population in 1959. By 1989, the top 4 percent had earned as much as the poorest 51 percent. In another 10 years, the top 4 percent will probably earn as much as the poorest 60 percent. The distance between the very rich and the rest is growing. Yet recall the figures earlier in the chapter: If we think of middle class as all of those above the poverty line and below $100,000, that group has grown in relative terms. While we can say that the richest and the poorest are growing farther apart, the middle seems to be swelling.

Although income poverty has declined slightly, the poor, those below the poverty line, get much more health care and other services than they did in the 1960s. The big success story is with the elderly poor. Their poverty has been cut by more than half during the last quarter-century.

Two last pieces of agreement among poverty researchers: We can't tell how much antipoverty programs have really decreased poverty, although some progress has been made. And we really don't know what causes poverty. How much is the result of macroeconomic failures, such as high unemployment? How much is an outcome of class, of people treated differently because of sex, race, family background, and age? How much is genetic or cultural inheritance? How much is due to birth defects brought on by parents who smoke and drink and take other drugs? How much is lack of the right services, such as education? How much is from bad choices?

No one knows the answers to those questions. When you hear an answer, you are hearing an opinion. It is likely that class has an effect on how we see class. Many people who have worked very hard for a small bit of security may justly feel that those who work less deserve less. It is possible that middle-class academics do not want to hear that much of the antipoverty program money ends up in middle-class pockets. People who see race and sex figure in employment decisions may regard those facts as the main feature of our economy.

Christopher Jencks and Paul Peterson summarize some of the evidence about poverty research and how it contradicts widely held beliefs about the poor:[20]

> Many believe that the percentage of the population persistently poor is large and rapidly increasing, that more and more unmarried teenage girls are bearing children, and that welfare rolls are exploding. It is frequently alleged that crime is on the increase, young people are dropping out of school in record numbers, and higher percentages of the population are withdrawing from the labor force. The poor are also said to be increasingly isolated in ghettos at the cores of our metropolitan areas.
>
> Yet none of these propositions is true.

The toughest poverty cases—those who live in neighborhoods where more than 40 percent of the residents are poor—amount to only about 1 percent of the poor. The biggest problem is a rise in children living in poverty, and most of them are in female-headed households. The young men who in earlier decades would live in those households and bring up the income of those families now earn less and work less than in previous decades. From an economic view, they are not marriage material.

Whatever your view of poverty, it is hard to see how education alone is going to make more jobs for these people. Education may have a lot to do with passing along the ability to live and earn at a certain level, but there isn't enough evidence to suggest that it can be used as an antipoverty program. At least, not the way we do education.

Diversity and Class

Do you believe that there are social classes in the United States, or do we simply have socioeconomic inequalities that seem to persist? Is it to your advantage to believe in social classes? Probably not. After all, if you do really well as an undergraduate and then do really well in some graduate program, there is every reason to hope that you will be on life's better track.

Is it to your advantage to ignore the remarkable inequalities? Or is it foolish to do so? Do you aspire to be asked to the Bohemian Grove some summer as a guest? Would you like to be in a position to have your son put on the membership list?

And what about the mix of equality, education, and excellence? Education seems to be the most obvious place to even the odds. Yet we saw that education seems to be the very place where we perpetuate inequality. Education, in many cases, helps keep people in the place their parents are in.

If you were going to invent a school system, is this the system you would invent? Would it be about work and jobs and social class? Maybe so. In your school system, would excellence ever come into play? Would the life of the mind be able to compete with Friday night?

Is education the place to solve social problems? And if it is, how? We use education to make up for the sins of our past. It can work. But one of the problems is that there does not seem to be enough good education to go around. What would you do as head of admissions for your college? If there is one place left in the incoming class, will you punish a middle-class person by accepting the equally qualified lower-class person? We will return to this topic in Chapter 10.

Different programs around the country are trying to provide better high school education.[21] Simon's Rock of Bard College, in Great Barrington, Massachusetts, takes bright and mature students after the tenth grade and lets them do college work. High school students in Berkeley, California, can take courses at the university, and those in Northampton, Massachusetts, can take classes at Smith College.

And every once in a while, a rich person will "adopt" a class of students in a ghetto school and promise to pay for their college education if they make the grades.

But those things happen on the fringes. Most of us, most of the time, muck around with the problems we had no hand in making. We went to the schools closest to our house, and those schools reflected the income of the neighborhood. The way we were taught had a lot to do with what our parents earned. There is much to be said about neighborhood schools—much good and much bad.

But here we are in college. Why? So that we can get a better job and earn more money? That is certainly understandable, but is education all about socioeconomic classes? Are we in school only to keep our place in the hierarchy, or move up a class or two?

College is not about excellence, equality, or socioeconomic classes—it is about all of these things. Until we each figure out exactly why we are in college, these three dynamics will be at war.

—5—

Gender Issues

I was discussing my work in a public setting, when a professor cut me off and asked me if I had freckles all over my body.

—an anonymous female student
quoted in *The Classroom Climate: A Chilly One for Women*

[M]ankind should all be educated after the same model, or the intercourse of the sexes will never deserve the name of fellowship, nor will women ever fulfill the peculiar duties of their sex, till they become enlightened citizens, till they become free by being enabled to earn their own subsistence, independent of men.

—Mary Wollstonecraft (1792)

S ex is one of the core parts of diversity and identity. This and the next chapter explore this part of who—or what—gets to define a person's identity.

The first question we ask you to consider is this: Are women and men really opposite sexes? We will look at the question by looking at the roles biology and society play in differentiating the sexes.

We review the history of women in higher education in the United States. We then discuss what everyday life is like for women going to college, and end the chapter with some common stereotypes of female students.

A case can be made that college life, college classes, and even the college campus are different for women and for men. In this chapter, we ask you to understand why this is the case.

This is very strange. Common sense seems to indicate that because our topic is diversity, we would concentrate on minorities of one kind or another. But this chapter is not about a minority at all. It is about women, the people who make up 51 percent of the population. One of the issues we have to understand is why this majority is treated like a minority. It should strike us as strange that the category "women" often means lesser status—less reason, less power, less money, less capability. Somehow, the majority is not the group that defines what is "normal."

In this chapter, we ask you to think about the status of women as an issue of identity, about who gets to define people, and about what is the content of that identity. At one level, it is clear that women and men do see the campus and campus life differently. We look at those differences as a subset of a wider debate on differences between women and men. The construction of identity may depend on how we see the relative contributions of biology and society to what we call women and men. Different views of those issues lead to distinct views of how we should organize colleges and work. There are meaningful biological differences between the sexes, but a history of women in higher education and accounts of attitudes and behavior on today's college campuses suggest that stereotypes powerfully shape the status of women and men. Some of the complications surrounding the status of women are explored in a section on sexual harassment. This chapter ends with unfinished business about women and men beyond the college campus, which is the subject of the next chapter.

If we use a circle metaphor of identity, it alerts us to a problem in understanding why this group, the majority, is not treated as the norm. Again, imagine the circle of 20 identical people, all different parts of one person's identity. There are a color part, an education part, a religion part, and so on. When someone breaks into the circle, what does he or she see most clearly? What is dim? Someone breaking into the circle might not see much more than a potential sex partner. Or the intruder might see a mom or potential mom. He or she may not see the many ways the person who is that circle wants to be seen or may see herself. In the two possibilities mentioned here, someone who sees mainly potential sex partners and potential moms will probably not notice the numerous differences among women. The standards of how we see ourselves, among our many possible features, have something to do with those who break into the circle.

One very common way of making sense of the status of women is to compare two simple pictures, presented as the way things used to be and the possibilities of today. The imagery here is out of popular culture and is found in many magazines, on television, in films, and in everyday conversations. The images are these: Women used to have a subordinate place in society, and now the ambitious, fully free women can have it all—career, kids, and a little power to exercise.

The images make us miss a lot of important parts of identity. To see women historically as subordinate is too simple and obscures what women in every society have accomplished. One of the important outcomes of the feminist movement of the late twentieth century has been the growth of fields such as history and literature to chronicle and help us understand women's activities.

The image of the have-it-all woman is also too simple. Having it all means, in part, letting others define identity. A woman may have to be all things to all people—the one who relates, a mate's lover, mother of children, keeper of the household, the person who knows which vaccinations the kids and pets have had, the mother who bakes and transports and reads bedtime stories, the career woman who makes lots of money, the aggressive and feminine athlete. It is a long list. If the list is a part of the expectations of those breaking into the circle of identity, those who love being mothers might believe they are not held in as much esteem as those who go to a job every day. Those who go to the job can be jealous of the mothers who have time for their kids. The ticking of the biological clock is now a cultural icon.

Neither stereotype, the subordinate woman or the super-woman, grants much basic humanity to women, but each gives us a clue to what we need to think about.

One would think that higher education would be the perfect place to work out the emerging roles of women. An institution dedicated to learning will help us learn about these issues, instead of separating sexes through stereotypes. If you believe that, it is time to think again.

School Life

It should be clear by now that colleges mirror the culture in which they exist. While weird and often wonderful things do go on in higher education, what goes on still happens mostly at the will of common American culture.

Fear and violence is an example. Most cities in the United States have areas that are unsafe for women to walk in after dark. That is simply a depressing fact.

Here is a little exercise about fear. Have everyone in the class draw a map of the campus. Two features should be on everyone's map: the places they normally go during the day, and the places they won't go at night. The bigger the campus, the more places most women won't go after dark.

In other words, men and women actually understand the same campus in different ways. Awful but true. On one of the campuses where we teach, there is a huge high-rise library with many floors. Women report that they are uncomfortable—are afraid—to be on a floor all alone. They won't study on those floors. They won't even look for books under those circumstances.

On the same campus, there is a science building that is really a network of several smaller buildings. It seems huge. There is a computer area that is set back behind the main building and away from the road. Women will use that building only during the day. It is just too dark and out of the way to go there at night. Men will use the facility at all hours of the day and night. Women will go there only before dark. In

_____ 82 _____

the winter, it is dark by 4:30 P.M. Certain science is over for women hours before dinner.

The university has police, has an escort service any woman may call, attempts to keep the campus well-lighted, and makes students take courses in civility and diversity. All of that is fine, but the bottom line is that the men and the women live in different spaces. After dark, women factor in fear when they think about going somewhere.

The point is that identity gets defined by the people around us. For women and men on campus, that seems to happen in different ways. Why? Do we simply say that women and men are different, and that women will always be more vulnerable? There is more to why identity gets defined the way it does, and different answers to the question.

Women and Men

Common sense tells us two things: first, that women and men are different, and second, that women and men are similar. We know that women are able to have babies. We also know many of the myths about men, such as that men are physically more capable and can do math better than women. We also know that our language puts us at odds—our sexes, we say, are opposite.

Let us explore the issue of how opposite we are.

Are we opposite? Is that true? Do we generalize the tension and titillation of sexuality into other parts of our lives? Have sex roles in our culture made us more opposite than we really are? Is biology destiny, or is culture destiny? Is the "weaker" sex weaker because of biology or because of society? Or is it weaker at all?

Currently, there are at least two important approaches to these questions. Both come out of research done by women. The first says that women are more like men than we think, and the other says that women are less like men than we think.

The first argument deals mostly with physiology and attacks the myth of biological determinism. The myth argues that basic biological differences are the reasons why the social roles of women and men are different. In other words, body size and strength, hormone levels, and maybe even brain development are so different in women and men that they dictate who should do what in society.

The argument in "Social Bodies: The Interaction of Culture and Women's Biology," by Marion Lowe, is that we hardly know that for a fact.[1] Given the data, Lowe argues that we do not know whether biological differences led to role differences or role differences led to biological differences. She states that "in contemporary American culture (and in most other present-day societies) women and men grow up and live in radically different social environments."[2] She believes that environment affects biology.

Molly Ivins gets us to the same point in a little different way. She writes, "Can't say I've ever come to any particularly cosmic conclusions about gender, but when you start out in a culture that defines your role as standing on the sidelines with pompons to cheer while the guys get to play the game, it will raise some questions in your mind."[3]

What Marion Lowe found was that as women's environments and activities become more like men's, the extent of many sex differences decrease.[4] For example, size, strength, and even some measures of aggression seem to become more alike when women and men have similar roles.

The facts and statistics and explanations for these arguments are both complicated and guarded. While this is not the place to review the entire argument, it is important to get a sense of what is going on.

There are all kinds of facts to remember. What is discussed are average values, and average tells us nothing about any single person. We need to remember that all traits vary widely for each sex. Indeed, the differences between groups are usually smaller than the variations within each group. Except for traits related directly to reproduction, there are extensive anatomical and physiological overlaps between men and women.

In the United States, men are about five inches taller, are heavier, and are more muscular than women. Women have a higher proportion of body fat (23 percent versus 15 percent) and have smaller and less dense bones than do men.

Why are these things true? What happens, for example, when women become more active? "In several studies in which non-athletic women and men were tested during training with weights, women's strength was found to increase faster than men's, and women's greatest gains were made in the muscles of the upper body."[5] And what about the lower body? "[L]eg strength per unit of lean body weight is actually slightly greater for women than for men."[6] The baseline averages for men and women are apparently a product of different types of activities.

Athletically, men do better than women in events requiring power and speed. But in tests that are primarily of endurance, such as super marathons (50- or 100-mile runs) and long-distance swimming, women have outperformed men. And since women began training and competing more seriously in swimming, almost all top female competitors routinely have broken men's records of the recent past.

If women keep improving performance at present rates, by 1998 the women's record in the marathon will equal the men's record.[7] Brian Whipp, a professor of physiology at the UCLA School of Medicine, writes that between 2015 and 2055, top female and male runners might be performing equally well in the 200-, 400-, 800-, and 1,500-meter races. Such comparisons were not possible under the old myths.

Is biology destiny, or is Title VII of the Civil Rights Act (the law that really created first-rate sports programs for women) destiny?

Certainly, there are still differences. When women work out, their muscles get stronger but not larger. When men work out, they not only get stronger, but their muscles also bulk up. Women's bodies have to be two or three degrees warmer than men's before they sweat. When women work out, they lose fat faster than men do.

Given similar environments, women's and men's bodies grow alike in many ways. What would happen if both sexes did the same jobs—what if women and men really were equal? We read:

In most contemporary societies, there is a tendency for men to perform the activities that require a great deal of exertion. Balinese society is an exception, since there neither women nor men traditionally do much heavy work, with the result that both are slender and show minimal sex differences in body build. European visitors have complained that they cannot tell the women and men apart, even from the front. However, when the Balinese men are hired to work on the docks loading ships for Europeans, they develop the heavy musculature we consider typical of males.[8]

Only recently have jobs in the "heavy" and often well-paying industries opened up for women. While some of the traditional women's jobs require strength (nurses, for example, lift, move, and rearrange patients all the time), nurses are rarely thought of as strong. What if women were treated the same as men? Would men's biological "superiority" disappear? Or mostly disappear? Which came first, the body or the culture? Which has influenced the other the most?

If strength depends on developing muscles, what about height? Mixed lessons here. We know that diet, diseases, the amount of sunshine you get, physical and emotional stress, and physical activity all influence how tall you are. That, and the height of your parents.

Immigrant families to the United States show surprising increases of height from one generation to the next. Prenatal and infancy care turn out to be key to one's height. So is exercise. In a long-term growth study of young women swimmers, it was found that their growth, as a group, was accelerated above established norms and that the acceleration was greater during their training years.[9]

There are two conclusions, each interesting and important. First, in cultures in which male children are treated differently from and better than female children, we can expect males to be much taller than females. Second, in cultures that have big class differences, we can expect children of the privileged classes to be taller than those of lower classes.

We do know that drug-addicted babies are smaller than average babies. That is also true of babies from malnourished mothers, as well as babies who are malnourished. But we also know this: Tall parents are likely to have tall children.

There is also interesting, conflicting, and sometimes confusing information about brain-power. Did you know that when IQ tests were first given, women scored higher on the verbal part, men scored higher on the mathematical part, and women scored higher when the two were combined? The people who wrote the tests, apparently dissatisfied with those results, put in more math questions so there would be no difference in the overall scores.

We know that the brain, like the body, responds to its environment. Even though most of the important studies were on rats (how stimulation and/or deprivation affected rat brains), the fact remains that people do respond to their intellectual environment. If that is so, then the more boys and girls are raised alike, the more alike they will be intellectually. That would mean, to take an easy example, that more women would major in math and science.

There is more. There are studies of how people raised in round homes (yurts or tee-pees) have a different sensitivity to vertical and horizontal than do Europeans, who are raised in rectangular rooms. The inferential leap here is that brains can be shaped by environment. If women are raised as if they are fit for only certain jobs (cave jobs, for instance), then their brains may not be suited for many other jobs. What if it turns out that the many hours some kids spend in front of video games result (as many parents may hope) in greater ability in learning to use more complicated computers in school and at work? If that happens, we may lament the strongly male orientation of the video game industry (nearly all of the subscribers to the main video games magazine are male).

Studies suggest that physiology can have something to do with occupational preferences and performance. Most recent summaries of sex differences in brains find differences in size and performance. Men tend to do better on spatial reasoning tests and in mathematical reasoning. Women tend to do better on tests of perceptual speed and in mathematical calculations.[10]

In the larger picture, cultural changes may literally reform what we look like, how we act, and how we think. If women and men are raised the same ways, we may assume that some of the differences in women and men will diminish and—at some point—no longer be important.

In conditions of equality, we can expect that women and men will become more alike.

We said there is a second argument. It is made mostly by a group of female psychologists. Nancy Chodorow argues that almost from the very beginning, girls and boys are different.[11]

According to Chodorow, the female child has far less ability to separate and differentiate herself from her mother than does a male child. The male child, after all, is different from his mother and so identifies himself with other males. The boy replaces the mother. Not so with the girl. Girls continue the relationship with the mother as well as having new relationships with others. Boys deny the attachment with the mother in order to have male identity. Boys naturally seek autonomy and separateness.

Girls do just the opposite: They connect with others to seek their identity. From here, it is easy to see how women and men will act differently when they go into the work world.

Of course, this all takes place in a context where the woman is the primary caregiver for children. In that sense, the difference in boys and girls is, ultimately, socially constructed.

The argument about difference extends to the workplace. Workers, after all, started out with the childhood differences. In the workplace, the typical organization is bureaucratic.[12] That means that each person has a well-defined role to play, a well-defined job to do, and a list of rules that must be followed. Those who do well in bureaucratic organizations are those who follow the prescribed rules, who believe in justice, and who are—in a word—judgmental. Near the heart of the bureaucratic structure is an inflexible arrangement of rewards and punishments that can be run by any competent manager.

All of those rules, all of that separation and reward and punishment is—according to this literature—how males act. It has everything to do with the male model of development. The boy separates and finds his identity (and his power) by being competitive. He is judgmental and has full faith and command of the rules.

Women, we read, seek connections. Although they are competitive, they do so in a way that will enhance cooperation. They build alliances and partnerships. Women try to empower others so that creativity, risk-taking, and openness are encouraged. The prescribed positions of a bureaucratic structure are undercut by the way in which women act. The separation between people is minimized; the connections between people are maximized.

Theory tells us that the male ego is comfortable with the hierarchy and the female ego is more comfortable with relationships. Mom goes to work and is egalitarian; Dad goes to work and thinks he is a ruler.

There is one more step to the theory that needs to be understood. The theory tells us that we live in a complex and changing world. It is a world in which the rigid bureaucratic structure—the male-dominated institution—simply cannot hope to survive. Inflexible male virtues cannot compete in a rapidly changing environment.

Well, says the literature, lucky us. The traits of women—connectedness, empowerment, and the like—are the very traits needed for our new world. Female leaders encourage participation, are comfortable with sharing power, and have the ability to get people involved. Those are just the things that are needed to compete in an environment that is continually changing.

The logic of the argument seems undeniable. We know that lots of large bureaucratic organizations, private and public, are in great trouble. We also know that for almost forever our huge bureaucracies have been run by males. If the developmental literature is true, girls should grow up to be women with values that are different from those of men.

The search for female qualities (and here we are talking about those found in leaders) has had mixed results. In a pioneering work,[13] Carol Gilligan argued that most psychologists who studied moral development and judgment defined maturity and development in terms of rights and independence of individuals. The ambiguities of context made mutual responsibilities too murky to form a clear basis for maturity. She argued that theorists were coming to understand the importance of attachment among people but had not fully under-

— 89 —

stood how that was in conflict with the definition of maturity as independence, autonomy, and individual rights. Gilligan studied women of all ages but noted some inconsistencies between findings for young and older children. Subsequent work[14] extended her studies to adolescent girls, and suggested that female identity goes through a crisis during that time as they must learn to work out a compromise between the ethic of care and the individualist values of the culture.

Other researchers have not found separate voices. In one study of the decision-making processes of women and men, it was found that three-quarters of the considerations by both males and females were about "rights" and "justice."[15] In other words, both men and women were using what Gilligan would call the moral reasoning of men.

Another study found that the higher the women went in an organization, the more "male" moral reasoning they practiced.[16] Other studies showed that executive women are not better able to reduce interpersonal friction, nor are they more understanding or humanitarian than their male counter-parts.[17] Researchers have even found a difference between lab and field behavior. Women exhibit more "female" traits in a laboratory setting than they do when they get to work.

This brief excursion through the literature about differences between women and men tells us something. There is no consensus on the differences or on the source of the differences. This turns out to be important, because what we look for, and what sense we make of what we find, says a lot about us. What do we want to find, and what do we want to do with that knowledge?

Data about sexual differences, we assert, are important only if they help us understand power, particularly the differences in power wielded by women and by men.

What do sexual differences mean? Do they mean that women and men are capable of different things? If we find differences in performance among athletes, would they mean that women shouldn't be fighter pilots or railroad engineers? Would knowing that many women care more about caring mean that there are some jobs that only women should have, or vice versa? If more women gain influential positions in organizations, will that constitute a dramatic change in how organizations operate?

These questions are important for a couple of reasons. The first has to do with our ability to appreciate diversity. If we want to see women as making a special contribution to organizations, we define them as alike in an essential way. That may be ignoring important differences among women. Women, like men, vary in where they are from, their religion, their class, sexual orientation, race, and cultural background. Are their interests always shared? If we do not recognize the diversity among women, do we limit the identity of individual women? It is axiomatic that the more one's identity is limited by other people, the less choice one has, the less freedom one enjoys, the less power one can use.

The second reason has to do with our standards for making sense of situations. If we are interested in justice and fairness in the distribution of power among men and women, how do we conceive of justice and fairness? Are they universal, gender-neutral standards of justice, or are they standards that define some aspect of maleness or femaleness as most desirable? This point needs some explaining.

In the past, ostensibly universal standards of justice and fairness usually pertained to the things men did. In Western cultures, sexual differences have been tied to the idea of what is public and what is private. The public things, such as politics and government, were run by men. Justice, we believed, was blind, and each case was to be treated the same. The private sphere was where women operated but it was also mostly run by men. But the standards of treating everyone equally did not apply there. Women had different responsibilities from those of men. Men had the opportunities to leave the private sphere for the responsibilities of the public. Men did justice. Women had a more difficult time finding acceptance in the public sphere and more difficulty getting the standards of justice and fairness applied to the issues that affected them, such as ownership of property, control of violence, and access to other institutions. To be universal, liberal standards of justice really have to apply to both the public and the private spheres.

But what if we reject liberal standards? If we believe that there are important differences between males and females, we do not want standards of justice and fairness that treat them alike. If we say that caring, nurturing, and connectedness among people are more the concern of females, we may have to give the social resources for those concerns more often to females than to males. A legal case, whether it involves property, child custody, or employment, would be judged differently if the person involved was a man or a woman.

If we see women as change agents, possessing special visions subversive to institutions, as emancipators from hierarchy and narrow privilege, we are getting close to the second position. We would have to take the blindfold off the image of justice and begin making judgments based on the sex of those being judged.

There are strong arguments for each position.

In the next section, we continue the inquiry into differences in another way. A brief history of women in higher education suggests that there is a long tradition of viewing females as less educable, less reasonable, and less deserving of education.

College

Higher education in early America was for men. As we have seen, it was set up in order to provide an educated religious elite. A male elite. A woman's place in the colonies was in the home and in the field. With the obvious exception of rich whites in the slave-owning South, even the women in more educated classes worked. Women raised the children and cared for the house. If they lived on the frontier, they were as rugged as their husbands. They often helped tend the family store or run the family-owned business. Women would sell, or keep books, or help with the harvest, or do whatever was needed.

Although women did go to schools as early as 1749, the real precedents of higher education for women were early women's seminaries. Seminaries were opened in Troy, New

York, in 1821, Hartford, Connecticut, in 1828, and South Hadley, Massachusetts, in 1836.[18] They were not quite colleges, but within a century they became not only academically reputable but also a powerful force for women.

The first college to become coeducational was Oberlin, in 1837. Oberlin enrolled four women and offered them a traditional B.A. as well as a special Ladies' Course. Before the Civil War, there were only a handful of coeducational colleges. What few colleges existed were mostly for males. Some schools were for women. The idea that men and women could be educated at the same institution seemed pretty silly.

It took the West and federal legislation to produce coeducational colleges and universities.

The legislation, both state and federal, created land-grant colleges and state universities. Public institutions of higher education in the West made coeducation a normal and accepted thing. The universities of Iowa, Wisconsin, Indiana, Missouri, Michigan, and California all became coeducational after the Civil War.

Women and men in the frontier worked equally hard. When state legislatures created schools that were coeducational, it had much less to do with radical politics than with acknowledging that in many ways women and men should be treated the same. No ladies-in-waiting in Iowa, no courtly balls in Missouri; life on the frontier meant hard work for everybody. When it came time to educate the emerging upper-middle and upper classes, there was no reason not to do it coeducationally.

While western colleges were open and coeducational, eastern colleges were private and separate. Exclusive male prep schools sent students to exclusive male private colleges. Schools for women did develop. Some of the women's seminaries, such as Mount Holyoke in South Hadley, Massachusetts, became very good colleges. The Poughkeepsie, New York, brewer Matthew Vassar established a women's college of his own.

The rich, deaf spinster Sophia Smith also founded a college. The Smith story is instructive. She had inherited a great deal of money from her brother. She had a reputation for being a little stingy, so as she grew older she still had all of that money. Her great friend and advisor, a man named John Greene, thought she should give her money to education. His idea was that she give it to his alma mater, the all-male Amherst College. Smith, who apparently had a little trouble making up her mind, had at least five different plans and wrote five different wills. The will at her death in 1870 established Smith College in Northampton, Massachusetts, still a women's school.

The great coed exception in the East was Cornell. In 1872, the school decided to become coeducational. On the whole, the rest of the East refused to go along. By 1872, there were 97 major coed colleges and universities in the United States. Of these 97, 67 were in the West, 17 in the South, 8 in the Middle Atlantic states, and only 5 in New England.[19]

Some schools, especially in the East, recognized the need to educate women but refused to become coeducational. Male schools created sister schools. Harvard "had" Radcliffe, Columbia had Barnard, Brown/Pembroke, Tulane/Newcomb, Tufts/Jackson, and so on. For a long time they were separate and not quite equal institutions. As we know, by the last quarter of the twentieth century, almost all schools had become coed. Later in this chapter, we will come back to the idea of coed and single-sex schools and see what makes sense. In this section, our main concern is women's access to higher education, and especially men and women being educated together.

In the history of women in higher education, several stories and quotes keep coming up. The reason they are repeated is that together they form much of the spirit of the place of women in the United States during the 1800s. What follows is a glance of the last century:[20]

After a visitor had seen Wellesley, he said, "All of this is very fine, but . . . how does it affect their chances [of marriage]?"

Proud daughter: "I have made 100 in algebra, 96 in Latin, 90 in Greek, 88 1/2 in mental philosophy and 95 in history; are you not satisfied with my record?"

Father: "Yes, indeed, and if your husband happens to know anything about housekeeping, sewing and cooking, I am sure your married life will be happy."

The Reverend John Todd said, "Must we crowd education on our daughters, and for the sake of having them intellectual, make them nervous, and their whole earthly existence a struggle between life and death?"

David Macrae was worried that coeducation would impair "the delicate modesty and refinement which constituted the opposite sex's great charm."

The vice president of Cornell said, "When I heard of a lady student calling one young man into the room, shutting the door, kissing him, it produced distress which embittered months of existence."

Finally, a Vanderbilt student said, "No man wants to come home at night and find his wife testing some new process for manufacturing oleomargarine, or in the observatory sweeping the heavens for a comet."

It is safe to assume that times have changed and that a kiss behind a shut door no longer embitters the administration for months. The idea of delicate modesty is also pretty much a thing of the past in many of our institutions of higher education. It is possible that the old Father did have a point: Someone has to cook. The Father assumed—rightly for those times—that women would do the sewing and the cooking. Things change.

Colleges and universities produced women who not only helped change the place of women, but also helped change the world. We need to understand how important higher education has been for women who want to become active in the world.

There were, according to Page Smith, three principle vocations of college-educated women.[21] First, women concerned themselves with domestic reform. The most famous example of this was the "settlement houses" for immigrants set up in most large cities. Jane Addams's Hull House in Chicago was the model. Second, women were school and college teachers. This was especially true in the South and the Midwest. Finally, women did foreign missionary work.

Women, during the times that they were supposed to be the weaker sex, traveled the world doing "good." By 1890, female missionaries outnumbered men almost two to one in the Near East. Many of them established schools for women in those countries and brought the word of Christ as well as John Dewey to people all over the world. The challenge to college students was put in the form of a question by Isabel Morrill: "Oh, girls . . . if we do not take Christ to the women and girls in Turkey, who will?"[22] Apparently not men.

College-educated American women helped bring education to women all over the world. Colleges, especially women's colleges, made it their mission to graduate people who would somehow make a positive contribution in the world. Colleges began to change when women became students. Liberal arts became female and the sciences became male. Home economics, domestic living, and health-related subjects were developed. Many of these subjects would later become part of high school curricula and a key in teaching immigrants basic hygiene.

There is an interesting tension in our history. There is an ongoing rub between the expected sexist attitudes that limit women and the rugged equality that developed out of the frontier tradition. Women on the frontier were often equal partners in the development of the West. Before political equality, state legislatures in the Midwest and West established coeducational universities. In the East, generations of well-educated women were produced by women's colleges. And while the dominant attitude was that a woman's place was in the home, college-educated women became reformers and educators all over the world.

As people understood more about how the world really worked—old-boys' networks from old-boys' colleges were the stuff of power—women wanted to attend men's schools. Economics also played a part as male students began to choose coed colleges. As the elite male schools became coed, they began competing for students with women's schools. There are now very few all-male schools, but many of the elite women's schools remain single-sex. Most students in the United States go to coed colleges and universities.

Higher education in the United States has been a powerful force. It has also carried the cultural stereotypes of the place of women in society. We have seen both good examples of the power of education as well as stereotypes that came out of those times. For example, Page Smith ends a chapter about women and higher education in this curious way: "Many of the women who graduated from Mount Holyoke, Smith, Wellesley, and Vassar became celibates, married to careers. . . . In the coeducational state universities, young men and women commonly found mates with whom they shared intellectual and/or career interests. They thus pioneered a new kind of marriage in which husband and wife . . . enjoyed a degree of mutuality seldom observed in traditional marriages."[23]

The stereotypes limit women's identity. Why would we care if women who graduated from college were celibate or not, married or single? We might care if we were concerned with the relationship of education to marriage. What does it mean if, when we encounter a woman in college, the first thing we think is this: How does she balance her education and career goals with marriage?

It may still often be true that when a woman marries, she chooses a life. Someone else's life. The point is that identity exists in a context and that context limits the possibilities one can choose. The "degree of mutuality seldom observed" says a great deal about the limits a culture can place on a sex.

Daily Academic Life

Are those historical attitudes about women in higher education still at work? The images of male and female relationships that you have in your heads from high school, or whatever life you lived between high school and college, are not automatically dumped out when you get to college. The mysteries of sex and gender do not disappear when you become 18—or even when you get to be 80. What we can see in campus life is that the stereotyping of hundreds of years gets routinely played out in everyday campus life. The tensions of those stereotypes help form the heart of this section.

One of the myths people have is that men's work is superior to women's work. In a series of tests, two groups of people were asked to evaluate particular works—articles, paintings, résumés, and the like.[24] The names attached to each item were clearly a woman's name or a man's name. The names were reversed for each group. In other words, one group was told something was a woman's and the other group was told that same thing was a man's.

In both groups, work that was believed to be a man's was rated higher than when it was believed to be a woman's. In all of the studies, women were as likely as men to downgrade the women's works. In another study, female college students rated scholarly articles higher if they believed the articles were written by a man than if they believed that they were written by a woman.[25]

Those are remarkable studies. They tell us disturbing things. How can women in college hope to get an equal education if people believe that men are smarter or do better work? Does that mean that when women do well they are lucky and when men do well it is because of greater ability?

It naturally leads to this kind of attitude: "I am even more ashamed to admit that out of my desire to be taken seriously as a physicist I was eager to avoid identification with other women students who I felt could not be taken seriously."[26]

There is another myth that leads us to believe that the essence of higher education is masculine. Higher education has traditionally been thought of as depending on rigorous reason, being intellectually aggressive and rational, and centering around science and mathematics. These are not the traditional female stereotypes. Indeed, the stereotype of female thinking that we read earlier in the chapter revolved around relationships and caring.

This myth follows a strong theme in Western philosophy and political thought.[27] Part of this theme is the notion that the male body is the prototypical human being and that women are a close but imperfect model of humanity, the weaker vessel. Building from this idea, the different roles males and females fill can be judged as natural, not socially constructed. The values females uphold come from their roles in the private realm, and their limited public roles generally involve helping others, caring for children, teaching the young, and so on. The values males uphold come from their roles in the public realm, as a recognized property-owning head of household, a citizen, an official of the state, church, or other important institution, or as a soldier. The dualism between male and female bodies is a part of many philosophers' arguments, even though the concept contradicts other parts of their theories (that all humans have reason, that reasoning humans can choose how to live, and that these choices are the foundation of the state).

A separate source of the myth of women's lower capacity for reason is the dualism inherent in most Western thought since the Enlightenment. Here are some of the main dualisms: reason/emotion, objective/subjective, fact/opinion, science/values, male/female. In crude terms, the first half of each dualism is considered better than the second. The first half is about knowledge, the second is about ignorance. The first half is about improvement and progress, the second is about the things we fight over. Coupled with the idea of the stronger vessel of the male body versus the weaker vessel of the female body, it is a short flight to the conclusion that males are better at reason, science, and education.

This dualism raises an important concern for those who argue for a distinctly female vision of the world, one that apparently would need a distinctly female epistemology. The idea relies on a renewed dualism of male/female knowledge. One of the artifacts produced by Western liberal thought is a strong reliance on rights. Would the female knowledge not rely on rights as strongly if at all?

This historical division of female and male intellect gets played out in college in the choice of majors and degrees: Nearly one out of four Hispanic women major in education, and almost a third of black and of Native American women major in education.[28] At the master's-degree level, more than 50 percent of white, Hispanic, and Native American women get their degrees in education; 66 percent of black women get their degrees in education. At the doctoral level, one-third of white and Hispanic women, half of Native American women, and two-thirds of black women receive degrees in education.

We know women go into fields other than education. In 1987, women received 24.3 percent of the Ph.D.s awarded.[29] They made up only 2.8 percent of the engineering doctorates, 9.6 percent of the math doctorates, 8.8 percent in computer sciences, and 2.8 percent in theology. The percentages were considerably higher in library science, fine and applied arts, letters, psychology, and public affairs.

The messages women get on campus about appropriate majors are often not subtle. A woman told one of us of the time she took an advanced math class. The professor counted the number of women in the class (it was six) and said that he expected six people to fail. Three of the women dropped out that day, and the other three passed. The story is not an isolated one. We read:[30]

> *"One woman earned high grades in a traditionally male field. Her professor announced to a mostly male class that this represented an unusual achievement 'for a woman' and was an indication, first, that the woman student was probably not really feminine, and, second, that the males in class were not truly masculine, since they allowed a woman to beat them."*

Put differently, but right to the point, there are female majors and there are male majors on campus. The majors with the highest status that will lead to the best-paid professions are the masculine ones.

The ranking of fields does not just appear. Any faculty survey will report the same basic biases that the undergraduate surveys show. Math and science on top, education and communications on the bottom. Hard sciences on top, social sciences on the bottom. Men on top, women on the bottom. Ask any professor.

Even as education strains to become more open, it is still true that women and men pursue different courses. Medical school classes are close to reaching parity when it comes to gender. It appears that merit, not gender, is the key to being admitted to medical school. Given that, we could speculate that the specialties in medicine are also reaching a female/male parity. We would be wrong. Women in medical school seem to choose obstetrics/gynecology (they will soon be more than 50 percent of the field), pediatrics, and family medicine. It is important to note that there are personnel shortages in these three specialties, and they are among the lowest-paid specialties. Women in medical school do not choose general surgery. Why? Certainly OB/GYN work has more than its share of cutting. It is reasonable to expect that women and men are equally qualified for any specialty, because they were admitted to the same school according to the same standards. Do women choose these particular specialties because they are more nurturing than other specialties? And if that is the reason, what does it mean?

Does the division have to do with our stereotypes of what women and men are capable of doing?

If the women choose their majors because of the nurturing values, is that also an artifact of too little encouragement to make use of other capacities, like aptitudes in biology or math?

The choice might also have to do with everyday language. What if, in every example, the man teaching statistics makes every statistician masculine? Is he trying to tell his class that he believes only men should be statisticians? If you happen to be a man majoring in elementary school education, how would you feel if the professor constantly used feminine words when talking about teachers? If you happen to be a man, generalize that to everything that goes on in all of your classes. Would it feel odd that every example everywhere was feminine? After a while, would something happen to the way you understand the world? Maybe so.

Until very recently, our language has been masculine. Does that bias seep into our brains? Can we assume that it means something to choose words that overlook more than 50 percent of the population? The point is not about politically correct language—that is discussed in Chapter 12—but about who we include and exclude in everyday conversation. Listen to your professors. Do they acknowledge that the world consists of men and women? Isn't it just as awkward if a female professor leaves men out of her language?

The phenomenon extends to talking in class. Two stereotypes are in tension here: Women talk all the time and men are smarter (school smarter) than women. To be honest, the word *tension* overstates the matter. The truth is that men dominate classroom discussions.

There is a sense that women are simply not taken as seriously as men. Faculty members are more likely to call a woman by her first name than a man by his. A woman is more likely to be less assertive in class ("I think . . . I was wondering"; "This is really important, don't you think?"; "Don't you think that maybe, sometimes . . .") than a man. That kind of language is often dismissed in a competitive classroom. The points made by women are less often developed, and more often interrupted, than those by men.[31]

Of course, any paragraph that begins with "there is a sense" tells you something; in this case, it is something that is worth remembering. Not all women are alike, nor are all men, all faculty, or all classrooms. Not all women use less assertive language, any more than all men are bright. The best any of us can do is see what the few studies say and then speak and write in either generalities or specifics. It gets tiresome for everyone, we hope, to read that all men are animals and all women are oppressed. Very tiresome.

But it does seem that men are more likely to dominate a classroom discussion than women. Here is what some studies have shown:[32]

1. Men talk more than women.
2. Men talk for longer periods of time and take more turns.
3. Men exert more control over the topic of conversation.
4. Men interrupt women more frequently than women interrupt men.
5. Men's interruptions of women more often introduce trivial or inappropriately personal comments that bring the woman's discussion to an end or change its focus.

A short review might be helpful. The topic of this section has been stereotypes about men and women and how they may get played out in class. The information indicates that men's work is more highly valued than women's work, that "male" majors are more highly valued than "female" majors, and that men are likely to dominate in class discussions. In all of this, it seems that everyone involved (students and teachers of both sexes) may contribute to what goes on.

By way of enormous irony, there is one obvious way out of some of these problems: women's colleges. The very problem—single-sex schools—that many women fought against for decades can be seen as the solution to another set of problems.

Women are not turned away from majors in women's colleges, they are not interrupted by men in class discussions, and their work is valued for what it is. Problems solved! But are single-sex colleges the answer? Do you really want to return to a world where the old boys go to all-boy colleges and women go to women's schools?

Is it realistic to believe that "Separate but Equal"—which is illegal when it comes to race—is workable when it comes to gender?

There are single-sex schools, and many of them are good. Should we have more of them? Are single-sex schools the best way to educate women in a world full of demeaning stereotypes?

One of the issues that illustrates the problems of the status of women on campus is sexual harassment, the subject of the next section.

Hormones on Campus

There is a very easy part of this discussion. The easy part is this: Everything that is illegal off campus is illegal on campus. There are laws against rape and sexual harassment. If employees at IBM or at the local video store or people who say no to their dates are protected by law, so too are all women on campus. That is not at all hard to understand.

But the topic of sexual harassment is hard to understand, because there are disagreements over what it means and what is behind it.

The U.S. Supreme Court recently defined sexual harassment in the workplace.[33] Sexual harassment is discrimination on the basis of sex, and it happens when the work "environment would reasonably be perceived, and is perceived, as hostile or abusive." No single factor is required, but it might consist of demeaning comments, sexual innuendos, vulgar behavior, or unwelcome touching. The Court said that the sum total of circumstances has to be considered, which might include "the frequency of the discriminatory conduct; its severity; whether it is physically threatening or humiliating, or a mere offensive utterance; and whether it unreasonably interferes with an employee's work performance." It is not necessary to demonstrate that the victim of harassment has suffered severe psychological or physical harm, although psychological harm may be one way of demonstrating that harassment took place.

It is wrong because it constitutes discrimination.

But there are ambiguities.

The standard announced by the court includes the word "reasonable," and the standard for judging whether harassment takes place is a hypothetical "reasonable woman." *Reasonable* presents an ambiguity.

Would a reasonable man see it differently from a reasonable woman? In earlier sections of this chapter, we have described serious people who do, indeed, see women and men judging situations differently. Is a reasonable person an individual in any role on a campus, or is it the affirmative action officer who is trained in equity and gender issues? Would someone in women's studies be more reasonable than someone in chemistry? Is reasonable at the University of New Hampshire the same as reasonable at Boise State?

A second ambiguity arises from our belief about the reasons sexual harassment takes place. It is not unusual for a violation of law to involve the state of mind of the perpetrator or the victim. Murder cases are often differentiated on the basis of whether the perpetrator meant to kill the particular victim and how much the crime was planned. Assault charges are often differentiated based on the context of the crime (whether the victim was in a fight with the perpetrator, whether "fighting words" were exchanged, and so on). If we see an incident as fairly routine sexual behavior, we see the situation very differently than if we see it as an abuse of power.

Everyday life contains a lot of flirting. Is something that happens between you and the bank teller O.K. at the bank, but not in a professor's office? Is an exchange that happens between you and the mechanic who changes your oil O.K. at the garage, but not in the classroom?

Consider this possible difference between the situations: Professors have more power than students. Supervisors have more power than their subordinates. Yet it is not just power that matters. It is more complicated than that. Otherwise, you could simply analyze the relative power of yourself and a person you wish to say something to, and if they "match," you could proceed with what would be otherwise unacceptable behavior.

Part of harassment involves ambiguities about the relationship between members of a profession and people they serve. Things have changed since then, but in the mid-1970s, the American Psychological Association voted, by the barest majority, that it is wrong to have sex with patients. About half the profession at the annual convention did not want to rule it out. There have been many instances of professors dating students. Suppose we have Professor A and Professor B: Professor A approached a student with a proposition. They eventually married, had three kids, and lived happily ever after. Professor B approached a student with the same proposition. The student was outraged and registered a complaint with the university's sexual harassment officer, and Professor B was fired. Is that possible?

Is it appropriate for students to date faculty?

Most harassment is probably not in the form of propositions, but that is just a guess. Claims about harassment that have gotten the most attention in periodicals professors read are about the cultivation of a hostile environment in the classroom, the office, or the library.[34] What if a professor is, in poor judgment, trying to be cool or hip but ends up offending people? What if the professor flirts or makes a comment that has a double meaning (one sexual)? Here is where the "reasonable" standard is supposed to apply.

We know this: Sexual harassment is wrong. We also know this: College is a particular environment and that environment has to be considered. The majority of students are beginning to understand themselves as adults, and more and more of them have been adults for years. College students certainly have adult appetites, adult freedoms, and adult bodies. Many, for the first time, are out on their own and beginning to figure out the relationship between freedom and responsibility.

And there is the faculty. Adults, with adult appetites, adult freedoms, and adult bodies. They also have adult positions of power. The power they have is directly over students. It's probably impossible to separate the power from the sex. The roles of professor and student were just not designed to handle the energy of sex.

You can see how professors can get defensive about this:

> *"We're continually being told by administrators that we'll be evaluated on the basis of how well we 'relate' to our students. We're supposed to be 'accessible.'. . . If you're a really good teacher you're going to touch them deeply. You're supposed to; that's your job. Many faculty members, male and female, sincerely believe, perhaps correctly, the best learning environment is one which is emotionally, even sexually charged . . . but it's also true that some professors take their D. H. Lawrence lectures out of the classroom and into the nearest motel."[35]*

While there are figures about sexual harassment on campus, no one knows what the real numbers are. Systematic data collection just does not happen. Some surveys of women who have graduated from college routinely show that between 20 and 30 percent report that they had been sexually harassed by male faculty during their college years. Because there are 6,500,000 women in college, that means between 1.3 million and 1.59 million women are sexually harassed while they are in school.[36] Puts a little different spin on college.

> *"I think he put me in the front row because he wanted to get his body near to me. I know that sounds conceited, but I guess I think it's true. He always came and stood right in front of me when he was lecturing and sometimes he would move his foot so it was*

*touching mine. He used to be standing right over me so I could
hear his breathing, and it was so awful, like some big jungle ani-
mal that was waiting to attack me."*[37]

Whatever the reasons why a particular episode takes
place among faculty and students, it is hard to believe that
they are consenting adults. Consenting adults have at least
roughly similar power. A professor has more power than a
student. Much more power. To use that power for some kind
of sexual favor—or to use that power to play sexual games—
can easily be harassment. Yet it does not seem realistic to
advise people to stop and think, "Who has more power here?"
and leave sexual conduct contingent on their answer. We
might need a better rule.

Does power make college different from going to a restaurant and flirting with the person who serves you? Is it all right
to leave a big tip after flirting at the restaurant but not all
right to change a "C" to a "B" for the same reason?

The subject would be big enough if it were limited to male
professors and female students. But it is not. As a psychologist
friend reminded us, homosexual professors hit on homosexual
students and female professors hit on male students. Hormones are active in all of us, and we know that both sexes
have the capacity to act foolishly, inappropriately, or illegally.
As gender and sexual orientation begin to even out in college
teaching, so too will the incidence of sexual harassment.

What follows is titled "a tentative list of warning signs" and
are possible "predictors" for recognizing sexual harassment.[38]
Does the list clarify what constitutes sexual harassment?

- Staring, leering, ogling
- Frequently commenting on personal appearance of the
  student
- Touching out of context
- Excessive flattery and praise of the student
- Deliberately avoiding or seeking encounters with the stu-
  dent in front of colleagues
- Injecting a "male versus female" tone into discussions
  with students or colleagues
- Persistently emphasizing sexuality in all contexts

If a faculty person does some or all of these things, the advice is to watch out. The above behavior is inappropriate and might be an indicator of other, worse behavior. If nothing else, it is a list of poor taste and social ineptitude.

Beyond the Campus

In this chapter, we asked you to consider the status of women as an identity issue. We suggested that women and men may see campus life differently and that there are various interpretations of where the differences come from. Our ideas about differences between women and men seem to be connected to distinct views about how we should organize colleges and work and how we should interpret problems such as sexual harassment. This all takes place in a context, a legacy of stereotypes and discrimination that has shaped the status of women and men. That legacy is played out in the society that surrounds college campuses, and that is the subject of the next chapter.

Earlier it was noted that our language sets us up for competition: Women and men, so says our ordinary language, are the opposite sexes. When she hears that kind of talk, Jacqueline Smethurst is quick to suggest an alternative. "Don't you think it's better," she says, "to think of us as the neighboring sex?"

Yes, Jacqueline, yes, and next-door neighbors at that.

—6—

Gender II: The Wider World

I myself have never been able to find out precisely what feminism is: I only know that people call me a feminist whenever I express sentiments that differentiate me from a doormat.

—Rebecca West

Only by grounding the idea of liberty in the collectivity—in the recognition that there has never been and cannot be any individual freedom unrooted in community discipline—can we hope to enact laws that recognize liberties as interdependent and as inseparable from social responsibility.

—Elizabeth Fox-Genovese

In this chapter, we present the idea that the role of women on campus is a mirror of the role of women in society. The world presents itself differently to women and to men. We explore this in several ways.

We see, in the world of work, unequal treatment of women and men. We see unequal pay, status, and opportunity to advance.

To get at the root of much of the inequality, we examine the idea of gender differences. The concept of gender invites us to see sexual roles as socially constructed rather than determined by biology. We explore how gender affects how we are treated and how we treat others. We ask you to consider how much identity is inherent and how much is taught.

Later in the chapter, there is a discussion of sex and violence, as well as a discussion of a community of women who seem to have few of the problems suffered by the rest.

In Chapter 5 and in this one, we ask you to think about how our sex affects our identity—and, equally important, where our ideas about the sexes come from.

It might be helpful to keep a couple of ideas in perspective in this chapter. First, much of the material will read as if women are treated as second-class citizens. Second, it is important to study and appreciate the enormous changes in the status of women during the last three decades. The changes have been so big that it is hard to imagine what life was like before. In a class one of us teaches, students were asked several questions that used to be the core of the feminist movement: How many of you believe in equal political rights for men and women (e.g., speaking, voting, office-holding)? How many of you believe in equal property rights for women (e.g., own and dispose of property as an individual, access to credit, equality in divorce laws)? How many of you believe in equal institutional treatment for women (e.g., access to education, resources for sports in educational institutions, equal employment opportunity)? Virtually all of the students, women and men, said *of course* they support those ideas. What democratic citizen wouldn't? Then, when asked "How many of you consider yourselves feminists?," only a few said yes. It seems that the feminist movement has won many victories over the last few decades, and what was movement politics is now mainstream.

Here is one other thing to keep in mind. With two chapters on women's issues, it may seem that this book is not about diversity and differences but is instead about how women (or any other group) are somehow the same. It is something of a paradox, but we can only appreciate the diversity women have to offer by considering them separately. College leaders often exhort their campuses to "embrace diversity," and when we hear a phrase like that, we should ask, "How? What do you mean?" This chapter is about what that means in gender issues.

Women and Men at Work

By the time you get to college, most of you have held a job. Indeed, most of you continue to work in order to afford school. We want to begin this second chapter on women by thinking about work. The world of work is where men and women have had ample opportunities to rethink the way they act. On balance, the evidence shows that change has come slowly. One concrete way to see that is to look at pay.

To begin with the simple measure of pay equity, women still make much less than men. There is a benchmark number: 59 cents. It stands for the money full-time women workers earn for every dollar men earn. The number has stayed with us, fluctuating a few cents over the years. As we write in 1994, it stands in the neighborhood of 64 cents.[1]

That number can get "better," meaning larger, in two ways. Women's pay can go up in relation to men's pay, or men's pay can go down in relation to women's. During the 1980s, probably more of the latter happened. Overall, women continue to be underpaid compared to men.

There are some bright spots. For recent female college graduates, the pay is more than 90 percent of comparable male pay.

The not-so-bright spots include growing numbers of women in traditional female occupations and falling proportions of women in traditionally male occupations. Not many women become carpenters or mechanics. In these highly skilled precision trades, the ratio of men to women entering the profession is about 10 to 1. Four times as many men as women become lawyers and judges. Three times as many men as women become natural scientists.

One important idea in work organizations is the glass ceiling. The idea is that women do not rise as high in organizations as do men, but the barrier is not easily seen. Men and women look up in their organizations, and they see higher positions. On the way up, women hit the glass ceiling.

There are, of course, more women in high positions than ever before. This is true in government and private industry. But that does not mean men and women progress at similar rates in organizations. And progress through organizations generally means more pay (and more status and power).

A number of things happen to people as they make their way through their careers. They learn the career ladders and appropriate behaviors from mentors. They get labeled as good workers or poor workers, good team players or bad, stars or bench-warmers. The important question here is, do men get these good opportunities and positive labels more often than women?

The answer seems to be yes.

One way to see that is to look at how people in organizations see men and women. In a classic study, done nearly two decades ago, Rosabeth Moss Kanter investigated the stereotype of the female manager.[2] Female managers, went the myth, were bitchy. They yelled a lot, bullied their coworkers and subordinates, acted emotionally, and were not good team players.

Kanter found that the stereotype was widespread. She then did a study of signs of bitchy behavior to see whether women were more likely to act that way than men.

They were.

Kanter was not satisfied that her search was over, so she compared the positions of people who acted bitchy with those who didn't. She found that people who act that way have positions with responsibility but not power. Men in positions like that acted the same way—they yelled a lot, bullied, acted emotional, and were not good team players.

What started out as a study of a widespread myth turned into a description of a widespread practice in organizations. The (wrongly) generalized myth tended to keep women out of positions of power.

Has much changed in the last two decades?[3] Women are still concentrated in the lower echelons of organizations. They tend to rise in career paths that are not close to power in organizations, such as personnel and public relations. Positions in budgeting and finance are generally more powerful.

When Change Happens

Another way to see identity issues for women at work is to look at a case of women entering a new field. A recent example is the U.S. Defense Department allowing women to enter training as fighter and bomber pilots.[4]

Pilots have been in our armed forces for more than 80 years. Female pilots have been in the armed forces for more than 50 years. They have flown fighters and bombers, but only to transport them from one place to another. Not for combat. Why haven't women been fighter and bomber pilots?

First, it is important to know that real integration of women into the ranks of the armed services did not really begin in the 1970s. The military was a male place. Now women serve at all levels of the military, with restrictions. Before the changes in the middle of 1993, women were not allowed into the Army infantry, armored forces, artillery, or combat helicopters. The Navy would not let women serve on destroyers, aircraft carriers, submarines, and combat aircraft. They could fly as instructors. The Air Force would not let women fly combat aircraft. The Marines would not let women fly anything, and their restrictions on ground roles were similar to the Army policy.

There was resistance to the idea of change, but not much. The armed services are good at taking orders, and they generally carry out policies accordingly. It will take a while to see large-scale changes.

The resistance seems to come from male members of the armed forces who see potential morale problems if women serve next to men. The skills, abilities, and decisions made by people in combat apparently, for these people, had a male aura around them.

Many of the traditionalists are nervous about what the changes mean for their organizations. What will the possible introduction of sex do to the behavior of the crew of, for example, a submarine? Will heterosexual sex somehow endanger the morale of the boat? Or, they worry, where do they go to the bathroom in a coed foxhole during battle?

Those are worries that, perhaps, commanders are expected to have. They do have responsibilities to accomplish their missions, and organizational changes may present challenges. These worries are signs of what it means to be in a male place and not to "embrace diversity." The identity of successful soldiers was, for a long time, exclusively male. The inclusion of women as fighter and bomber pilots marks a fairly dramatic change in the identity of people in those organizational roles. We can think of it as adding another figure to the circle of identity of some women—and changing what that circle looks like in men.

We get a glimpse of the politics of changing rules in the military from the Tailhook scandal.[5] The Tailhook Association is a group of current and former Navy and Marine aviators. They take the name from the hook under the tail of carrier-based planes that catches a cable upon landing. The name is important. A tailhook is a small piece of metal that separates a safe landing from a serious crash. People who handle tailhooks well are a small, highly skilled, and elite group. Members of the Association like associating with each other, and they have an annual convention. The Association, drawing its numbers from aviators in the Navy and Marines, is mostly male. During the 1993 convention in Las Vegas, Nevada, more than 100 of the attending Association members took part in extensive drunkenness, lewdness, and debauchery. One report by the Pentagon's Inspector General said that 83 women were assaulted at the convention. On one hotel floor in particular, women who happened to get off the elevator or walk down a hallway were mauled, as if running a gauntlet of pawing, grabbing drunks. That, as well as public sex and fights, led to charges being filed against 140 men who attended the conference.

At first, the Navy resisted an investigation of the conference behavior. They eventually did complete two investigations. The Navy's own investigations were regarded as incompetent by the Defense Department's Inspector General's office, which in turn did its own. None of the investigations produced much evidence against those charged with crimes and conduct unbecoming of officers, and virtually all of the charges were dropped. The events of the 1993 Tailhook convention don't happen at the rest of their annual meetings. Those things don't happen very often in military organizations. They are rare, but the fact that they happen is important. Politically, the convention scandal was important. This happened at the same time that the armed services were wrestling with the question of whether women would become fighter and bomber pilots. The Tailhook scandal caught the public's attention, and it showed one of the chief defects of an all-male elite in the armed services. Congress and top Pentagon leaders got the message. Traditionalists who resisted opening the new positions to women had this stark fact, this ugly event, to explain away. They couldn't.

In 1992, it was true that the all-male fighter and bomber specialties presented a problem about justice and access for women. But the public, Congress, and top Pentagon officials did not have a Democratic president and the Tailhook scandal to underscore the point.

Politics brought about the pressing need for Defense Department officials to rethink their positions on women in the armed services.

The pace of change is often slow. This is because the changes have had to take place not only in attitudes, but in the institutional processes of change. This is illustrated in the changes in the law and court cases affecting women and work.[6] The major pieces of legislation aimed at bringing about equality for women in the workplace include the Equal Pay Act of 1963 (which was largely symbolic—few people at the time believed that women and men did equal work), Title VII of the 1964 Civil Rights Act (which prohibited workplace discrimination and segregation based on sex, race, color, religion, or national origin, and remains the most important piece of equal opportunity legislation), and Title IX (1972) of the higher education amendments to the Elementary and Secondary Education Act (which extends Title VII protection to education). Each of these laws passed because key leaders, national events, interest groups, and occasionally public interest coincided in a consensus that there was a problem of inequality, and legal remedy was necessary. What is surprising is how infrequently that has happened over the last generation. The issue of comparable worth helps show us the complex politics of equality in the workplace. The example suggests that politics can lead to a change in how we see the work of women and men and that this change may be more important than legislation.

The idea of comparable worth is an expansion on the notion of equal pay for equal work. A fact of workplace segregation is that many occupations are either mostly male or mostly female. Another fact is that the mostly male occupations tend to be paid more. How should we compare these occupations? In a classic comparison from an early comparable worth case, how can you compare the work of nurses with the work of tree-trimmers? We have to be able to answer these questions to understand diversity. Job segregation means we deal with differences among people by keeping them apart. It's the opposite of "embracing diversity" in organizations.

One way to answer those questions about jobs is to use the tools that organizations have in place to rate their jobs. Virtually every organization has some kind of position classification plan, and the plan rests on some method of job analysis. A job can be classified, for example, on the basis of how many people are supervised, how much money is handled, danger to the worker or to the people served by the worker, and so on. Nearly all organizations do this.

In Washington state, some women who worked in an agency looked at the job analysis data and noted the pattern of male and female occupations and apparent differences in pay. This happened in 1974. They requested that the next round of job analysis include enough data so that they could make comparison across a larger range of jobs. The information was collected over the next two years, and here is what they found. For those jobs where the workforce was segregated (a female occupation was defined as one where more than 70 percent of the workers were women, a male occupation as one with more than 70 percent men) *and the job analy-*

sis results show the male and female jobs were worth about the same, the men made almost 20 percent more money.

The women who discovered this wrote a report. State officials who had before supported the strong job analysis methods used by the state suddenly found weaknesses in them. Pay policy did not change. The women studied the problem again and again and got the same results.

A group of female employees sued, claiming they were paid less on the basis of sex. In 1984, a federal district court judge found that the women were right and ordered the state to pay damages and back wages for the previous eight years (since the state officials reasonably knew about the problem). The state suddenly owed women employees and former employees in the predominantly female occupations nearly $1 billion.

The state appealed the case, of course. Appeals take time. In the two years of the appeal, the state negotiated with the major labor unions and agreed to a comparable worth settlement of about $150 million. Most local governments in the state followed the lead and put their own comparable worth plans into effect.

The compromise between the state and the unions came one week before the appellate court overturned the finding of discrimination.

Comparable worth did not become law, but it did become reality. It is an example of how a change in thinking about identity, about how women and men work together, can be at the root of real change.

In an important sense, that is what happened in the larger U.S. workforce. During the 1970s, a large number of women entered the workforce. They did so out of choice and necessity. With real family incomes falling (mainly after the oil price shocks of 1973 and 1979), another adult had to work in most households. Demographic and other changes enabled women to leave the home and enter the labor market.

Men who had never worked beside women found themselves having to understand a new set of rules. Traditional male occupations had male humor and insignia. Calendars with nude or scantily clad women, for example, were common in traditionally male trades. The calendars and the jokes surrounding them make the workplace an unwelcome environment for women.[7]

The point is this: Where men set the standards for behavior and have access to power in organizations, women may not feel welcome, and job segregation can prevail. Attitudes and actions affect identity.

In an important way, people get part of their identity from their work.[8] Particularly in the professions, an individual identifies himself or herself as a physician, a college professor, a social worker, an attorney, and so on. In bureaucracies, the control relationships of supervisor and employee encourage members to personally identify with their work and the approval they get through salary, promotions, and encouragement from supervisors. In so doing, they adopt important values of the organizations where they work.

This raises an important gender issue. It matters who gets the jobs and who sets the standards for proper behavior in the organization. One suspects that, at least for a while, new female trainees for fighter and bomber pilots in the military will find encouragement to behave like the most successful people who went before them. Those women will act like the men have.

The point goes further than particular organizations. One of the most common questions asked among newly acquainted middle-class people is, "What do you do?" The question serves to classify people in several ways. Money is one way. Surgeons make more than just about everyone else. Child-care workers make less than just about everyone else. Status and respect is another way. In a survey of the occupations adults in the United States most and least admire,[9] the ten most admired were, from the top: firefighter, paramedic, farmer, pharmacist, grade-school teacher, mail carrier, Catholic priest, housekeeper, baby-sitter, and college professor. The ten least admired occupations were, from the bottom: drug dealer, organized-crime boss, TV evangelist, prostitute, street peddler, local politician, member of Congress, car seller, rock and roll star, and insurance seller.

Is access to status and wealth tied to gender? In the previous chapter, we noted that different majors seem to draw more men or women, and that these choices are connected to access to occupations. The segregation by sex of the work-force begins earlier than the time of job application. It starts with the way we learn gender.

Gender

Even the briefest account of males and females at work brings out the fact that they are treated differently. The big question is why.

The idea of gender helps us sort out the different ways men and women are treated and get along with each other. It starts with this: Gender is not the same as sex.

Sex is a fairly clear criterion for classifying people. Men have male sex organs; women have female sex organs. Females can bear children and lactate. Males can't. When men and women use these parts together, they can have children. There are some other tendencies about male and female bodies, but the topic, with sex, is biology. An extraordinary amount of art, music, commercial activity, popular culture, and behavior revolve around sex.

Gender is a much narrower topic. Here the focus is on the *roles* occupied by men and women. In the previous section, we used the example of fighter and bomber pilots—males could fill the role, females could not. That was the rule. If some roles are closed to women and some roles are closed to men, gender segregation takes place.

The interesting question is whether sex and gender are at all related. That's why the word gender was used in the first place: to emphasize the conceptual possibility that they are not.

Ask yourself this: What social roles are closed to men or women because of sex? What social roles are better taken by a man or a woman? Make a list, then think about it. Why is each item on the list?

There are really very few things men or women do that the other can't do. Beyond the fact of having babies, work and social roles seem within the capabilities of either sex. But in the real world they are not.

How many female presidents have we had? Vice presidents? Senators? Supreme Court justices? Heads of Fortune 500 corporations? Managing editors of major newspapers or magazines? University presidents? How recently have various churches admitted women to the clergy, and which still have not? In some fields, the numbers of women are increasing, such as attorneys, physicians, scientists, university teachers, and military officers.

But there is no denying that men and women have different doors open to them. Men are much more likely to fill some roles; women are much more likely to fill other roles.

The patterns of social roles, gender, start early in life. Males and females have traditionally seen different roles open to them. Parents and friends, the media and teachers, all sorts of influences encourage youngsters to see the roles available to them in certain ways.

It might start as early as we can imagine.[10] People who look at newborn babies believe they can see boys acting masculine and girls acting feminine—even if they are wrong about which babies are boys and which are girls. By the time boys and girls get into kindergarten, they see each other as different—boys like to play with cars, hit people, and will be bosses; girls like to play with dolls, talk a lot, and will grow up to be teachers.

To point out and criticize the way we support these differences, a group of performance artists did something during the Christmas 1993 shopping season. They bought G.I. Joe and Barbie talking dolls (300 was their claim), swapped their voice machines, and smuggled them back onto store shelves. Unsuspecting consumers got a G.I. Joe doll that held a weapon and said in an enthusiastic lilt, "Can we ever have enough clothes?" and "Let's plan our dream wedding." They also bought Barbies that said, in a gruff voice, "Eat lead, Cobra!" and "Vengeance is mine!"

In the early years, children learn such things at home, and they quickly learn from peers once in school. Identity touches every aspect of behavior. For example, why is it that little girls do as well in math as little boys until they reach puberty, and then fall behind?[11] There is no evidence that female brains become slower in math. This is about learning an identity of feminine or masculine behavior.

Learning to be a heterosexual female in a gender-segregated society might include learning that the boys do better at math.

If we accept the argument that context structures how children learn gender roles, it might be possible to deliberately change the context. One place to see this is in the family.[12] The Family Leave Act of 1993 is an example of a very recent change in the public debate about the roles of women and men. For at least a generation, we have seen a growing recognition that women play two roles—the primary caregiver at home and a worker in the job market. The two roles will conflict, and that usually means difficulties at home and at work. At home, it means pressure on relationships and children. At work, it means less commitment to career, with less pay and other rewards.

The law was changed in 1993 to allow women *and* men time off from work, unpaid, to attend to the other role, giving care in the home. Another recent change, in the Pregnancy Discrimination Act of 1978, forbids employers from discriminating on that basis. The argument is that if women and men occupy the caregiver roles and the roles in the workplace, children will not pick up the stark differences represented by Barbie and G.I. Joe.

It may help to compare this to the experience of other countries that have more deliberately made policies aimed at accommodating many roles women and men can fill. In most of western Europe, for example, women are legally recognized as having both home and work roles. That means employers are expected to give *paid* leave time for parental and maternity leave, extensive health coverage, and child-care benefits. Paid vacation periods are typically four weeks long. Men participate in these benefits as well.

At a simple level, the comparison seems stark. We are behind. It only seems that way if we agree that meaningful change will head in that direction. In this country, that is not yet clear.

The western European model shows that it is possible to publicly institutionalize and compensate both roles for men and women. Women most often are the primary caregiver in European homes. In the United States, women are usually the primary caregiver in the home, but that is regarded as a private matter. We seem to believe that that is the business of each family, and we will not publicly change it. If women want to have a different role in the home, in this country that is a *private* matter. Not political.

Is this a private or a political issue? Your answer probably reflects how you see this next idea.

One of the core ideas in the study of gender is *patriarchy*. Briefly, it means the rule of the father. In Western culture, authority is traditionally hierarchical, and the authorities at the top have usually been male. In the early modern period (the sixteenth and seventeenth centuries), it was seriously argued that political power was in some way related to parental power. Just as the father rules the house, so a father must rule the polity. Theorists such as Thomas Hobbes and John Locke dismantled the theory but left in its place an argument that modern societies emerged from the action of men asserting their natural rights. They were creating a public arena where rules for society could be made. They were creating the space for men, not women. Until very recently, few people looked seriously at where women were at the creation of the modern political order, and why their roles and duties seemed to take place in a private space, not the public space of politics. If you start asking questions about these things, you are asking questions about patriarchy.

There are two general trends in response to patriarchy. The first is firmly in the liberal tradition and relies on individualism and free expression. If we think that modern history, at least in our culture, is a gradual unfolding of human freedom and that it finally includes women, then our course is clear. If we pass laws that say it is illegal to discriminate on the basis of sex, gender neutrality is possible under the law and true human freedom is available to both sexes. Freedom will take the form of free expression and individual choice (meaning, importantly, women's choices) in sexuality, reproduction, careers, and living arrangements.

The second response seeks an entirely different answer, and the course is not so clear. This response is called radical feminism, and it rejects parts of the liberal tradition. The hierarchy in politics and society is a product of patriarchy, goes the argument. Gender-neutral laws are only paper and ignore the background of power and authority that excludes women from roles and labels them as inferior. Laws about equal credit, for example, ignore the larger reality of why women have had less access to credit. Marriage and prostitution, dating and rape, domestic violence and careers, the fashion industry and pornography are all institutions that are part of the web of patriarchy. Far-reaching changes in all of these institutions, including a radical rethinking of the nature of sexuality, will not happen overnight. It is going to take a long time to fully understand and change the hierarchies that confer on women second-class citizenship.

The liberal and radical views have very different implications for identity. The liberals believe that we must learn to think of women the way we do men—as full of possibilities, as having inherent inalienable natural rights, as being individual moral agents who get to choose how they live. Freedom and equality are found, for liberals, in universal standards. The radicals believe we must learn to understand distinctly women's interests, such as an ethic of caring and connectedness (discussed in Chapter 5). Women's interests are subversive to, and capable of liberating us from, the rules of traditional hierarchies.

The underlying question when studying gender is this: Can we abolish it?[13]

Perhaps we can start this way. Does gender qualify anyone for anything? Is reason found more in males or in females? Is strength needed to do a job or fill a role found in males, but not in females? Are different kinds of strengths gender-related? Is virtue found more in females than in males? Are you better suited to some things than others because you are female or a male? Are you gendered?

There are several ways of thinking about those questions. One is that gender impairs a person. We might think, for example, that men are simply incapable of a certain range of emotional response. They are not good at nurturing. Or we don't like the idea of male nurses or female topologists. In other words, we think that gender implies weakness and, at the same time, different strengths. This way of thinking asserts a natural division of labor—possibly more by the biology of sex than by the social construction of gender.

This seems to explain a lot of the world around us. Try completing these sentences: Women just aren't good at ____ . Men just aren't good at ____ . Fill in whatever you believe. Because women have traditionally filled fewer roles than have men (for example, they couldn't be fighter pilots), we have to think that it was men who effectively labeled the other as inferior. We can look at who does most of the driving on family trips. We can observe who does most of the shoveling or moving rocks when working in the garden. When tragedy strikes, we can see who does most of the comforting. We can ask male and female parents when their children and pets had their last vaccinations and whether they are up to date on all of them. If we see differences in these situations, we can ask why they happen. This approach to observing gender roles focuses on who gets the roles that confer power and control. If we see these to be distinct gender roles, we have taken the first important step to showing that the context determines our roles.

A second way of thinking about gender questions has to do with choice. Assume we turn out the way we do because of particular choices we each made. The choices are made in a context, of course, but consider the context as just background and not a determinant of your choices. A woman who excels at mathematics, for example, can simply choose to do so and ignore the fact that more women than men abandon higher math. A woman might think the Three Stooges are funny or might like Clint Eastwood movies. A man may prefer cooking and baking to football. A man may love to shop for jewelry. The key to seeing gender this way is to assume that the context does not guide or limit you very much.

A third way of thinking about gender issues is to focus on particular issues that seem to be central to patriarchy. For example, family roles are at the core of the analysis of patriarchy. In our current politics, they center on another intersection of sex and gender: the control of reproduction.

Control of reproduction decisions can be used to illustrate how apparently gender-neutral rules can instead be an outcome of patriarchy.[14] It was not until 1965 that the U.S. Supreme Court, in *Griswold v. Connecticut*, overturned state laws that outlawed the use of contraceptives, even by married people. They argued that basic protections for individual rights found in the Constitution created a zone of privacy where the state had no business. Conduct in the bedroom clearly was private. (Notice that the issue was framed as a liberal interpretation of freedom, not a radical critique of domination of women.) A similar argument was used by the Court in the 1973 decision about abortion.[15]

Before changes in the law between 1965 and 1973, women had much less control over reproduction. Is this control an important part of freedom for women? At stake is who gets to control whose body. One possibility is that physicians get to decide whether a woman has access to contraceptives or whether a woman can have an abortion. Another possibility is that a legislature decides who makes these choices in their particular state. There is the question of whether the man involved gets to decide anything. Advocates of reproductive choice argue that the control of women's bodies is the first order of business in establishing equality for women. Nothing is more basic. Advocates of social controls on reproduction argue that other rights, such as the rights of fetuses and the rights of male parents, need protection. Reproductive rights are at the core of women's identity (how they define themselves and how the wider society defines them). The issue is still contentious and is not likely to go away in this generation.

No matter how we see issues of gender and patriarchy, we know that change has happened, and more change will happen.

Here is one sign of a change over the last quarter-century. When one of us was in college a professor asked a class of about 125 people, including about 60 women, how many of the men planned a full-time career. All raised their hands. To the same question, less than half the women raised their hands. We ask the same question today of our classes, and all the women raise their hands.

Sex did not change. Gender did.

Gender differences are a strong theme in our history and philosophy.[16] It was not until 1792 that the first strong statement of women's rights and gender issues was published.[17] It was met with derision. Perhaps the clearest indicator of the

status of women in our politics and social thought is the nineteenth amendment to the Constitution. It was ratified in 1920.
It says, simply:

> The right of citizens of the United States to vote shall not be
> denied or abridged by the United States or by any State on
> account of sex.

Voting in 1920. Fighter pilots in 1993. That means all the
big changes are within living memory, and that the changes
are not over.

Gender goes much further than jobs, but jobs are important. Perhaps all the other social roles, the rights, and the
way men and women think about men and women are connected to jobs and the economic independence they confer.
Mary Wollstonecraft made that argument in 1792. Economic
independence is the key. Until women have that kind of independence, men will hold the power in society. It remains
true.

Still another way to see gender roles and the way they
define identity is to observe that the way people dress and the
way they do their hair says things to other people.[18]

People can say things to others by what they wear. A man
can wear a western shirt, string tie, and pointed-toe boots. He
can wear athletic shoes, brand-name shorts, and a tank top.
These are "marked" styles, styles that say something about
what this man thinks of himself and what he wants others to
think of him. Dress can be a statement of identity. The man
could also choose a style that says virtually nothing. Standard
hair, standard suit and tie, dark comfortable flat shoes. He
can choose to be "unmarked" and say simply, "I belong to the
mainstream group." He is "a suit."

Women may not have the choice. Few people notice if a
man doesn't wear makeup, but they do for women. There is
no standard women's haircut. Many of the widely used styles
of women's hair mark women. The same goes for shoes. Birks
say something, as do heels. The message of heels might
depend on how high they are. The length and cut of a skirt or
blouse say something. In our culture, women's bodies and
styles are always on display.

Here is the comparison to make. Through clothing, how easily can men choose not to say things about their masculinity or attractiveness? Through clothing, how easily can women choose not to say things about their femininity or attractiveness? Who has the most freedom, and why?

If gender is the strongest part of identity, we may see the whole world through either pink or blue glasses.

Individualism

Gender studies in the United States take place in a culture of individualism. Is full human development for women possible in a strongly individualistic culture?

The question is taken seriously by Elizabeth Fox-Genovese.[19] She argues that feminism has been part of an American tradition of political struggle and change. The dominant feature of that tradition is individualism. In a liberal culture like ours, we emphasize individual rewards and accomplishments. Although feminism embraces concepts such as sisterhood, the differences between women have been stronger than the things that bind them together. Women may claim that their own personal gains make the world better for all other women, but that is different from a collective purpose. They make it as individuals.[20]

An individualistic approach to freedom says that all individuals deserve equal rights and enlarged opportunities to allow room for each person to develop his or her talents and to receive the appropriate rewards. That is one of the main threads of feminism.

A sometimes competing claim in feminism is that there are distinct women's values. Women stand for things that men do not seem to care enough about. Women stand as the victims of patriarchy that has relied on the control of women's bodies, the setting of standards for thinking and learning, and the building of a culture of war.

This second thread of feminism is also informed by individualism, says Fox-Genovese. The nurturing and maternal values assigned to women came from a division of labor that had men organizing social power and women doing the household work. The mining, manufacturing, shipping, fishing, and most other parts of building a civilization were in the hands of men. The fact is that women were and continue to be involved in the building of civilizations. "To teach the French Revolution as an exclusively male story is not merely unfair to women, it is to distort the French Revolution itself, which touched all aspects of society and the polity, including gender relations," writes Fox-Genovese.[21] But that does not mean women were only adding nurturing and caring. We have to understand that men did not create everything, and that women did not merely sit and watch men make the world. Women's experience has included more than oppression, and men's experience has included more than the oppression of others.[22]

Fox-Genovese argues that in studying and rewriting history, in criticizing and reforming power, feminism has to break away from the strong individualism of the culture. She believes that this individualism is a value that has us see male and female as absolute categories, as essential parts of an individual's identity. Instead, she believes feminism should reflect "the multiplicity of female experiences, the range of female consciousness, and the varying strategies for coping with what remains overwhelmingly a man's world."[23]

To take this thought a little further, those experiences point to a need to guard the values of the whole that individualism too easily overlooks. The collective has needs too. Absolute individual freedom is a value that can abolish slavery in its many forms, but it can also neglect the need to raise children, to build communities, and to nurture the people around that free individual.

Fox-Genovese suggests that liberals may be wrong about the sources of individual rights. The rights of individuals may come from the society, not from an abstract nature or a powerful God. This means that the differences between men and women are important and subject to joint and constant reinterpretation.[24] Men and women are interdependent, not polar opposites.

The argument is a strong one, but we have to ask a serious question: How helpful is it to blame individualism when so many women and men believe in, enjoy, and prosper in it? What does it mean to attend to the collective needs if we like individualism?

If women and men are interdependent, there is a question we should ask: What if the ways of thinking and communicating among men and women are different?[25] It might mean that personal relationships and work organizations, to name two possibilities, will be places where conflict between styles emerges.

What if it is true? The developmental argument, reviewed in Chapter 5, alleges that men end up with a focus on independence. Their center, if you will, is about avoiding taking orders from others and maybe having the ability to give them. Women focus on intimacy. Their center, to use the same metaphor, is about avoiding isolation and maintaining connections with others.

This is how that might play out in a typical situation.[26] A man and woman who live together will talk about their own experiences. If the woman tells about troubles at work, she tends to look for understanding. The underlying message is about connections, and the response she seeks should affirm those connections— "We are the same, you are not alone." Men tend to hear stories of troubles as problems, and propose solutions. Their underlying message is about independence. The woman may hear this response as a denial of connections— "We are not the same, you have a problem and I have a solution." This can be a frustrating play: The women don't like the denial of connection, and the men don't like the women's unwillingness to take advice.

Studies of male and female patterns of conversation tend to bear out the fact of difference. For example, by counting instances of the styles noted above, we can find out who adjusts more in mixed conversation. Women change more to the male pattern than vice versa. Women interrupt more in same-sex conversations, and do so as a way to include more people in the conversation. Although men interrupt less, they resent the interruptions. Male stories tend to be about contests and their role in them and rarely feature women. Women's stories tend to tell about incidents, about norms and groups, and more often feature other people and men.

Again, what does it all mean, even if true? It means at least this: Relationships will have to be negotiated, and men and women will have to understand that conversational clarity is not automatic. Men and women may see the world in different ways and are seen differently by others. Put differently, there are powerful contextual limits on your identity. This possibility takes on startling proportions when we think about the links between sex and violence.

Sex and Violence

The United States is a violent place. We set the standard for murder and violent crime in the industrial world. About 1 in 10,000 people is murdered each year. We know, of course, that not all groups suffer the same murder rates. College students are not likely to die of murder. But if you are black, male, and between the ages of 16 and 40, your most likely cause of death is murder. For our entire population, a person is more likely to be killed by a gun than in an automobile wreck.

Violent crime, including rape, robbery, and aggravated assault, strike about 76 out of every 10,000 people.

Sex and violence seem to go together in our society.[27] The campus is just a microcosm of the ongoing epidemic of sexual assault in the United States.

No one knows the actual number of rapes. The FBI's *Uniform Crime Reports* show that out of an average 10,000 women, about 8 will be forcibly raped in a given year. That adds up to about 95,000 rapes each year in the United States. But that number is suspect. First, rape is probably the most unreported serious crime. How much unreported rape occurs? No one knows. It might be four times the reported amount. It might be 14 times the reported amount. Second, there is no agreed-upon definition of rape. The FBI forcible rape statistic is about reported rapes in which violence was clearly used, as in the case of the criminal using a weapon, or that occurred during another crime such as a break-in. We might think of all rapes as forcible, but the FBI does not. Many rapes reported on college campuses are not listed as forcible rapes.

The FBI's *Uniform Crime Reports* for the last decade show a steady increase in the number of rapes. Some of this may be due to an increase in the number of young males in the population. But if we look at the number of calls to rape crisis centers and talk to the people who work there, it seems that violence against women and rape has gotten worse in general.[28] But no one has done a systematic survey of the number of rapes on college campuses. Colleges are, as yet, uneven in required reports of crime on their campuses.

A study by Diana Russell, done in the early 1980s, found that about one quarter of a random sample of 900 women had been raped.[29] One in three had been sexually abused as a child.

This certainly is a serious problem, but there isn't a consensus among lawmakers on what they can do about it. They work within the liberal framework of law and individualism. The rules of behavior have to be precise. Is rape within marriage a crime? Not in all states. Is acquaintance rape a crime? Not in itself—the ambiguities of acquaintance rape usually are sorted out through laws geared to rape by strangers. If we want to use law to reduce rape, we need to clarify legal definitions of rape, to increase the likelihood that rapists are arrested and convicted, and to protect the rights of victims.[30]

Those changes are significant. One of the ways that rape can be clarified is to change its name. Sexual assault and sexual abuse, for example, are gender-neutral terms. They are crimes that can happen to men or women, and so are less frequently regarded as just a women's problem. The name changes also get away from the idea that women are property of men and that the damage done in a rape is to the man whose woman was sullied. (Does that idea sound ridiculous? Why weren't rapes of prostitutes and of wives by husbands vigorously pursued until recently?) Rape is a crime committed against a human being protected by the law. One sign of the change in attitude is that more states, about 40 percent, permit prosecution for violent rape by a spouse. Most states will allow prosecution if the couple is separated or divorced. About three-quarters of states have such gender-neutral definitions of rape.

The evidence needed to prove rape has changed in many states. Women in most states do not have to prove that they used specific amounts of physical resistance to demonstrate that sex took place without consent. Defense attorneys in fewer states can inquire about a woman's sexual history for evidence about character.

The issue of acquaintance rape on campus is an instructive example of the difficulties of sorting out rape in the law. In most states, there is a legal difference between rape by a stranger and rape by an acquaintance, such as a date. Vigorous police pursuit and state prosecution are mainly for rape by strangers.

Does that mean that women who go out on dates, have a man in their room, or go to a fraternity party are less able to say "no"? If the law does not help you say "no," does "no" mean different things in different places?

Because of the problems of definition and the lack of systematic data, it's unclear how often acquaintance rape occurs. Responding to students, parents, and lawsuits, many colleges now have special codes of conduct and disciplinary systems to deal with cases of acquaintance rape.[31] Yet, this is not about law and justice. This is about administering a college. First, the ability of colleges to deal with the problem of rape is severely limited. What can a college disciplinary system do, as an ultimate penalty, to someone found guilty of rape? The answer is, throw them out of the college. Students who use the college disciplinary systems are seeking extremely limited remedies to their assaults.

Second, there is a debate on college campuses over just what entails rape. As one student complained, "Administrators think that date rape is sex gone bad. . . . They don't think there are criminals on campus."[32]

That point is strongly argued by Camille Paglia.

> Today, these young women want the freedom that we won, but they don't want to acknowledge the risk. That's the problem. The minute you go out with a man, the minute you go to a bar to

have a drink, there is a risk. You have to accept the fact that part of the sizzle of sex comes from the danger of sex. You can be overpowered. . . . Women have the right to freely choose and to say yes or no. Everyone should be personally responsible for what happens in life. I see the sexual impulse as egotistical and dominating. . . . Women have to understand this correctly and they'll protect themselves better. If a real rape occurs, it's got to go to the police.[33]

That's one way of looking at it. It points to a problem with the liberal understanding of freedom and the law. Women simply have less freedom. Because they "can be overpowered," women have to keep themselves away from such situations. Then, if a "real rape" occurs, the legal system can get the bad guys. This, according to the argument, is a fact of life.

A different argument about rape rejects this entire line of reasoning. Acquaintance rape is real rape. No means no. The law, and colleges or any other organization, will not settle this as long as women are dominated by men. As Susan Brownmiller wrote in 1975, "rape has played a critical function. It is nothing more or less than a conscious process of intimidation by which *all men* keep *all women* in a state of fear."[34] Rape is thus a central part of patriarchy. To see women as property, to assess the damage in rape as sustained by the husband more than by the victim, to turn a blind eye to acquaintance rape, all contribute to domination of women by men.[35]

The subject of violence and women seems to flow from a discussion of gender issues. Both are connected to the experience of women in the workplace. The world seems to be a different place for men and for women. The fact of violence forces itself on identities.

Is peace possible?

A Community of Women

Here is a description of a group of women.[36]

They are the longest-lived occupational group in the United States. They live in a community that gives them a great deal of moral and spiritual support. They are not worried about paying the bills. Probably their biggest concern is whether they are on the right track to fulfill their mission. Their work takes them all over the country, and over the course of a career they will live in several different regions. They are highly educated and tend to change career tracks several times in the course of their lives. Often this means getting new advanced degrees or learning new skills. They run hospitals, social services, and a college. They frequently get together from all over the country to celebrate as a community. Their average age at death is 84, and they stay active in some way all their lives.

The women are nuns.

They have trouble finding new members for the order. A year that brings two new vocations, as they call members' vows, is now unusual.

They are serious, thoughtful, caring, and hard-working people.

The women are rarely faced with serious identity questions. The big questions of "Where do I fit in?," "What is my purpose here?," and "What is my relationship to other people?" are settled most of the time.

The bonds of their community might be strong partly because they come from all over the world. The people they live and work with are likely to be of different ages, from different regions of the country or from Nigeria or some other far-off place. This means they have experience dealing with diversity when it comes to making all sorts of community decisions. They have to make decisions about who works where, where to get money, how to spend money, how to run the hospitals and the colleges, and so on.

One enjoyable part of community life is they have friends of all ages. A 45-year-old member of the community will be close to others who are 30 and 75 years old.

They work with men. Under church law, women cannot provide the necessary sacraments by themselves, so they work with priests. Their bishop is a man. They also work with men in their hospitals and their college. They are in the wider world.

If you happen to pass through South Bend, Indiana, visit the campus of St. Mary's College. If you can, see the new chapel. It is not shaped like most churches. There is no space that separates people into leaders and the led. There are not many icons or stained-glass windows to remind people of stories that teach lessons. Instead, it is a space made to share and worship together.

The story is offered as a comparison. Relations between men and women will always be subject to negotiation. We can see a nation where individualism and power, community and support, are not comfortably balanced. Questions of identity are often answered in a context of narrow limits, even violence. It is instructive to realize that some people have constructed a community that enables them to live long and productive lives.

— 7 —

Sexual Orientation

The heart has its reasons, of which reason knows nothing.

—Blaise Pascal

In humans and other mammals . . . the overall male or female phenotype is an outcome of many interactions of different gene products (hormones) with autosomal and with X-linked gene loci.

—Cecie Starr and Ralph Taggart

This chapter is about sexual orientation and its relation to identity. In important ways, sexuality defines who you are, what others think of you, and what you think about others. Sexuality is often thought of as a private matter, and we start by looking at our concepts of what is private and what is public. It seems that, today, very little remains private.

Much of the chapter is about why we are attracted to whom and what that might mean. We discuss the biology and politics of defining how people think about sexual orientation, and explore how the opinions of those around us help determine our own attitudes and actions. It seems that, for most people, defining identity depends on labeling and distinguishing the self from others.

Do you care what other people do, in private, with their own body parts? Who really cares whether Dick loves Jane or Tom, or both of them? Why should Linda's loving Mary concern you at all?

Return, for a moment, to the metaphor of the circle of identity. Of those 20 beings that make up the identity of one person, how important is sexual orientation? You can begin answering that question with yourself. How many times during a day will you notice something about yourself or other people that has something to do with physical attraction? The encounters with attraction can vary from arousal toward another person to feeling comfortable with the way automobile advertisements are presented in a magazine.

Sexual orientation is part of our politics. As we write, the mayor of Seattle, Washington, has just appointed a committee to help him select a new chief of police. The mayor said, "involving a broad cross-section of the community, through this committee, will make my selection process stronger and more complete." He included people from different parts of the city, representatives of major activist groups, people of different colors, and people of different sexual orientations.

The mayor was careful how he used language. He did not say *sexual preference*, he said *sexual orientation*. Sexual preference may imply, to some, that people choose the way they want to be. Some people reject that notion and reject it publicly. The mayor did not want a gay rights demonstration over his police chief search committee.

Who we are attracted to and how we understand sexuality are parts of our identity. In this chapter, we will begin to sort out the issues involved. The issues might start with notions of what is private and what is public.

Ancient Greeks

Perhaps the best (but certainly not the most obvious) place to begin our discussion—in terms of context—is with the ancient Greeks.[1]

Much of Western culture began with the Greeks. Many of our myths, as well as much of our language, rest heavily on their ideas. Eros, after all, was the son of Aphrodite. He was not careful about the way he dispensed attraction and, usually, the agony that went with it.

The Greeks had definite ideas about what was public and what was private. The Greeks believed that people appear in public. There, in the presence of other citizens, people could speak and act, and others could watch and listen. If a person was to be immortalized—if that person was to be remembered—then it would be a result of what was said and done in the public space.

The idea was that there were things of importance to the whole community. There were public issues that united all citizens. If a person—if, to be precise, a citizen—could say the right thing at the right time, if a citizen could do the right thing at the right time, then the community would be better off for it. That citizen would be immortalized for doing something great in the presence of others.

An obvious example of this in recent times is the "I Have a Dream" speech by Martin Luther King, Jr. His were exactly the right words at exactly the right time. The nation was better off because of them. King has been immortalized—in part because of what he said that day.

There was, for the ancient Greeks, a special sense of what was public. Public was a place where a person could be defined by speech and action.

Private affairs were literally kept out of the sight of others. Boundaries were walls that divided the private from the public. A home was the place of children and slaves and sex and private matters. If a family was disgraced, that family's home would be destroyed and plowed under. The private place was simply destroyed; it was taken from the face of the earth. We can think of nothing like that in our society.

Wealth was, in moderation, a good thing to have, but its acquisition was mainly private. Wealth was not the point of a life well-lived in Greece; it simply allowed a person the opportunity to have free time to spend in the public place. Wealth gave a citizen the chance to say and do the right thing in order to be immortalized in stories and in myth.

Sex was not a public topic. We do read that powerful men loved their families and also loved beautiful younger men. This was as much a political as a sexual matter. We also read that women stayed inside. Men were public and had the opportunity for immorality. Most women were above slaves but stayed within their boundaries. Some women were allowed into the public spaces and allowed to choose their casual and intimate friends. Some were prostitutes and others were not tied to a man's home. The public person was literally one who owned his or her own body.

But the point here is not about how women and slaves were treated in ancient Greece. The point is that there were things public and things private. It is a distinction worth considering.

Differences Now

Have we changed so much from the Greeks?

One of the most important things that happened was that the business of government changed. Household affairs—things that were once private—have now become the business of government. We have become a national family, with government having become something like a parent.

In modern times, there are few things that government does not care for and even fewer places where government does not go. Our public debates are about private matters. Republicans and Democrats argue about who has the power over a womb. There are laws about just where a penis can go and who may have access to whose vagina. In a recent confirmation hearing of a Supreme Court justice, we listened to talk about Long Dong Silver and pubic hair on a can of Coke.

Are those really affairs of state? Is it right that these topics have become part of the great debates of our time? Who really cares what Jesse Helms, the ultraconservative senator from North Carolina, has to say about lust and physical attraction and art?

But let's take it one more step. When we look around on campus, it seems that one of the more organized and maybe even more interesting sets of groups are organized around their body parts. On some campuses, gays, lesbians, and bisexuals have an enviable kind of community. They support causes, have parties, hang out together, and keep each other company.

They seem to have formed a kind of community and created a public place to act, as the Greeks had sought, about important things. Perhaps they understand that if they stick together, they can fight off oppression while publicly playing off the routinely homophobic attitudes so many people have.

Do straight students need gays and lesbians to bring up the topic of sexuality? The answer is yes, if we mean by that to bring up the topic so that we can see it in fundamental ways. Plenty of people routinely think about sex. Studies show that men think about sex six times an hour. Once every 10 minutes. Six times during a normal class. College-age people are, physically, at their sexual peak, fertile and virile and physically about as prime as you're going to be, so once every 10 minutes might be a conservative number. But the routine thinking about sex is generally not about asking fundamental questions.

If a visitor from Mars spent time on the two campuses where we teach, sex would appear to be lesbian, gay, or bisexual on the East Coast and straight on the West Coast. At the University of Massachusetts in Amherst, straight sex seems prim. At Pacific Lutheran University in Washington State, one of the few public acknowledgments of sex is the jar of condoms in the health center. Is there a right and a wrong here? Of course, there are other kinds of East and West Coast campuses, but the point is that there are differences.

There is a book by an anthropologist named Michael Moffett.[2] The idea of the book is interesting: The young-looking Moffett lived in a dorm at Rutgers and pretended to be a first-year student. He studied the students. He actually continued his study in the culture of students for several more years.

Near the end, Moffett spends two chapters on sex. It reads a little like the letters to *Penthouse* magazine—lots of stripping and throbbing and the like, focused on genitals, and students who want fast action. For those two chapters, almost all of the sex is heterosexual.

Are we to believe that Rutgers, a state university in New Jersey, is straight? Are we to believe that everyone sees sex the way it is presented in *Penthouse?*

Let's look at each of these two questions. For the first, do we care about the incidence of homosexuality? For a long time, most writers on the subject believed about 10 percent of the population to be homosexual. Are all 10 percent in the closet at some colleges—Rutgers, for example? It is possible that some campuses attract more gay students, or that proportionately fewer homosexuals attend college. Reliable data about the number of gays in the general population and on campuses are hard to find. Recent reports place the frequency of homosexuality in the general population closer to 1 to 2 percent.[3] There is a lot of controversy over the different estimates. Advocates of the larger number seem to think it shows an added importance to gays and lesbians, as if that means their concerns are more valid. Advocates of the smaller number seem to use it in the opposite way. Does it matter?

The numbers researchers find will differ with the way questions are asked. If you were taking a survey, would you simply ask whether someone was gay or straight and leave it at that? Or would you *not* rely on self-reports? Would you ask about behavior, like when and how often the subject does what? Would you focus on behavior, gender identity, or both? Would any homosexual behavior qualify, or would only sustained behavior count? Who would you ask? Would you do a random survey of the population or ask the people who came into a clinic that dealt with sex? Where would you ask them? How would you get people to trust you on what might be a delicate and private subject? It is not surprising that survey results, especially about sex, can vary tremendously.

The fact is, no one really knows how many people are doing what and with whom.

Would we treat people differently if the group they belonged to constituted 1 percent, instead of 10 percent, of the population?

The second issue here is what people mean by sex. Does sex mean The Act and the specific uses of body parts? Magazines like *Penthouse* and most pornographic films are aimed directly at a heterosexual male audience. Does that group get to define sex for everyone else? Might sex mean intimacy and trust and caring for someone else? It might include both, and there are serious questions about what happens when either side is left out.[4]

What about Michael Moffett? At one point, he muses about being 30-something and hanging out in a younger world. Did he accurately tell us what was going on?

The questions about who is doing what are important for those who run higher education. More and more, the people who run higher education are finding they must have—excuse the pun—a hands-on policy when it comes to sex. Again, more questions come up. Should students set policies? Should bisexuals and lesbians and gays set the agenda? Should we go back to the fifties and play out those strange times; should we go back to the sixties and play out those even stranger times?

On today's college campuses, sex seems to take up more mental energy than any other three topics combined. But we are caught in the very strange situation—sex is about as private a matter as you can imagine, but it has become part of our public life. If that is so, what should we in higher education be doing about it? Should sex be the one activity in life that we ignore?

What people do with their bodies seems to be of great wonder to just about everyone in higher education. It makes sense to understand something about sexual orientation and what, if anything, it means.

Figuring out your self, your body, and someone else's body is not easy. There are times we may want to kill for love and other times we want to die for love. We go through a lot with the great hope that, someday, we finally get it right. What follows is a discussion of some of the psychology, physiology, and politics that lace love and attraction. Although it is an incomplete account of each particular group, by the end of the chapter, much of the important material will be—how best to say it?—exposed.

Women

Imagine.

You have a secret. You have never really been comfortable dating men. In fact, you seem attracted to women—to people of your own sex. You know all of the things that society says about women who love women. You know that your parents expect you to marry and have children. You don't *look* like what a dyke is supposed to look like. You don't have a crew cut. You don't wear leather. You like to "dress." You even shave your legs.

But you are attracted to women.

After forever—or what seems forever—you decide to talk with your best friend. The two of you have known each other from high school and decided to go to the same college. So, one night, the two of you talk. You tell her that you think you might be a lesbian.

She looks at you as if you were from another planet. She leans away from you a little. Without thinking, she crosses her legs. She stares.

The conversation isn't very helpful. She's clearly uncomfortable. From what little she says, you figure out that she thinks you are a pervert. A *pervert!* From your best friend. Well, from your former best friend. And then what does she do? She blabs all over campus. Imagine your surprise—you're out of a closet you weren't even sure you were in, and you feel awful.

Or, imagine this.

College has been great. You did pretty well on the first round of exams. The classes are so much better than anything you had in high school. Being away from home was kind of hard at first, but you like being on your own. Anyway, there are phone calls and letters that really help. There is always something to do and there are always people around. There are a bunch of guys to hang out with, and you think that there is one who could be special.

The dorm is fun, but never exactly quiet. And some people are so messy you wouldn't believe it. Yuck. What would their moms say? And talk about luck—you got the neatest roommate. She's a little quiet, but very definitely neat. Life is good.

One day, in the student union, you're hanging out with your roommate's best friend. She can't wait to tell you this: Your roommate is queer.

You go back to your room and don't know what to do. You like your roommate. She's been great. But what if she is a homosexual? How are you supposed to act? Is it OK to undress in front of her? Should you look away when she undresses? Suddenly, in your head, life in your very own room will never be the same.

What is going on? Here are two normal, average women. They are college roommates. If you did not know their sexual orientation, you would have a hard time telling them apart. But the point is that there are a lot of people who make a very big deal out of sexual orientation. Men and women. They make other people's sexual habits their business.

Can you imagine?

Let's go back and do a little history. It was not until the 1890s that we even had the word homosexual or lesbian. Things are even more curious than that: The word *heterosexual* did not come into being until 1892. Originally, it meant an "abnormal or perverted appetite toward members of the opposite sex." It didn't take long for heterosexual to take the meaning that we now know.

Does that mean that there were not women who loved women before 1890? Don't be silly. Same-sex love has always been with us. So how was sex described? Until the last century, there were two kinds of sex: natural and unnatural. In natural sex, you would create babies; in unnatural sex you wouldn't. That is one of the ways society still teaches us about sex—it is either natural or unnatural. There are those among us who don't stop there. We hear that natural sex is right and unnatural sex is wrong. Go to heaven, go to hell.

Can you imagine what it is like if you have the "wrong" feelings? If it seems that everyone important says that you somehow have gotten love and sex wrong? If the moral law is heterosexuality, then to be homosexual is to be an outlaw.

Two things, at least, are going on here. The first thing has to do with people who are attracted to people of the other sex, people who are in the great 90-something percent of the population. Heterosexuals grow up with the absolute support of the institutions of society. From religious self-righteousness to role models, being heterosexual is just the thing to be.

But something happened. It turns out that not everyone is heterosexual. Not only that, homosexuals are individually as different as heterosexuals. Tall, short, fat, skinny, funny, grim, smart, dumb, long-hair, short-hair, no-hair, pink, yellow, red, black, and so on. Who knows who is lesbian or who is gay or who is bisexual? Unless a person flaunts it, who knows? The lipstick lesbian looks straight, but the stone butch looks lesbian. Looks lie if all that is in your head are stereotypes.

History

A short history of lesbians in the United States shows some important changes in how society has treated them. The times—this is no great surprise—have been the dominant force in shaping how we see sexuality.

During the 1800s, there was a notion of romantic friendship. Basically, that meant women could live together as friends and lovers and no one would notice. Same-sex love, for women, was not a public issue. There seemed to be a category of women who lived together who were great friends, and no one thought too much about it. People did their best to ignore the fact women slept together.

Biographers of the last century did their share to promote the idea of female friendship without sex. For example, Jane Addams, a pioneer in American social services, had a relationship with a woman named Mary Rozet Smith that lasted for 40 years. They lived together, and when they traveled together they wired ahead and asked for a double bed. Given such evidence, one recent biographer wrote:[5]

> [She] remained largely untouched by the passionate currents that swirled around her. The crowning irony of Jane Addams' life, therefore, was that she compromised her intellect for the sake of human experiences which her nature prevented her from having. Life, as she meant the term, eluded her.

What the biographer should have said was that life as he meant it (heterosexuality, marriage, and family) eluded her. What we know is that passion and love did not elude her. She had a 40-year romantic relationship—people sometimes called two women who lived together "devoted companions"—that we should assume was very satisfying. The modern notion of lesbians and the term *being in the closet* had yet to be invented.

That does not mean that the surrounding culture was sympathetic to a lesbian life. Society was robustly heterosexual, and heterosexual assumptions were part of nearly every institution. Attitudes about sexual orientation become concrete in countless small ways, from marriage laws and customs to rules for social clubs, from faculty spouses' teas to medicine. This is all still true. Although the idea of being in the closet may not have been invented, lesbians were certainly not welcome to be themselves in the parlor.

Around the turn of the century, things began to change. Sexologists began to write about homosexuality. They began to study lesbians, whom they called "sexual inverts." Before, people who loved others of the same sex were thought of—if at all—as sinners. Sexologists began to describe these people as "homosexuals" and as victims of inborn "contrary sexual feelings."[6] These were new categories. They had the effect of defining same-sex love as something sick or abnormal.

Once "lesbians" were "discovered," people apparently found them very interesting. In the Index Catalogue of the Library of the Surgeon General's Office, there is only one article on lesbians between 1740 and 1895. But between 1896 and 1916, the same catalogue lists almost 100 books and 566 articles on women's "perversions," "inversions," and "disorders."[7]

All of a sudden, there was a word for—a concept of—lesbianism. Lesbians were believed to be born with an inverted sexuality and have many masculine traits. All of those women who were called devoted companions in the nineteenth century were to be called lesbians in the twentieth century. By the 1920s, there was another turn on how lesbians were seen.

The twenties were wild times. During the twenties, a sociologist named Catharine Bement Davis studied 2,200 women. She found a little over half of them (50.4 percent) admitted intense emotional relations with other women and half of that number said that those emotions experienced were either "accompanied by sex or recognized as sexual in character."[8] Many of the women studied eventually married and settled down to have a family, but the twenties were a time to experiment.

Being a lesbian, in certain social circles, was chic. It was the in thing to do. It was a form of rebellion that fit in perfectly with the times. Bisexuality, in particular, seemed to be accepted. Freud himself thought that bisexuality had a physiological basis. In trendy social circles—especially in New York City—many people tried it and liked it.

Lesbian chic was trendy, and the most trendy place to flaunt it was in Harlem. We read: "Made braver by bootlegged liquor, jazz, and what they saw as the primitive excitement of Africa, they acted out their enchantment with the primal and the erotic."[9] Although blacks had the same basic attitudes about homosexuals as whites, there were clubs in Harlem that catered to homosexuals. It was, to use the language of the day, everything naughty. Harlem was the place to go.

If the twenties were open, the thirties were closed. The nation shut down in a remarkable number of ways. The Great Depression affected everyone. Society returned to traditional values. One of the key traditional values was that men worked and women stayed at home. There was a lesbian population, but it was generally a working-class population. It was a population that wandered the country looking for work. During the thirties, being a lesbian was, in part, an adventure.

Many lesbians settled for the safety of marriage and, possibly, a bisexual life. But not much is known about how many women did this or what it was like for them. During times when such stories are not told, people don't share understandings on what it means to be lesbian or bisexual. For example, Eleanor Roosevelt—easily the most admired first lady in our history—apparently had an affair with journalist Lorena Hickok.[10] It was not common knowledge until about 50 years after the affair. Did that make Roosevelt a lesbian? A bisexual? She didn't write down what she thought about these questions.

Lesbians, in the thirties, were in the closet. Lillian Faderman writes:

Sandra, who worked in a Portland department store during the '30s, tells of having been part of a group of eight women—four couples—who went skiing every winter between 1934 and '37. "I'm sure we were all gay," she remembers, "but we never said a word about it. Talking about it just wasn't the thing to do. Never once did I hear the L word in that group or any word like it— even though we always rented a cabin together and we all agreed that we only wanted four beds since we slept in pairs."[11]

World War II changed things. With so many men fighting, women were again an important part of the work force. Also, women served in the military. One estimate suggests that about a third of the one million women in the military were lesbians. Although the military did not really want lesbians, they did need people to do work. If lesbians did work, then so be it. The military had a giant "who cares?" attitude until the end of the war.

The tolerance ended when the war did. The military loaded thousands of homosexuals onto "queer ships," gave them "undesirable discharges," and took them to the nearest U.S. port. A huge number decided not to return to their hometown. Instead, they stayed in those port cities and established homosexual enclaves. That is what people in social science call an *unintended consequence*. The port cities of Boston, New York, San Francisco, and Los Angeles became home for gays. According to historian Allan Berube, "The government sponsored a migration of the gay community."[12]

In post–World War II America, the psychoanalytic community decided that homosexuality was an illness. Luckily for their profession, psychoanalysts also decided it was an illness that could be cured. They seemed to agree that the "sickness" of homosexuality would respond to the right kind of therapy. Psychoanalyst Edmund Bergler actually promised his patients that same-sex love was reversible. The treatment would be at least three appointments a week with a psychiatrist for a year or two. The cost, in today's dollars, was about $60,000.[13]

Women who loved women had gone from being called devoted companions to being called sick. By the 1950s, things got worse.

During the fifties, especially the early fifties, there was an effort by the U.S. Congress—in the form of Senator Joseph McCarthy—to purge the government of "undesirables." Undesirables were communists and homosexuals. (It is more than a little ironic that two of McCarthy's aides were openly homosexual.) When Dwight Eisenhower took office in 1953, one of the first things that he signed was an executive order calling for an investigation of people in government who were suspected of being homosexual. It also called for the screening of applicants for new positions. The military had investigations looking for gays and lesbians it could discharge. To sum up the times, Lillian Faderman believes that "[t]he 1950s were perhaps the worst time in history for women to love women."[14]

By the beginning of the sixties, lesbians were in an almost unique position. Sixty years earlier, love between women hardly had a name—and it certainly was not considered a pathological condition. Women who loved each other did so in a quiet way, and most of society, most of the time, ignored them. While it might have been thought of as sinful, it seems that it was rarely thought of at all. But the days that women could be romantic friends or devoted companions were gone forever.

By the sixties, lesbians had a name and were treated as sick, subversive people. Just as bad, in terms of politics and identity, they had no real history or customs or mores. Other minorities have those things—blacks and Jews and Catholics have a history; they have a past to give them identity and direction. Lesbians had none of those things.

Come the sixties. The whole decade seemed, in large part, devoted to liberation and being, wherever possible, offensive to existing standards. One of the first things to be liberated was sex. Premarital sex, group sex, mate swapping. There was the pill, there were miniskirts. It was in-your-face time. Heterosexuality now looked like homosexuality—it was done for love and for fun, but not necessarily to make babies. A remarkable number of young people experimented with what seemed like everybody. Genital life was an adventure. With it came an epidemic of sexually transmitted diseases. It is hard to imagine the spread of herpes and chlamydia in the seventies and AIDS in the eighties and nineties without thinking about the sixties.

The women's movement reemerged. The idea of equality began to spread from repressed group to repressed group. There were sit-ins and marches and lawsuits and legislation that helped push the idea of equal rights. The push for liberation and subverting existing standards did have real effects. During the sixties, homosexual activity was more in the open, and more people were experimenting with it, but it was not until the end of the sixties that the idea of a large, active, and political homosexual community emerged.

This brief history of the interplay of society and homosexuality ends with Stonewall.

Stonewall was the turning point in homosexual politics in the United States. On June 28, 1969, the police in New York City raided the Stonewall Inn. Stonewall was a gay bar in Greenwich Village that called itself a private club. The raid was one of many on gay bars during that time.

As always, the patrons were put out in the street after being questioned. Unlike previous raids, they did not go home. They stayed in front of the bar and began a riot. They threw bottles and garbage and anything they could find to throw, including an uprooted parking meter.

Four policemen were hurt. The riots continued the next night. Fires were started all over the neighborhood. The *New York Times* reported it on page 33. The Stonewall Rebellion was the first gay riot in history. It was the turning point, the event that identified homosexuals as a group that needed to demand equal rights. It was the beginning of the politics of sexual orientation . . . and possibly sexual preference.

Politics

Two things are going on that need to be made clear. The first thing is that there continues to be prejudice against lesbians. Not from everyone, and those who are biased are biased in varying degrees, but it is safe to say there is prejudice. In reaction, there is an impulse for any oppressed group to band together. Individuals are almost forced together by the way they are treated.

The second thing is that there are lesbians who believe they see and understand the world in a different, unique way. It is their intention to separate themselves from mainstream life and to create their own community and their own culture, separate from heterosexuals and gay men. This is very different from feminism. Feminism is a much more straightforward attempt to make society safe for women and for sexual orientation. Not all lesbians take kindly to feminism:[15]

> Lived and practiced feminism has been a constant source of pain for so many lesbians because of heterosexual women's continued loyalty to men and because of feminism's failed promise of friendship among women.

There are those lesbians, then, who concentrate their energies on other lesbians and lesbian issues. These are intensely political attachments. How they understand themselves and what they call themselves is important—it helps define what they are.

Do labels count? They do to Julia Penelope. In *Call Me Lesbian,* she tells how her identities changed as she was growing up. She has called herself Republican, beatnik, existentialist, Leninist, Ayn Randian objectivist, libertarian conservative, feminist, lesbian-feminist, and separatist. She has also been a homosexual and a stone butch. She reports that she had a "heterosexual phase" that lasted "maybe three seconds."[16]

For people outside the community, these definitions do not seem compellingly important. A stone butch, for example, is a lesbian who will not allow other lesbians to make love to her— she insists on being the active partner. Do you care? Maybe not. But if it were your sexual identity, maybe you would care. For the separatists, the politics of being a lesbian is central to much of what they do. It helps make up their identity, and they certainly do not care how they look to outsiders.

One of the debates in the community revolves around why women become lesbians. It is a kind of nature/nurture debate. Is a person a lesbian from birth, or does society "make" a lesbian? Gay men seem more into this particular debate, so we will take it up later. Just know that it is a political (and medical) matter people take sides on.

To choose to be a lesbian is to choose to live a certain way. It is to choose to be who you are. It is a choice that defines what you do. It is a declaration. It is an act.

Some define themselves as separatists and choose a separate community. That means exclusion. Political communities, especially those that feel oppressed, tend to isolate themselves. In order to feel safe from outside oppressors, it is necessary to build boundaries and exclude. In order to develop a separatist lesbian identity, there must be as little outside interference as possible.

Politically, separation makes good sense if one feels the prevailing norms are hostile. Here is a question that mimics that sense of hostility for heterosexual white women: Would you feel more uncomfortable in a lesbian separatist meeting or a white supremacist meeting?

"The Lesbian stands against the world created by the male imagination. What willfulness we possess when we claim our lives!"[17] There is an extreme to exclusion. Here is a sense of what community can mean:

In 1989, Lesbian mothers brought at least four male children to the first East Coast Lesbian Festival even though the festival brochure said specifically: "Lesbians and Girl Children Welcome." . . . Why . . . do a few mothers insist that we tolerate their sons? For one thing they have millennia of heteropatriarchal dogma behind their demands: Because breeding is considered "normal" and "natural," those mothers expect to take their offspring wherever they wish. . . . Some Lesbian mothers persist in demanding that we allow them to bring male children to wimmin- and Lesbian-only events. Their insistence on giving males access to wimmin- and Lesbian-only spaces reaffirms the breeders' privilege they enjoy in the heteropatriarchy.

If Lesbians want to raise males, they should be teaching them that wimmin have the right to establish our spaces; that no man has any right to be where we don't want him; that "No" doesn't mean "Yes" . . . "wimmin-only" space means wimmin only; "Lesbians only" space means lesbians only. There is no ambiguity in either phrase. Sons are, by definition, inherently male; otherwise, they would be daughters.[18]

In the politics of oppression/identity/community, the above is a pretty clear statement. The underlying emotion is this:[19]

> Picture for yourself the map of the "known" world presented to us every moment, every day of our lives. Label that map HETEROPATRIARCHY out to the very neatly trimmed edges. Now read the warning signs along the edge: "Dangerous," "monstrous," "sick," "sinful," "illegal," "unsafe," "Keep Out! Trespassers will be violated!"

If that is how a woman who loves women sees the world, it is no great surprise that coming out as a lesbian is not an easy thing to do. For anyone considering coming out, the uncertainty and fear are grim facts. How does a lesbian on the verge of coming out approach a telephone call that could very well mean her parents will never speak to her again? Or how does one decide to act openly in a way that may move best friends or employers or the dentist or the neighborhood kids to suddenly grow hostile? One answer, one political answer, is to separate yourself from everything that is dangerous, monstrous, and the like.

The extreme separatist view does give us a better sense of some of the emotions behind what a homosexual might go through, but it is clearly not the whole picture. The fact is that there is no agreed-upon definition of the word *lesbian*. It is silly to believe that a mere sexual act (or acts) defines a human being. Many lesbians have sexual attractions but never act on them. Some remain celibate all of their lives. Some come out as lesbians as soon as they can; some come out after years of marriage and raising a family. Some come out when they are at college—when they are 18 or 28 or 38 or 48. Some are militant separatists and are happy, and some have baby boys and are happy.

Men

As we saw the politics of homosexuality with lesbians, we can see the biology and psychology of homosexuality with gay

men. Certainly, gay men are political and have created different communities. We also know that lesbians debate psychology and biology. The oppressed vision of the world that some
lesbians have is shared by some gay men. There are lesbian
communities, there are gay communities.

There is the story of the professor who began his class by
saying, "Today, we will discuss the theories about why some
men are gay." A student—a loud-voiced student—said, "Who
cares?" The rest of the class cheered.

The class cheer may be a sign of disgust at homosexuality,
but it might mean something else, too. Why should we care
about theories of the origins of sexual orientation? In a liberal
society, where we value individual rights and liberties, what
matters most are behavior and institutions. If we see that
some people are denied the exercise of their rights or are
oppressed by the state or by what John Stuart Mill called the
"tyranny of the prevailing opinion and feeling," we have identified problems with behavior and institutions. Freedom and
equal treatment today, regardless of the origins of our differences, are what should matter.

But the question of origins is hotly debated. It matters to
people on both sides of the debate because they want to make
statements about themselves and about the other side. The
quest for facts is taken up in the defense of values.

Here is one way of thinking about why a person finds
another person attractive. Suppose you see two people
together, obviously enjoying their attraction to each other. You
conclude, They have found each other. Lucky them.

There it is. You don't bother to judge the people, no matter
who or what they are. You don't think much about the origins
of their feelings.

Would it make a difference to know the reasons they preferred each other to other people? Their sexual identity is a
fact.

The whole question of whether homosexuality is a choice
or something that cannot be changed seems to be connected
with approval or disapproval of homosexual behavior.[20] The
public is evenly split on whether they believe homosexuality is
a choice. Among those who think it is a choice, 64 percent
object to having a homosexual doctor, compared to 34 per-

cent of those who believe it is not a choice. Among those who think it is a choice, 78 percent say homosexual relations are morally wrong, compared to 30 percent of those who believe it is not a choice. Among those who think it is a choice, 71 percent object to having a homosexual as a child's elementary school teacher, compared to 39 percent of those who believe it is not a choice. Among those who believe it is a choice, 30 percent say laws should be passed to make sure homosexuals have equal rights, compared to 58 percent of those who believe it is not a choice.

It seems that belief of cause and effect is connected to moral judgments.

Some argue that homosexuality is an illness that can be cured. For a long time, that was the consensus among psychoanalysts. To understand this point of view, it is useful to start with Freud.

Psychology and Homosexuality

Freud did remarkable work, inventing much of what we know as modern psychology. He believed he was a scientist, and he set out to discover and prove the science of the human psyche. His followers claim that is exactly what he did. Some of his ideas are very useful when trying to understand human motivation and behavior. Not only that, Freud the scientist and inventor was probably more interesting and open to different ideas than many who have tried to adapt his work.

Freud did not know a lot of things—in a famous passage, he confessed his ignorance of what women wanted, for example. But he did know a lot of other things. The following quotes are from a letter to an American mother whose son was a homosexual (this was in 1935) and from a newspaper interview (published in 1903).[21] The first quote is to the mother:

> Homosexuality is assuredly no advantage, but it is nothing to be ashamed of, no vice, no degradation, it cannot be classified as an illness. . . . Many highly respectable individuals of ancient and modern times have been homosexuals, several of the great-

est men among them (Plato, Michelangelo, Leonardo da Vinci, etc.). It is a great injustice to persecute homosexuality as a crime, and cruelty too.

I am . . . of the firm conviction that homosexuals must not be treated as sick people. . . . Wouldn't that oblige us to character-ize as sick many great thinkers and scholars . . . whom we admire precisely because of their mental health? Homosexual persons are not sick. They also do not belong in a court of law!

Although Freud did equivocate about whether being a homosexual was pathological, he was clear that he believed that homosexuals were not sick. Interestingly, what he believed, wrote, and said apparently had little effect on the profession he still dominates. Until 1973, the American Psy-chiatric Association listed homosexuality as an emotional dis-order. The group did not come to the decision easily. In 1974, the decision was bitterly debated and voted on again. Thirty-seven percent of the APA members voted to reinstate homo-sexuality as an emotional disorder. Thirty-seven percent believed that being gay was being sick.

If you are gay and feel awful about it, there are still those in the helping professions who will help you try to "get over it." Joseph Nicolosi, a psychologist, is one of those "helpers."[22] While he believes that no one is ever "cured," there can be "a diminishment of homosexual feelings" to the point that some gay men can marry and have families. He says that treatment is "probably a lifetime process."[23]

A psychoanalyst, Charles Socarides, believes that human beings were "anatomically made to go in male–female pairs." He writes that "the homosexual is ill, and anything that tends to hide that fact reduces his chances of seeking and obtaining treatment."[24] In an interview, Socarides said that he has a flourishing practice turning unhappy homosexuals into "happy, fulfilled heterosexuals."[25]

Traditionally, homosexuals have been excluded from psy-choanalytic training. The bias continues.[26] In order to under-stand the bias against homosexuals, it is necessary to know a little about psychoanalytic theory. To understand the theory is to see the bias against homosexuals.

Freud, as we saw, did not believe that homosexuality was a sickness. Indeed, he was open to the idea that there was a genetic predisposition to bisexuality. From there it would not be so difficult to consider the possibility that being homosexual was also a product of nature and not of nurture. But many of Freud's followers liked the psychological explanation much more than the biological one.[27] Briefly, the psychological explanation of why men are gay is as follows:

The psychoanalytic theories of homosexuality agree that gay men suffer from "a deficiency in their masculinity."[28] In psychological terms, that means something went wrong in early childhood and that the "normal" development did not take place. Psychoanalytic thinking holds that if "normal" development does not take place, the person is, almost by definition, abnormal.

The reasons why normal development does not take place—for the arrested development of the homosexual—have to do with the father or the mother or both of them. We read:[29]

> Either a distant father fails to help his son separate from his mother or the mother pathologically binds the boy to her, sometimes because of her own ungratified needs to be mothered. She attempts to get what she lacks by giving, but does so with enormous rage that is emotionally draining to her and wounding to the child. In both scenarios, gay men are believed to have either a conscious or an unconscious feeling of femininity. To put it simply, traditional analysts believe a man cannot be homosexual without also being and/or feeling effeminate.

> Distant (or weak or detached or hostile) father + smothering (or dominating) mother = gay son.

Can this really be true? What about heterosexuals who have weak dads and dominating moms? What about homosexuals with normal parents? What about well-adjusted and healthy homosexuals? Wouldn't all gays exhibit signs of mental illness if they did not develop "normally"? The problem with this theory is that studies tell us the percentage of homosexuals and heterosexuals with psychological pathology are the same.[30] Gays, in other words, are no "sicker" than straights.

To be fair, not all psychotherapists believe that homosexuals suffer from abnormal development. Although many analysts continue their belief that how a person is raised is the key to sexual orientation, most psychologists seem to have rejected the idea. Smothering mothers and distant dads do not automatically produce gay sons. Maybe they never do. No one quite knows.

If psychology does not give us a clear understanding about why some men are gay, then maybe we should look at biology.

Biology

Biology, in truth, is not much more helpful than psychology.

Some very recent studies seem to say that biology is a piece of destiny in terms of sexual orientation. There are many holes in the evidence, but one summary puts it this way:

> [S]cientists must sift for their conclusions through ambiguous results from a disparate group of studies that are excruciatingly difficult to interpret. Yet even at this relatively early date, out of the web of complexities it is becoming ever clearer that biological factors play a role in determining human sexual orientation.[31]

Here are examples of some of those studies.

Neuroscientist Simon LeVay, working at the Salk Institute, studied the brains of 41 male cadavers.[32] Nineteen of them were homosexuals. He found that the tiny area believed to control sexual activity—the nucleus of the hypothalamus—was less than half the size in gay men as in straight men. Difference does not mean cause, but something seemed to be different in the brains of homosexual and heterosexual men.

In another study, this one of identical twins, it was found that if one of the twins is gay, the other is almost three times more likely to be gay than if the twins were fraternal. Of the

56 identical twins studied, 52 percent were both gay, as opposed to 22 percent of the fraternal twins. Fraternal twins have weaker genetic bonds. To take it a step further, of adoptive, nongenetically related brothers, only 11 percent were both gay.[33]

A study of one set of identical twins who were raised apart found that both were homosexual.[34] Another study showed that gay men have significantly more homosexual or bisexual brothers (22 percent) than do heterosexual men (4 percent).[35] Similar findings come from studies of hormones and genetics.

Is it nature or nurture? Is it biology or politics? Is it a combination of each? And does it matter? Does it matter to you why you, or your roommate, or your uncle, or the person sitting in front of you is sexually attracted to his or her same sex? Is it important to you if homosexuality is born or bred?

What if, right now, the phone rings. You answer it and it's your parents. They want to tell you something. Maybe you want to sit down, they say. For all these years, they tell you, one of them has been a closet homosexual. Now that you are in college, you should be old enough to understand. They are going to divorce. Of course they will always be friends, but one of them can no longer stay in the closet. You will have a new parent—Pat.

They both still love you. You hang up.

What is your reaction? What are you thinking? Does this say anything about your identity? Why?

Let's take it one step further. Let's say your homosexual parent is a career officer in the armed forces of the United States.

Bill Clinton, while he was running for President of the United States, promised your parent and everyone else that he would overturn the military's ban on homosexuals serving in the armed forces. It was one of several things he said as campaign promises, promises that he used to influence voters and to win the 1992 presidential election.

He could have easily made the change by himself. In purely formal terms, all he had to do was sign an executive order and overturn the ban. He could have done that as commander in chief of the armed forces.

But the President chose not to do that. Had he done so, Congress almost certainly would have overturned his order. Instead, he raised the issue with people in the Defense Department, notably the Joint Chiefs of Staff, and with people in Congress, and found little support for lifting the ban. Many people in the military and Congress openly opposed lifting the ban.

The Senate Armed Services Committee held extensive hearings on the subject and heard influential opinions supporting and opposing the ban.[36] The politics came down to whether the issue would cost the president too much if he went ahead and lifted the ban. It was clear that it would. He had to compromise on his original idea.

The eventual compromise is called "Don't Ask and Don't Tell." It is not clear just how it will work in all situations, but the basic idea is this: Homosexuals may not openly serve in the military, but may do so if they keep quiet about their sexual orientation. Supervisors should not go looking for evidence of whether soldiers serving under them are gay or lesbian. Advocates of lifting the ban are not pleased. One not-very-funny joke about the new policy is that the government, concerned with the plight of homosexuals in the military, gave them a lot more closets.

And your parent—the career officer—can stay in the military as long as he or she keeps quiet.

The example shows that policy about issues of personal identity and about issues of what is public and what is private is attached to strong feelings. Change in these feelings seems to come slowly and painfully.

Bisexuality

One of the amazing things about being bisexual is this: There are times when it seems that *nobody* approves. In a way, that makes almost no sense. After all, if you are attracted to both men and women, it would seem that both men and women would approve of you. But that's not the way it works. Greta Christina writes:[37]

The idea of purity is a pervasive one in the lesbian and gay community . . . an insidious one. The notion is that, because we're all queer, we must be essentially the same at heart with no fundamental differences, no real diversity or vagueness of definition. This conformist ideal makes our politics and controversy particularly divisive and vicious. . . . If we feel there's only one right way to be queer, then seeing someone who does it differently forces us to either condemn them as a traitor or perceive of ourselves as failures. . . . How can we demand of the straight world, "We will love whom we choose and in the way we choose, you must accept us as we are," and then turn around and tell others (bisexuals) in our own community, "The way you love is misguided and wrong; we will not accept you because you are not exactly like us." Craziness.

Stories about exclusion are easy to find. In Boston, there are separate networks for bisexual men and for bisexual women. Every year in Northampton, Massachusetts (dubbed "Lesbianville, U.S.A." by *Newsweek*), for 17 years at this writing, there has been a gay/lesbian/bisexual march. Every year, it seems, there has been a vote about whether bisexuals should be included. Some years, the vote went against them, and there was a gay and lesbian march. Recently, there has been a lesbian fair about the same time, and it is only for lesbians. The newspapers treat it as serious news.

In some ways, bisexuals seem to be the most threatening group of all. For those who take much of their identity from homosexual communities, bisexuals just don't fit. To recall the extreme reaction to male babies at a separatist function, imagine how a woman who liked men as well women would be treated? At times, it seems to be easy for gays and straights to believe that bisexuals just don't belong.

When AIDS came along, things got even worse for bisexuals. The great fear was that bisexuals would pick up the virus from one sex and deliver it to the other. Blood and needles aside, to hear the gossip was to believe that bisexuals were the reason why AIDS spread to heterosexuals. That just wasn't true (the main ways heterosexuals have contracted AIDS, according to the National Center for Health Statistics, are by sharing drug needles with infected people and by having sex with people infected through drug use).

One of the criticisms of bisexuality is that it is "trendy"; another is that it is a way for homosexuals to fit into the straight world. It might be, in other words, a cover for someone who does not want to come all the way out of the closet. A last criticism is that bisexuality is just the result of confusion, and when the person grows up it will go away.[38]

What are we to believe? What is true, if there is a truth in all of this? There are psychologists who believe that fantasies and dreams are the true indication of a person's sexual preference. If you happen to have a really sexy dream about your roommate or some remarkably attractive person of your own sex, then it's possible, say these doctors, that you are bisexual or homosexual. Anna Freud (Sigmund's daughter) believed that whom you think about when you masturbate is the way to discover sexual orientation.

If we adopt those rules for defining bisexuality, does one encounter make it so? Is one dream a definition? Is one year a definition? Camille Paglia asks, "Why do I have to give myself a label? Why can't I just respond from day to day and just go with the flow in a Sixties way? . . . Stop imposing the heavy burden of 'identity' on people. Just let them live and breathe!"[39]

What the studies imply is that stereotypical queens or butches are not the only people in the room who have different sexual tastes. They are saying that it is possible most of us have some desire for both sexes.

There are tests and scales that help us understand sexual orientation. There is, for example, a scale from zero to six in which zero is exclusively heterosexual and six is exclusively homosexual.[40] In the well-known Kinsey studies, 50 percent of the males were exclusively heterosexual and 4 percent were exclusively homosexual. That means 46 percent of the males studied were somewhere between the extremes. If we are going to apply labels, what does that make them?

There are more recent and more revealing measures. The Klein Sexual Orientation Grid, for example, is an extension of the Kinsey scale. The idea behind the test is, in part, that people can change over time. Instead of believing that sexual orientation is fixed for life at childhood, Klein's grid looked at the idea that sexual orientation might change.

There is no doubt that some people stay the same all of their lives. But we read this: "There is a significant trend in the direction of the bisexual norm with the heterosexuals moving toward a more homosexual orientation over their lifetimes, and homosexuals moving away from a homosexual orientation. One might assume that these changes over a person's life span would hold true for bisexuals and homosexuals only. In this study, however, heterosexuals also changed."[41] What you are, the studies imply, is not necessarily what you are going to be.

There is a possibility for more ambiguity. The idea of *intersexuality* holds that for some, there is a degree of maleness or femaleness in phenotype.[42] As many as 4 percent of births result in some variation from the pure male and female physical forms. Most of the time, when a baby is born it is clearly classified as boy or girl. But not always.

Up for Grabs

This chapter began with the idea that there is a politics to sexual orientation. In our version of what is public and what is private, all of us have done our best to make more private things, such as love, the business of the public. That may have been an awful mistake. It matters a great deal to some people that there are others who think of sex differently from the majority. There are facts about differences, but most of all there seem to be harsh judgments about the differences. The politics of sexual orientation seems to be over disapproval, exclusion, and a search for certainty. We found some examples of approval, inclusion, and uncertainty. There are even reasons for tolerance.

One purpose of this book is to help to put some of this in perspective. Diversity is about identity. Is it important for you to stake out sex as part of your identity? Judging by all the energy expended on the subject, we think it is for most people. Does your own identity depend on labeling and distinguishing yourself from others? For your own identity to be acceptable, do people who are different from you have to be unacceptable?

Take yourself as an example. Here you are in college; you have unpacked your identity and have gotten to the subject of sex. What are you going to do with it? How active are you, and are you going to trust it to anyone else? It is part of figuring out who you are, and it does not matter how old you are, what color you are, or where you were born.

Many of you did not wait for college to explore your sexual identity. But there seem to be more options as well as opportunities in college—more people offering a variety of experiences. For many, it is not an easy choice.

The choices might be even more difficult than you had imagined. What if your sexuality really is not fixed in the womb? What if your sexual orientation changes over time? What if the very things that today you believe are perverted turn out to be your activities of choice in 15 years or the activities of your children? What if sexual orientation is as out of control as everything else seems to be?

Perhaps it would help if you were to learn more about sex. Maybe you could look at the latest studies of sexual behavior, good studies that describe what people are doing, how they think about it, and what seem to the consequences of acting this way or that. That would be great information to have.

Why don't we know more about human sexuality? The first and most famous study about human sexuality was done in 1948 by Alfred Kinsey, Wardell Pomeroy, and Clyde Martin. One would think that our sexual activities might have changed with the changes in our social life. But no one has done the great study that describes just what people are doing, how they think about it, and what seem to be the consequences of acting this way or that.[43]

The study hasn't been done because of censorship and oppression, which started a long time ago and are still happening. In 1897, there was a book written by a German that treated homosexuality in scientific and neutral tones. The British publisher of the book faced criminal prosecution for printing a "lewd, wicked, bawdy, scandalous, and obscene" work.

A German institute was founded in 1919 to house works on the study of sexual behavior. By the 1930s, there were about 80 clinics that offered professionals and lay people medical and sexual information. By 1933, the Nazis attacked the institutes, took all of their books and papers into the street, and burned them.

The United States did not do much better. In 1954, Kinsey was attacked by the American Medical Association for contributing to "a wave of sexual hysteria." A congressman, Louis Heller, called for an investigation of Kinsey and wanted to ban all of his books from the U.S. mail. Heller said Kinsey helped cause "the depravity of a whole generation." Because of political pressure, the Rockefeller Foundation withdrew its funding for Kinsey's work.

In 1989, the National Research Council warned that our state of ignorance was such that we did not know enough to win a war against sexually transmitted diseases, including AIDS. But that did little to stop the censorship.

Several years ago, the National Institute of Child and Health Development, a government agency, awarded a research contract to Edward Laumann. Laumann is the dean of social sciences at the University of Chicago. The research project was a high-powered, methodologically sophisticated, sensitive attempt to understand how people's sexual activities change during their lives. The study seemed to have taken into consideration just about every variable you could imagine. It was a remarkable research model. The idea was to learn enough about sexual behavior to make sensible policy about sexually transmitted diseases. It was fully funded and ready to go.

The first question never got asked. Senator Jesse Helms and Representative William Dannemeyer heard about it, got very angry, and were able to cut off funding for the project.

In 1990, Laumann tried again, this time for a more limited project based on the larger one. The application got great reviews, and the proposal ranked in the top 2 percent of all proposals received. The director of the funding agency told Laumann that it would be "political suicide" to give him the grant.

In 1991, a study was funded to survey 24,000 teenagers and their parents over a five-year period. It received a high-priority score from the funding agency. This time, Helms and Dannemeyer pressured then Secretary of Health and Human Services Louis Sullivan to cancel the project.

In 1991, Helms proposed that all money earmarked for sex surveys in the National Institute of Health budget be transferred to the Adolescent Family Life Act. The AFLA is devoted to encouraging premarital celibacy. In other words, Helms decided that research about sexual activity was not as important as just saying no. His colleagues in the Senate are not willing to stand up to his attacks on sex surveys.

This is what Jesse Helms had to say on the floor of the Senate.[44]

> The NIH funds these sex surveys . . . to "cook the books," so to speak, in terms of presenting "scientific facts"—in order to do what? To legitimize homosexual life-styles, of course. . . .
>
> [L]et me just say that I am sick and tired of pandering to the homosexuals in this country. . . .
>
> The real purpose is to compile supposedly scientific facts to support the left-wing liberal argument that homosexuality is a normal, acceptable life-style. . . . As long as I am able to stand on the floor of the U.S. Senate, I am never going to yield to that sort of thing, because it is not just another life-style; it is sodomy.

But that is no place to end this discussion. The heart of this chapter, in important ways, is not merely physical attraction; the heart of this chapter is love. Love is a very curious thing. It may be our most central emotion, but it is not one that people can teach other people. It may be that each new couple invents love. It is new and fresh with each new couple. Love finds its own rhythm as individuals find each other.

One couple's rhythm may be no good at all for another couple.

And the right rhythm sometimes seems impossible to find. There are all of those people you have dated and broken up with. There are all of those divorces. There are all of you from "broken" homes. Hopes dashed. Lives made unhappy.

The diversity of the world begins with who we are attracted to and who we love. To be ashamed of it, or phobic about it, does not seem very wise at all.

— 8 —

Race

It takes an entire village to educate one child.
—An African saying

Human beings are meant for life and not death. They are meant for freedom and not slavery. They were created for each other and not against each other.
—James H. Cone

This chapter is an introduction to issues of race and problems of racism. We begin by asking you to consider the idea that race—the basis of racism—is not a fixed biological category. It may be, in fact, more of a political idea. It turns out that race means much more than mere color.

We borrow a definition from Robert Cahill that divides racism into two parts: plain and fancy. The plain racism consists of small everyday incidents, such as insulting words or offensive jokes. The fancy racism is openly declared and hostile. We suggest that the two types need and feed off each other.

Next, we examine issues of race on college campuses. We look at admissions and affirmative action policies.

Finally, we ask you to consider racial stereotypes. Are Asian-American students high achievers? Can even positive stereotypes be destructive?

So here we go—race and culture in the United States— the most troubling questions of our country.

Race

We can define racism in a couple of ways. One is: Racism is a system of thought based on the idea of race. The other is: Racism is the belief that one's own race is superior.

We could do more, but all such definitions hinge on belief in the idea of race.

Race is a very straightforward topic until you begin to think about it. It turns out that race might be more of a political category than a fixed biological one. What we will see is that race is a changing and evolving concept that is much more inclusive than we ordinarily think.

Research on racial differences has led most scientists to agree on three major conclusions.[1] First, skin color, hair texture, and facial features are only three of many differences between people. There are dozens of physical differences ranging from body chemistry to shapes of bones to consistency of ear wax.

The second agreed-upon point is that one of the reasons for the great evolutionary success of the human species is its genetic variability. In other words, as humans moved around the globe, their large variety of physical traits greatly enhanced their chances of surviving.

Finally, no one has ever discovered a reliable way of distinguishing one race from another. That seems hard to believe. We all have our ideas about race, and which race is which. Kurt Vonnegut, in the novel *Hocus Pocus,* writes that human beings come into the world color-coded. Well, what's right for *Hocus Pocus* might not be exactly right scientifically. Skin color does not tell us everything about race. Although we know that most Africans from south of the Sahara, and their descendants around the world, generally have darker skin than most Europeans, that doesn't tell us much. There are millions of people in India who are classified as Caucasoid (or "white") who have darker skins than most Americans who call themselves black. Biology books and professors will probably tell you that skin color is determined by *polygenes*, or on several locations in your DNA, and the effect of the many genes is roughly additive. Humans run along a continuum of skin colors, with no clear lines between light and dark.

There are Africans who have skins no darker than Greeks or Lebanese or Italians. So, skin color cannot be the universal test for race. Neither is height, eye color, or the shape of your nose. The biological point is that there is no one reliable way of distinguishing one race from another.

Did you see the movie *Mississippi Masala*? It's an interesting movie. The two women behind the movie, the screenwriter and the director, are Indian-born and Harvard-educated. The movie is about an Indian (India Indian) woman who was born in Uganda.

Her parents were successful in Uganda, but because of racial bias, they were kicked out of the country. They moved to Greenwood, Mississippi. These nearly nomadic people manage a low-rent motel. Nomads running a motel—working in our cultural artifact for being on the road.

The heroine, Mina, has no interest in college, a career, or any of the Indian men who hang around the Monte Carlo Motel. A little grumpy, a little lazy—not very happy. Until, by accident (actually, a minor car accident), Mina meets our hero, Demetrius, who is black.

Even if you did not see the movie, you can begin to imagine just how thick the plot gets, and why. We have an affair of two people of color, and they are roughly the same color. Of course, color is not the issue.

The white middle-class admires the Indians for their work ethic, but certainly does not admire them enough to believe they are social equals. Whites in the United States have not traditionally treated blacks as equals. We also know that black Africans threw the Indians out of Uganda because of prejudice. Racism is racism.

If we get some sort of identity from our color and our old homeland, the movie is revealing. None of the black Americans in the movie has ever been to Africa. Africa may be the source of most of their color, but only some of their identity. When Mina's father returns to India, he is bitterly disappointed. How can Mina think that India is her home if she has never lived there? Part of what is going on is the fact that these people of color are Americans, like it or not. But even if they are all Americans, there is still a current of difference. Mina's father warns her to "stick with her own kind." Demetrius's half-deaf uncle somehow chooses to hear that Mina is a black girl "from Indiana."

The movie is an excursion through the problem of color and just how misleading and meaningless and meaningful it can be.

Notice how we started talking about race and ended up talking about color. That is no accident. It seems to work out that way in real life, not just in books and movies.

It might help to unpack some of the colliding ideas about race by starting at the beginning. There is one human race. *Homo sapiens.* We're all it. Anthropologists use terms such as "group" and "tribe" because they allow flexible definitions to fit actual human populations, without some of the baggage that accompanies the term *race.* There is a lot of variation in sizes, colors, shapes, technologies, mobility, histories, religions, family practices, and on and on. But all one race.

There are people today who make much of the variations, and scientists try to explain the variations. Let's start with the scientists.[2]

Two schools of thought are in a fight right now. One holds that humans evolved in several regions around the earth, pretty much where they are now in Europe, Africa, East Asia, and Australasia. Strong genetic similarities among these populations result from connections between the populations over the last million years.

The second theory suggests that an "Eve," a single common ancestor, lived in Africa about 200,000 years ago. All human populations, goes the argument, can be traced back to one woman. That's why she is called Eve. The humans all over the globe spread out from Africa and replaced previous populations in the new regions they settled, and human variation is the result of recent evolution.

Why is this a controversy? That might be the most interesting question. The means of calculating Eve is uncertain (it is based on estimates of the rate of change in mitochondrial

DNA), and could easily be off by more than half a million years. The estimate of the time of parallel evolution could be off as well. The two theories could be talking about the same thing, only Eve lived a lot earlier. Both theories agree that populations evolved and continue to evolve.

There is a controversy because of how people interpret the theories. Would you take the existence of a recent Eve to mean that all humans are more closely related than previously believed? Or, to take the other side, do you believe that the groups that evolved in the different regions are at different levels of evolution, some having evolved more? Would you take the parallel evolution theory to mean that races were distinct and, at some point, "pure," or that the parallel quality of the evolution shows a long-term pattern of genetic mixing among the regional groupings of populations?

If you are worried about race, it raises a lot of questions.

Most questions about race start with distinctions between groups of people. There is an explanation for most of them.

Color is a good example. Generally speaking, if you start at the equator you will find people who have the darkest skin. The farther you get from the equator, north or south, the paler the skin. Your skin color is a function of the intensity of a dark brown pigment called melanin. Skin cells have varying amounts of melanin granules. All races can increase the melanin in their skin by exposure to the sun. Populations that evolved closer to the equator produce more melanin.

We have known for some time (as the ozone layer is getting holes in it, we are painfully aware of the fact) that the human body can tolerate only a narrow range of intensities of sunlight. Too much sun causes sunburn and cancer, too little deprives the body of vitamin D and can cause rickets.[3] Albinos who live near the equator have a high rate of skin cancer and dark-skinned children living in northern latitudes had a high rate of rickets before their milk was fortified by vitamin D.

The dark skin limits the skin's production of vitamin D in northern latitudes, while light skin lets in more of the sun. Dark skin protects against too much sun near the equator, and light skin lets in too much. (The white of polar bears lets more sun in than the fur of black bears.)

Simply put, one reason we survive as a species is that our skin color has adapted to different regional demands.

What about the nose on your face? Accident? Racial characteristic? Maybe a kind of adaptation? The job of the nose is to warm and humidify air before it gets to sensitive lung tissues. Given the job, it is no great surprise that people native to colder or drier climates tend to have longer, more beak-shaped noses. The colder or drier the air, the more surface area is needed to make sure that the air gets to be the right temperature and humidity.[4]

There seem to be explanations for height and eye pigmentation and scent glands and so on. But scientists are far from understanding why there are so many differences between us. Why do bushmen of the Kalahari, the !kung, have small noses? Why do many of Nigeria's Wodaabe have more beaky noses? Why are Aleut noses more like African or Asian noses than like Lapp or Celt? There seems to be no compelling reason why Indian men in one part of South America have blue penises. Maybe it was just a genetic mutation that women found wildly attractive.[5]

The idea that there may never have been "pure" races fits well with the fact that contemporary races continue to mix. For example, it can be argued that American blacks are a distinct race. They are a combination of African blacks and European whites. According to Boyce Rensberger, it has been "calculated that whites contributed 21 percent of the genes to the American black population. The figure is higher for blacks in northern and western states and lower in the South."[6]

Indeed, in many Latin and South American countries, the native populations are stable mixes of two or three races. They have become new races. These races are continually adapting to their environment.

We can now circle back and make the point that began this section, but make it a little more clearly. Races are not fixed biological categories. Indeed, they may never have been. Races are intermingling and interacting and evolving all the time. That constant evolution is one of the reasons the species is so successful. Given that all people are the same species, it seems silly to try to classify people according to race. When it comes right down to it, racial classification is more political than scientific.

Race is a nebulous idea, maybe even a nonidea, but it is an important nebulous nonidea.

The Real World: Plain and Fancy

Enough facts. All too often it seems that common sense has no place in the world. What we know is that our world is full of racism. Although we are painfully aware of the racism in the United States, certainly racism is not limited to here. Germany has a pretty serious racism problem. South African politics are about race. The Balkans used to be at war over race, and now they are at it again. Most of the countries in East Asia do not like "outsiders," and that includes people from other countries in East Asia. What makes the United States so interesting is that we are committed to understanding how different races can live together. It sometimes seems that the health of the republic depends on how well we answer the question.

Robert Cahill says racism comes in two versions: plain and fancy.[7] Fancy, he argues, is openly declared and assertive. The compound of the Church of Jesus Christ Christians, Aryan Nation (they like to call themselves the Aryan Nation) wasn't far from where Cahill used to live. They are fancy racists because they propound theories of racial separation, publish propaganda about how race mixing destroys the country, and live in a community of like-minded separatists. Racist skinheads are fancy. They shave their heads, wear military boots, and often have Nazi tattoos, swastika armbands, and German Iron Crosses hung around their necks. They blame social problems on race. (It should be noted that not all skinheads are racists.)

The Aryan Nation people dress the part and they think the part. They are proudly explicit about their racial beliefs and are intendedly political about them. They believe that it is important to restore America to what they think of as its origi-

nal state—white and Christian. Fancy racists are serious about stopping what they understand to be the "dangerous" trends in the United States toward racial amalgamation and equality. Those tendencies are, for the fancy racists, clearly un-American.

These fancy racists are committed enough to the great restoration to use violence. It is their belief that white supremacy—or white separatism—is necessary. These fancy racists (properly and routinely called hate groups) preach white pride and point to what they believe are the superior accomplishments of whites. It is their basic belief that whites need an area of the country that no one else can enter.

These people divide the nonwhite world into roughly two groups: predators and parasites.

Predators first. These are strong and intelligent groups that are powerful but evil. They use their considerable force to prey upon the "too-innocent, too-trusting white race, seeking to paralyze its will and bring it to destruction."[8] The predators want to destroy the white Christian world.

Predators are clever. They are insidious. They infiltrate American institutions, all the time claiming to have American values while devoting their time and energy to private and vile ends. They are happy to encourage the intermingling and even the intermarrying of the races. The predators are out to dominate the world. In order to do this, they have decided to first enslave America and then the entire planet.

These predators are political progressives. These predators are liberals. These predators are Jews. No matter what their complexions, the fancy racists consider all Jews nonwhite.

The other group of nonwhites are considered parasites. These people are considered weak, powerless, stupid, and dependent. They live entirely on the productivity of the white race. The fancy racists believe that the parasites help the predators by systematically sapping the strength of the whites. They take, take, take. The parasites encourage the whole dynamic. They are known to the fancy racists as "mud people." They are black Americans, Hispanic-Americans, and Native American Indians. The distinctions of *Mississippi Masala* are lost on fancy racists. The ideological answer for what to do with the parasites is easy enough: Make them slaves. A straightforward and simple solution.

To the ends of eliminating the Jews and enslaving the "mud people," the fancy racists organize, demonstrate, march, broadcast radio programs, hand out literature, print newsletters, magazines, and books, and periodically engage in violence. They actively recruit new members in "prisons, colleges, high schools, and even elementary schools, organizing 'white pride' groups and 'white student unions.' "[9] They incite racial tension. They practice political terrorism.

Plain racism is still racism, but it is not openly proclaimed and not openly confrontational. It is everyday behavior, according to Cahill.

This kind of racism can be understood in two ways. The first is to look at access to the basic necessities of life. The second is to focus on the seemingly endless humiliations and indignities of everyday life. We are all familiar with plain racism.

If we think about basic necessities of American life—equal justice, good housing, suitable employment, and education—then we can argue that plain racism is common.[10] Consider these facts:

- About 30 percent of black Americans, around 9 million people, live in segregated housing, isolated from other groups. Housing values are the main reason the median wealth of black families is one-tenth that of white Americans.
- Although two-thirds of black Americans can be characterized as middle class, average individual black income is 59 percent that of whites. Well-educated young blacks earn 85 percent of what comparable white Americans earn.
- The so-called urban underclass is disproportionately black. About 10 percent of working-age blacks are simply not at all in the work force and earn no money. Nearly 40 percent of black Americans aged 20 to 24 who dropped out of high school haven't worked in a year. Most social programs and income support programs are aimed at people with children and some earnings.

- Nearly two-thirds of black children are born out of wed-lock. About half of them live in poverty, largely because they live in households with at most one income. About one of every four black men aged 20 to 29 is somewhere in the criminal justice system—under arrest, awaiting trial, in jail or prison, or on probation. In our criminal justice system, black Americans are more likely to be arrested, convicted, go to jail, and in states with capital punishment, to be executed.

Enough facts? There are more like them. The point is, what do the facts mean? Do they mean that racism is thriving? It could be that these facts are outcomes of pervasive racial prejudice that denies black Americans a chance, right from the start. There are other explanations for these facts. Some of them are the subject of the next chapter. For now, consider that disagreements over the meaning of facts have to do with how we define racial prejudice and racism.

Consider these definitions.

Racial prejudice has to do with a person's attitudes about races other than his or her own. First, it means that we have a concept of race, and who is in what race. Second, it means that a person's race has much to do with whether that person is liked, feared, and so on. It is an attitude; actually, racial prejudice is a complex of attitudes. It is how we think about "others." It is, importantly, a private matter and a piece of identity.

Racism is public and it is political. Racism is how we act. Racism is deliberate, purposeful, hurtful action that is intended to oppress someone of a different color. Although racial prejudice and racism are certainly closely tied, they are not the same thing. Racism is not directly about your atti-tudes—your private self—but is about how you act.

You should know that not everyone defines racial preju-dice and racism this way. We would like to be clear about the way we use words, but the fact is that we are using words that mean different things to different people. Some define racism the way we define racial prejudice, and say the actions are outcomes of racism. By this different definition, unintended outcomes can be racist, and ostensibly innocent people pursuing benign purposes can be racist. How deep racism is will have something to do with policies aimed at racism. People disagree over those policies.

People disagree on what the facts mean. Plain racism and the necessities of life are the stuff of argument in America.

A second way to understand plain racism is the everyday variety of slights and insults about race. Everyday racism ranges from ugly graffiti on rest room walls to subtle jokes and epithets to run-of-the-mill discourtesies that "just happen." All of it is somehow woven into our lives and seldom noticed, commented about, or acted upon.

We have different myths about plain and fancy racism. We believe that the "fancy" racists are simply know-nothing fools, a fringe of crackpots that are so far out of the mainstream of American life that we can ignore them. We dismiss "plain" racism by believing that almost everything was pretty much "fixed" in the sixties and subsequent affirmative action policies (more on affirmative action later in the chapter). Satisfied by our myths that tell us everything is fine and getting better, we can look at racism straight in the face and ignore it.

This is one place where those definitions of racism matter. If we believe that only purposive, hurtful actions, aimed at oppressing someone of another group, are racism, there may be no plain racists. A judge may invalidate an affirmative action program because it costs whites too much and classifies people by the color of their skin—by one interpretation, a racist act of government. Since the action is not aimed at oppressing someone, it is not racist. But it is part of the calculus of the numbers that show some groups making less money, getting fewer jobs, and so on.

What needs to be understood is that plain racism and fancy racism use each other to exist. Most of us are self-satisfied because we aren't violent, aren't cross-burning, hood-wearing, Nazi-loving racists. But for the plain racists, the public expression of racism serves a purpose. Their feelings get shown, even if they do not show them. There is no genuine effort to stop the hatred because it plays out the fantasy of too many people.

This is a real dilemma in a liberal society. We value individual liberty and above all freedom of expression, and that extends to newsletters and computer bulletin boards and leaflets on car windshields that are filled with racist ideas. It means that the overt, assertive acts of racism get tolerated. And, says Cahill, it allows us to ignore more of the plain racism.

The fancy racists take heart in all of the plain racism. They felt good that David Duke was almost elected governor of Louisiana. They nodded their heads yes when Pat Buchanan visited the graves of relatives who fought for the confederacy in the Civil War and when he told Jewish demonstrators to go away because his speech was "only for Americans." They counted it a victory when then-President Ronald Reagan visited a German graveyard where members of Hitler's SS troops were buried. They knew who their candidate was when George Bush ran an advertisement calculated to incite racial fears and the Democrats seemed to have no response. (The creator of the infamous Willie Horton ad said he was sorry he did it, shortly before he died.)

Both kinds of racism are ugly. Each kind of racism is dangerous. And this is the bottom line: Each is stronger because of the other.

Higher Education

When looking through literature for this chapter, we came across an article titled "The Admission and Assimilation of Minority Students at Harvard, Yale, and Princeton, 1900–1970."[11] It originally appeared in the *History of Education Quarterly*. The title sounded interesting. This essay, we thought, will explain how people with different skin colors have been treated badly by three very powerful schools. But it turned out that the article was about how these schools discriminated against Jews. Jews! We're looking for racism and find nothing more complicated than religious prejudice. Or so it seemed. It turns out that the *Oxford English Dictionary* defines a Jew as a member of the Hebrew race.

Part of the reason the author decided to concentrate on Jews is clear: There were too few other minorities to write much of an article about. Until fairly recently, these schools worked hard to limit the number of Jews they would take. Racial minorities were seldom even considered. Numbers help tell the story. By the early 1960s, for example, only 2 percent of Harvard undergraduates were black. At Yale, the Class of 1964 had 10 blacks.[12] We know that since the mid-sixties, efforts have been made by colleges and universities to encourage racial diversity on campus. It has been a struggle. It might be best to think a little about education so we can see what the struggle is all about.

Education occupies a central role in the United States. We ask it to do many things. Traditionally, education is supposed to embody a disinterested search for knowledge. It is the one institution whose sole purpose is the pursuit of excellence. But we—and, in truth, most societies—expect more of education than the mere search for knowledge. We expect education to provide the brain-power to lead the world in technology, as well as to provide the country with a sophisticated work force. Finally, we want education to help solve our social problems. It seems perfectly reasonable to believe that well-educated people will know how to be good citizens.

So here sits education—and higher education in particular—right in the middle of most of our critical national problems. Excellence, jobs and inventions, civility and citizenship—that is a powerful set of expectations. Any one of those things would be a full-time job. But the biggest problem is that these three aims seem, at times, to be mutually exclusive. We can see those tensions more clearly by understanding affirmative action on campus.

There is a remarkable book titled *Illiberal Education: The Politics of Race and Sex on Campus*. It was written by Dinesh D'Souza.[13] What makes the book remarkable is that D'Souza writes about almost all of the right topics. Many people have strong disagreements with what he writes, and disagreements about his conclusions, while sharing an interest in his topics. His politics are angry, so when he talks about the politics of race and sex on campus, he believes that they have led the university away from all that it should be about.

His is a powerful statement of how some whites feel about what has been going on in the United States for the last 30 years. He makes us try to come to terms with what is fair and why it is fair. He takes on several very powerful universities and asks them to rethink what they are doing. It is a strong statement of Western values written by a native of India.

The topic is affirmative action and the example is the University of California, Berkeley.[14]

In D'Souza's dramatic version of affirmative action at Berkeley, we are told the story of an Asian-American student named Yat-pang Au. He had applied to Berkeley—the school his father had graduated from—and by every measure believed he would get in. He had gotten straight A's in high school, gotten 1340 on his SATs, lettered in cross country and track, and on and on. He had good grades and extracurricular activities, and was a nice person. He could not believe it when he was rejected.[15]

He thought about it and concluded that he had not been accepted because the university's admission standards were too high. Then he learned that 10 people from his school had been accepted and none of them seemed to have as good a record as he had. Some had lower test scores and some lower grades. At that point, Yat-pang didn't know what to think.

His parents began to suspect that he had not been admitted because of discrimination. He asked to be reconsidered and Berkeley said no. He was told that he "was good, but not good enough."[16] That seemed unlikely to his family, because his SATs were 50 points higher than the average of the incoming class. His father, Sik-kee, decided to fight. Sik-kee organized the Asian community and they raised a little hell.

What they found out was this: Yat-pang was not as well prepared as other Asians. Put differently, there was a quota, and other Asians had stronger applications.

Berkeley was in a jam. Here were the pressures on this remarkable state university. In 1974 and again in 1983, the California legislature instructed the university to create a student body that more accurately reflected the diversity of the state's high school population. They wanted, roughly, the same percentage of Hispanics, Asian-Americans, and others who attended high school. The university concluded that it made good democratic sense for its students to represent the diverse population of California. That, they believed, was the way to guard against Berkeley's becoming an elite school that would be monolithic in perspective and monochromatic in color. Each group, according to the policy, would get its fair share of positions in the incoming class.

What was Berkeley like before these policies? In the 1950s, Berkeley was almost all white. Even by 1968, the student body was only 2.8 percent black and 1.3 percent Chicano/Latino, and the Asian immigration of the 1970s had yet to happen.[17] In the 1960s, almost every applicant with a 3.25 grade average was admitted. By the fall of 1989, about 5,800 people were accepted of the 21,300 who applied. Is Berkeley competitive? In that year 2,800 students with straight A's were not admitted.

That is a little of the background in D'Souza's chapter about Berkeley. A good, white undergraduate state university (with a world-class graduate school) in the 1960s had become the most competitive kind of undergraduate school with a very diverse student population by the late 1980s.

This is how Berkeley goes about accepting its incoming class. The first 50 percent of the admissions spaces in the College of Letters and Sciences are filled by using an academic index that combines grade point average and test scores. Berkeley tells us that the majority of these places are filled by Asian-Americans and whites.[18]

For the second 50 percent, the academic index is not weighed as heavily. Other things are considered, such as whether the student is a gifted athlete or musician, or is from a rural area, or is disabled, or is from an underrepresented minority—defined as African-Americans, Chicanos, Latinos, and Native Americans.

D'Souza argues that these are quotas. So did Sik-kee Au. So did many in the Asian community. It is important to remember that for many in the Asian-American population, education is highly regarded. Acceptance by Berkeley, especially, is seen as a status symbol, a sign that a person (and his or her family) has "made it." How serious is that? In 1980, a total of 8,000 people applied for admission to Berkeley; by 1988, 7,500 Asian-Americans alone applied. As we have seen, thousands of those who applied were first-rate students.

So Berkeley got a mandate from the people who fund them and they devised a new admissions policy. D'Souza writes: "Given Berkeley's definition of diversity as proportional representation, the university's mandate seems clear: more blacks and Hispanics, fewer Jews and Asians."[19] His point is a direct charge: Berkeley—whose sole reason for being is the search for truth and excellence—is punishing the very people who should be rewarded. Because Asians and Jews tend to do better academically, D'Souza strongly believes that they should be rewarded for their accomplishments. He quotes a Berkeley official as saying, "Merit is no longer the predominant factor in admissions."[20]

In 1991, the entering class at Berkeley was 35 percent Asian-American, 30 percent white, 13 percent Chicano, and 8 percent black. One percent of the incoming class of 3,300 was Native American, and other groups made up the rest.[21] Think about it. From an almost all-white school less than 25 years ago to an incoming class where whites are not even the largest group. The new admissions policies may have actually kept the white group from being even smaller, and overall the policies seem to have increased diversity. But are they right?

Given the different groups on campus and the different ways of being admitted, it is reasonable to wonder what campus life is like. D'Souza—no surprise here—paints a bleak picture. He believes that students are angry because some of their friends were not admitted while people with poorer academic records were accepted. Others believe that they are treated as second-class citizens because it is assumed they are not qualified simply because of the color of their skin. On the other side, an Asian student believes that there is a backlash against Asians. She says that with "the influx of Asians, it's the whole thing of Yellow Peril."[22] To read only D'Souza, one can get the idea that no one is happy with affirmative action at Berkeley.

After many arguments about lower standards, injustice, bitter campus relations, and the like, D'Souza ends with this evaluation: "Berkeley's abandonment of an effort to apply a neutral standard of academic excellence has cut the university off from the moorings of just principle; now it is buffeted about by the tides of racial pressure groups."[23] Not a ringing endorsement.

Troy Duster thinks that "ideologues like Dinesh D'Souza and his imitators" are wrong. Duster is a black sociologist at Berkeley. He argues that much of D'Souza's arguments are merely myth and in the end are nothing more than a wrong-headed reaction to the fact that the world is changing.

One of D'Souza's myths, according to Duster, is that "Diversity Means Dumber."[24] Duster asks, Dumber than when and dumber than whom? If we think of comparisons between entering students of a given year, then yes, some students who are not admitted are higher academic achievers than some who do get in. Duster argues that a longer view gives a different perspective, that current students at Berkeley are much better—using SAT scores and grade-point averages—than when the university was all-white in the fifties and sixties. He argues that, for the first time, white students are not getting in because there are stronger students who happen to be a different color. The demographics of California (and the rest of the nation) are changing. By the year 2000, whites will barely (52 percent) be a majority in California. It is no longer reasonable to think that the percentage of white undergraduates at the university will ever approach what it was as recently as the early seventies. Now diversity is reasonable, as the legislature found.

The second myth has to do with "Good Old Meritocracy: GPA + SAT = MIT."[25] D'Souza constantly comes back to the point that judging on merits is true equality. His argument is that a meritocracy is truly just. It is a powerful point, but Duster believes that it ignores reality. Are all grades equal? Hardly. We know that some high schools are hard and some are easy. Is it right to compare grades between the two? We also know that some classes are more difficult than others. Should a 3.7 in advanced placement courses and other heavy electives count the same as a "3.7 piled up via Mickey Mouse courses"? Duster thinks not.

SAT scores are not quite merit either. "What we know about SAT scores is that they correlate almost perfectly with zip-code and economic status."[26] We know that socioeconomic class has a lot to do with academic achievement—wealthier, better-educated parents tend to pass those things on to their children. If we went strictly by the numbers, think of the advantage someone from a well-educated, upper-class family who happened to go to an easy high school would have. Would the higher numbers mean the entering students were smarter?

You may recall from Chapter 4 that class gets mixed up with other issues in higher education. Here, the mix is with affirmative action. Do all people have a right to a good education? Do the people who get higher grades in high school and higher scores on the SAT deserve it more? Does it make a difference if those numbers tend to follow class lines? Affirmative action programs must deal with your answers to these questions.

D'Souza fails to mention that no first-rate college or university ever judges solely on grades and SATs. We just saw that for decades, Jews were kept out of Harvard, Yale, and Princeton because the admissions procedures were set up to keep Jews out.

The point Duster makes is that colleges and universities have never relied simply on grades and test scores to admit students. He believes the rub is that Berkeley is now using a method to benefit people of color (but not Asian-Americans). The great cry about meritocracy sounds to Duster like an argument "on behalf of privilege, one more time."

The third myth is about "Terrible Tribalism." There are tensions on campus, and people do tend to group themselves by color. Duster offers two bits of background to help understand what is going on. First, he writes that it is not unusual for new groups to form organizations. When Catholics and Jews were the minority students on WASP campuses, they organized Newman Centers and Hillels. It made sense. That the new minorities on campuses are doing the same thing should come as little surprise. Second, Duster reminds us that most minorities come to campus from high schools that are not racially integrated. The university is their first experience with multiculturalism. There is no reason to believe that it will be easy for them.

Duster and D'Souza look at the same thing and come to different conclusions. It would seem that all D'Souza sees is tension and its destructiveness. Duster writes "what strikes this sociologist as remarkable is how well and relatively peaceably it works."[27]

On Campus

Being a college student is not easy. Most people come to campus carrying the baggage of their home, neighborhood, high school, and life. To take higher education seriously, both academically and socially, it seems that a person's very identity is questioned. The academic part is hard. The pace, the workload, the pressure, the deadlines are cranked up from the easier high school life. Good higher education is tense. And whatever racial baggage you bring with you to campus is likely to get opened up.

People are tense, and there is trouble. No group goes untouched. At the University of Massachusetts, Amherst, 3,000 white students attacked 20 African-Americans in 1986. What started it all? A disagreement about the World Series.

A black fraternity house was burned down at the University of Mississippi.

The African-American Center and the Holocaust Memorial were damaged at Yale.

In 1987, at the University of Connecticut, six or seven white male students spit tobacco juice on the hair of eight Asian-Americans. The whites called the Asians "Oriental faggots," "chinks," and "gooks." The taunting continued throughout a dance. The Asian women at the party were so frightened that they hid in a closet most of the evening. The proctor at the dance told the Asians to just "relax," that the white males were "just having fun."

In 1987, the National Institute Against Prejudice and Violence reported that 20 percent of all minority or culturally different students who attended traditionally white schools had been the victim of some ethnic violence.[28] The violence ranged from blatant physical attacks and property damage to subtle harassment (both in and out of the classroom), to name-calling and insults.

Reports of racial violence on campuses are almost routine.

We know that there are tensions on campus. That is not news. We know that there is racial tension on campus. Again, not news. We even know that some of the reasons why these things happen on campus. Where do we go from here?

Cultural Stereotypes

We have seen that race is not the most helpful place to look; it's possible that we can learn something by looking at culture.

Let's begin with a group that has been extraordinarily successful in higher education. Asian-Americans have been academically dazzling for the past decade or so. In 1986, all of the top five recipients of the prestigious Westinghouse Science Talent Search were of Asian descent. A minority of less than 2 percent of the population had produced the top five prize winners. As the Jews had done earlier, Asian-Americans became successful in education and because of education.

Yet it seems that Asian-Americans pay a price for their success, a price beyond the fancy racism of being spit on or the plain racism of being called names. Some of the very best schools have quotas that limit the number of Asian-Americans admitted.[29]

In the Berkeley case, it is not hard to see a backlash against the success of this group. Asians, goes the reasoning, are taken care of and are getting their share. It is easy to hear on the Berkeley campus that they are "taking over" or not deserving of any special attention. It is a widely discussed cultural myth that Asian-American students are bright, work hard, and succeed in school.

The heart of this cultural myth comes from generalizing to all Asians from ideas that pertain to some. Three key ideas are explained by three different writers.

Stephan Graubard writes that Asians have the advantage of coming from stable families and that Asian mothers rear their children for success.[30]

Robert Oxnam tells us that "it is the story of a broader cultural interaction, a pairing of old Asian values with American individualism, Asian work ethics with American entrepreneurship." Oxnam writes that the success can be traced to "the strong family ties and powerful work ethics of Asian cultures" as "key factors in Asian-American achievement."[31]

Finally, Malcolm Browne quotes a corporate executive as saying "tightly-knit families and high respect for all forms of learning are traditional characteristics of Asian societies . . . as they are for Jewish societies."[32]

Unless you are Jewish, it is easy to be jealous or angry at Asian-Americans for these built-in cultural advantages. There is an uneasy feeling that somehow everyone else in the United States just does not measure up to this one group.

There are, not surprisingly, problems with the myth. The first problem is that it is foolish to lump all Asians together. There are 48 countries in what we call Asia, and each of those countries has a distinct culture. There are no data to support the claim that the various cultures involved share common values about the family that are significantly different from those of non-Asian cultures. Remember, only in the United States is it assumed that Asians share a common culture.[33] The Asian families in the stories about great students are generally first- or second-generation East Asians.

The second problem is that the myth assumes that all Asians who come to America are remarkably successful. That is just not right. While we focus on individuals who do well academically, we forget that there are "deep pockets of poverty, exploitation, and despair" in the various Asian-American communities.[34] What are we to think of those who are not doing well? Do we somehow believe that they are less Asian than those who are successful academically?

The third problem with the cultural myth is that it is wrong to generalize about a culture from people who immigrate. Ezra Vogel, a scholar of China and Japan, writes that the Asian immigrants to the United States "are a biased sample, the cream of their own society." Put differently, a surprisingly large number of Asians were successful even before they got here.[35] Those would probably be the people who rear their children for success, have strong drives to work hard and succeed, and have a strong respect for education. Perhaps the most surprising fact is that East Asian children who spent a year or two in refugee camps perform significantly better than average. These children come from families who in their former lands emphasized the need to study and do well in school. Is it a big surprise that success transfers from one culture to another? We know that if you were born in the United States, your chances of going to college are greater if your parents went to college than if they did not. What we learn is that the mind-set of a high percentage of immigrants from Asia revolves around success and education.

We have a cultural stereotype of Asian-Americans. But Asian-American is a category only in our heads. Our great generalizations about dedication to family and the work ethic have everything to do with who is attracted to the United States.

Divisions and Combinations on Campus

Here are some stories that paint a picture of race relations on American college campuses.

Every year for the past 76 years, the Kappa Alpha fraternity at Auburn University in Alabama has held an Old South parade.[36] Its members dress up in Confederate uniforms or period dress, break out the Confederate battle standard (the crossed blue bars with stars, on a red field), and march through the town. It is a long-standing tradition at Auburn. In 1992, students opposed to the parade took the unusual step of demonstrating and blocking the parade route. They said the parade was offensive, celebrating an era in which many people's ancestors were slaves. Administrators at Auburn don't like the parade very much. It makes it difficult to attract more minority students to the campus. Yet the parade goes on, because the fraternity is not directly under the control of university administrators.

After the police trials in the Rodney King beating in Los Angeles, which we discuss in the next chapter, students at campuses all over the United States protested the decisions.[37] At the University of Massachusetts at Amherst, students took over the office of the school newspaper, which had earlier fired three minority editors, and the chancellor's office. In Washington, D.C., about 400 students, mostly from Howard University, marched to the White House. In Los Angeles, 28 campuses shut down during the riots that followed the verdicts. In Atlanta, students from Clark University and Spelman, Morehouse, and Morris Brown colleges started a march into downtown. They were joined by people they passed, and the growing group threw rocks through windows, and some protesters attacked white onlookers. The next day, another gathering on one campus was contained by police, who did not want them going downtown again. A couple of stores were torn up, two cars were set on fire, tear gas drifted across the campuses, and about 70 students were arrested.

Campus protests take place in a context of events, changing policy, and divisive attitudes. Events like the Old South parade and the protests over the Rodney King affair take on meaning as the context changes.

A second type of story comes from changes in national policy about minorities on campus during the Reagan and Bush years. For example, in 1990 through 1992, the U.S. Department of Education changed its policies on minority student scholarships.[38] Because it is against the law to discriminate against people on the basis of race, reasoned department officials, exclusively black or Native American scholarships violate the law. Advocates of affirmative action were upset, not only for the change in what they regard as already too-small programs, but for the overall message it sends to colleges. The message is clear to minorities: You are on your own, and don't expect help from institutions. At Winthrop College in Rock Hill, South Carolina, administrators changed their program from African American Honor Awards to President's Scholarships, which will serve to bring any kind of diversity to the campus. They made the change to stay ahead of the apparent direction of national policy.

Attitudes have grown more divided. A survey of 15- to 24-year-olds found that 50 percent of young people in the United States regard race relations as "generally bad."[39] Two-thirds of the black respondents said so. When asked whether whites or minorities are more likely to be harmed by discrimination, 49 percent of whites said whites are; 68 percent of blacks and 52 percent of Hispanics believed minorities are more likely to be harmed. Fifty-one percent of whites said colleges and universities should not give special consideration to minority students, but 74 percent of blacks and 57 percent of Hispanics said colleges should do so. When the wording of the question was changed from "special consideration" to "special preference," the number of whites who said no increased to 64 percent. The blacks and Hispanics who said yes decreased to 52 percent and 56 percent, respectively. When asked about special preferences for minorities in employment, 78 percent of the whites were opposed. The current college-age population is divided by race on policies toward minorities.

Black college students generally see the United States as essentially a white nation, and their place in it is a constant fight with prejudice.[40] The undercurrent of black nationalism on campuses may appear to be separatist, but members of nationalist organizations see it as a set of moorings from which they will operate in the center of American society. The balancing act does not sound easy.

Some programs are in place to address diversity on campus, but the attitudes of people are still divided across races. Events in the wider society affect the campus, and the same divisions are found in town and gown.

This raises, again, some questions about what we expect from college. In very general terms, college should enhance one's preparation for life. Does that include preparing people to take a place in the economy? Does it include building a more cohesive society? A more peaceful place? If encouraging more minorities does not seem to dramatically affect attitudes about race, should colleges do more to promote respect and understanding? Should teachers include in their curricula things that strike at racial divisions?

What is the sum of these and similar stories?

Diversity and Identity

What is important to see in this chapter is that colleges and universities are in a unique and central position. If and how the United States intends to deal with different colors and cultures depends in no small part on what goes on and what is taught in higher education. If you are in college, that means you are involved whether you want to be or not. We have scholars telling us that there is no such thing as pure races, yet we have people willing to do violence because of color. Race is at the core of a good deal of campus politics, and there are policies meant to overcome problems of racism.

We name people and create myths about them—Asian-Americans for example—that distort reality.

We acknowledge that for hundreds of years, there have been laws and social customs that were brutal and unequal. To right the wrongs, legislation was passed to help ensure chances for people who formerly had no chance. Now we read that some of the very people who were helped by those laws say they are no longer needed. Was affirmative action merely a phase? Is it time to rethink it? Is affirmative action righting a wrong, but are quotas merely another form of racism?

Colleges and universities have always had quotas. Catholics and Jews were kept out for decades. They probably still are at some schools. Should we consider the proportional representation at Berkeley a quota system, or merely one method to make the student body reflect the diversity of the culture? Does your opinion about this depend on your grades? Your SAT scores? Your color?

The bottom line is that color, race, and culture have been a central problem for the United States from the beginning. Probably our most difficult problem. The issues are deeply rooted in misconceptions, misunderstandings, and all too often hatred. One hopes that higher education will be one of the centers from which the answers emerge.

— 9 —

Race II: The Wider World

So the tensions which we witness in the world today are indicative of the fact that a new world order is being born and an old order is passing away.
—Martin Luther King, Jr.

We don't believe that we can win in a battle where the ground rules are laid down by those who exploit us.
—Malcolm X

P olitics in the wider society is tied to politics on campus. We cannot understand how to deal with problems on campus if we do not know about the events that produced them. Current events make little sense without the context of history, so we begin this chapter with a history of the recent past of race relations in the United States. We concentrate on movement politics of the last 40 years.

We then move to more current issues and ask you to think about what they mean. Two events—the nomination of Clarence Thomas to the Supreme Court and the Rodney King beating and trials—are harsh reminders of the role race plays in our society.

In this chapter is the reminder that there are many racial minorities in the United States. As an example, we discuss issues in the history of Native Americans since the arrival of Europeans.

We end the chapter with a discussion of affirmative action. Affirmative action is one way we, as a society, have tried to address the problem of ongoing racial prejudice. To work through the tensions of affirmative action is to begin to understand how difficult it can be to address the problems of racism.

Movement Politics

A detailed understanding of race in America really begins with the first contacts between the European explorers and the natives here. It includes the nearly 350-year experience with slavery. It includes the Civil War, Reconstruction, segregation practices, the Indian wars, the movement west, and the acquisition of land. The detailed understanding moves from there to policies of this century, policies about segregation and desegregation, about letting people into the country and keeping people out, about moving people who are already here, and more.

We are not going to do such a detailed history. We start with the movement politics of the 1950s and 1960s.

The movement of the fifties and sixties can be understood as events that happened in different places that we now lump together as the civil rights movement. Although some of these events live in our collective memory, there are many others that should also be remembered.

We should remember A. Phillip Randolph. He was a leader who organized people and tried to get powerful people to integrate society. He got President Roosevelt, in 1941, to set up a federal Fair Employment Practices Commission to look at charges that black Americans were not being treated fairly. He got President Truman to ban racial discrimination in the nation's armed forces in 1948.

Most people remember Branch Rickey as the Brooklyn Dodger executive who "broke the color line," bringing Jackie

Robinson to the big leagues of professional baseball in 1947. Few can name any of the people who persuaded him, and put pressure on politicians at the time, to accept such a change.

Those events were part of the movement.

A central part of the movement was the Supreme Court's 1954 decision in *Brown v. the Board of Education of Topeka*. In that case, the court ordered the desegregation of the nation's schools. The slow pace of compliance with the policy led the court, more than a dozen years later, to endorse a policy of forced busing to achieve desegregation.

The court was responding to the movement. The *Brown* case was a product of a long campaign by the National Association for the Advancement of Colored People (NAACP) Legal Defense and Educational Fund. This group of civil rights leaders and attorneys built up, over several decades, expertise and a history of case law in lower courts that enabled them to bring the *Brown* case to the Supreme Court. The general counsel of the NAACP at the time, leader of the Legal Defense and Educational Fund, was Thurgood Marshall, who would later become the first black American to sit on the Supreme Court. The NAACP's first victories in the courts were about segregation in graduate and professional schools. Once case law made it clear that separate but equal schools were illegal, the NAACP's lawyers were ready for a test case on public education. *Brown* was the product of decades of hard work.

The Montgomery bus boycott, starting in late 1955, galvanized the movement in new ways and spread it beyond the courts. The city buses in Montgomery, Alabama, like virtually all services and places in the city, were segregated. Seats in the front of the buses were reserved for white riders, and black riders sat in the back. If white passengers ran out of seats in the front, black passengers were supposed to give up their seats and move farther back. If the bus got too full to seat everyone, black passengers were supposed to stand while white passengers sat.

On several occasions, black riders refused to give up their seats. On one occasion, the passenger who refused was Rosa Parks. The bus driver called the police, and Parks still refused to move. She was arrested and released on a bond of $100.

Local black leaders, in particular E. D. Nixon, state chair of the NAACP, suggested to Parks that her case could be used to change the rules of segregation in public transportation. She agreed. Parks was a seamstress who also worked as secretary in the local NAACP.

Nixon and others organized a one-day bus boycott. It successfully showed that the black citizens of Montgomery could act together politically. They organized a committee to keep the boycott going until the buses were no longer segregated. They asked a young new minister in town, Dr. Martin Luther King, Jr., to lead the committee.

King was smart; he was a minister and a stirring public speaker, and he had justice on his side. Although his talents were special, his story is, in an important way, typical of the civil rights movement of the 1950s and 1960s. His father was a Baptist minister active in civil rights issues. King followed in his father's footsteps to become a minister. The leaders in Montgomery were all ministers or important figures in local congregations. This makes sense: The only institutions where black citizens could act freely were the ones of their own making—the churches. That is where most leaders of the civil rights movement came from during that period.

The Montgomery bus boycott lasted more than a year. It took a Supreme Court decision, as well as intense local politics, to bring about an end to segregated buses in Montgomery.[1]

The Montgomery boycott was important for the momentum it gave to the civil rights movement. Black citizens, acting together, could bring about change. This fact alone meant that history was being made. A new group of black leaders, mostly from churches, gained a national audience.

An important lesson for the movement came out of Little Rock, Arkansas. Arkansas, like several other Southern states, declared open resistance to the *Brown* decision. One of their tactics was to grant local school boards the authority to assign students to classrooms. This meant, in practice, that organizations like the NAACP could not win statewide suits against desegregation orders, but would instead have to fight the battle through each school district.

In September 1957, Little Rock's schools were under a court order to desegregate, and the local board was apparently willing to comply. The governor of Arkansas, Orval Faubus, used white fear of desegregation to help his reelection bid. He ordered the National Guard to block the entry of black students into a high school. He calculated that this would energize local segregationists into active resistance. He was right.

President Dwight Eisenhower was displeased with Faubus's action and talked to him. Faubus told the president that no further problems would occur. But after Faubus called off the National Guard troops, a mob of white citizens blocked the black students' entry to the high school.

Eisenhower retaliated by nationalizing the Guard troops, and ordered them to accompany the students to school. The students did win entry to the school, but with soldiers at their side during gym class and in the hallways between classes.

The next year, Faubus closed the city's schools *for the entire year.*

Little Rock taught leaders of the movement that they could not rely upon white leaders to achieve full civil rights for black Americans. Change would have to come from massive political participation and widespread change of attitudes.

Another important ingredient of the movement came from Greensboro, North Carolina, in 1960. Lunch counters in drug stores, like most public facilities, were segregated. Four students at North Carolina Agricultural and Technical College had been raised during their teen years amid talk of the *Brown* decision, and especially of the Montgomery boycott. Ministers at their churches and associates in NAACP chapters had talked about justice for years. Martin Luther King, Jr., had visited Greensboro and given a speech on civil rights issues. The students took it very seriously.

On a Monday in February 1960, the four sat down at the Whites Only lunch counter of the local Woolworth drug store and asked for service. They were refused. They sat at the counter in silent protest. Other students at the college came to support their sit-in. Each day, more students came and stood in line to be served until, by the end of the week, nearly 1,000 students were standing in the street outside the drug store.

The drug store closed the lunch counter rather than desegregate, but the lesson had been learned.

By mid-April, demonstrations like this, massive disobedience of unjust segregation laws, had occurred in more than 50 cities throughout the South. Local officials put protesters in jail, and civil rights organizations instructed demonstrators how to act in an organized fashion, how to behave when arrested, and, most important, how to take a beating while minimizing serious injuries. The key to the tactic was nonviolent disobedience. Local communities and a national audience would not be moved by elected leaders—change would have to come from mass participation and new attitudes, taught to a nation by people willing to risk even their lives for civil rights.

A series of marches, mostly centered around voting rights, took place over the next few years. Some civil rights workers were killed for attempting to register voters. One tactic used by protesters was the freedom-ride. Civil rights activists got on buses bound for cities in the South. The buses started in Washington, D.C., where white and black passengers were not segregated, and headed into territory where the laws separated riders by color. They were met by mobs who beat the freedom-riders.

The mass marches, the sit-ins, the freedom-rides, and the arrests were part of the movement that captured the interest of the news media. The whole nation watched peaceful marchers, asking for justice, get attacked by police dogs and knocked down by blasts from fire hoses. There was little doubt about who was right and who was wrong.

The marches and sit-ins continued for nearly four years.

The Civil Rights Act of 1964 and the Voting Rights Act of 1965 came out of that newly galvanized movement. The 1964 Act outlawed segregation in public places, discrimination by employers or unions, and unequal rules for voters in federal elections. It allowed federal agencies to withhold funds from states that violated the law, and instructed the U.S. Attorney General to pursue discrimination cases. (See the appendix for the full scope of the 1964 Civil Rights Act.) The 1965 law extended the equal voting rules provisions to state and local elections. These laws, which changed our society, were signs of the movement's success; they showed that public attitudes had changed enough to move their elected officials to pass antidiscrimination laws.

It was a remarkable time in our history.

Of course, there was resistance to the movement. While much of it was local, there was also resistance among national leaders.

The 1964 Republican candidate for president, Barry Goldwater, was an opponent of the 1964 Civil Rights Act.

The movement changed in the 1960s, too. The triumphs of the legislation in 1964 and 1965 simply covered the basic rights that we assume every citizen should have. We all get to vote, and laws and practices that keep black Americans from voting are very wrong. We are entitled to equal justice under the law, and laws and practices in which states treat white Americans and black Americans differently violate that principle.

Justice requires more than voting and equality under the law. Martin Luther King, Jr., argued that freedom for black Americans would come only when they have access to decent jobs that will support families. He was murdered on April 4, 1968, in Memphis, Tennessee. He was there to support a strike by city workers.

The truth is, America in 1968 was divided over civil rights. The early victories that culminated in the 1964 and 1965 laws were the easy part. Fighting poverty and the war in Vietnam were not as popular as fighting for voting rights.

The movement expanded into concerns about political power and dignity. Malcolm X agreed with King on the goals of human dignity and freedom, but had a different message about how to get it. He showed that black Americans had a separate, African history. He had a way of keeping the history of Africans in America in everyone's face. He said that the nonviolent approach, which relied on the moral conversion and the goodwill of white Americans, is not the only way to freedom. Malcolm X helped to energize the movement, but he scared people—especially white Americans, who wanted to know what he meant by black nationalism and black power. He was murdered in early 1965.

The movement also changed the way laws were carried out. Federal courts supported busing to desegregate schools, and in some cases federal courts took over local school districts. Affirmative action became federal practice and then law, eventually spreading to state governments and private employers. People are still divided over these issues.

Talking About Racism—Events

Over the last decade, several events stand out as defining the state of race relations in the United States. Here are two recent examples.

The confirmation hearings of Clarence Thomas, who was nominated to the Supreme Court, and the accusations raised by Anita Hill.

The beating of Rodney King, the two trials of the police officers who beat him, and the trials of people who rioted in the aftermath of the first police trial.

Neither of these is easy to talk about. They are not easy because too many issues are opened up at once. A simpler issue helps make the point.

If one-third of white Americans believe that black Americans are poor, and one-third of black Americans believe that white Americans are rich, we can discuss that fairly easily. We can find a set of facts that lays out how many black citizens are rich and poor, and how many white citizens are rich and poor. We can talk about where those attitudes come from, but we can ground the discussion in a set of facts.

But these issues—the Thomas/Hill hearings and the Rodney King affair—have no clear set of facts. Each raises many issues, and we know that tens of millions of people were interested. Each raises issues that reflect our history and our different perspectives.

These events have to do with who we are and what we think. Our identities are not simple things. Touch one part of it, and the rest starts moving, too.

Clarence Thomas and Anita Hill

First, let's start with a few facts.[2]

Thurgood Marshall was the first black American to serve on the Supreme Court. He had a distinguished legal career before his nomination (he was the lead attorney who argued the *Brown* case before the Supreme Court in 1954, and he later served as Solicitor General of the United States), and was a strong voice for civil rights and liberalism on the Court. In his words, he just got old and decided to retire. He made no secret of the fact that he stayed on longer than he otherwise would have because he was concerned that conservative presidents would appoint justices who would move the Court too far to the right.

George Bush was president when Marshall announced his retirement. Bush nominated Clarence Thomas to replace Marshall.

Thomas was a graduate of Yale Law School. He worked with John Danforth, first when the latter was the attorney general of the state of Missouri, and later on Senator Danforth's staff in Washington. In between, he worked for a large corporation. His government service included working in the U.S. Office for Civil Rights, a term as head of the Equal Employment Opportunity Commission (EEOC), and appointment to the Federal Appeals Court.

A fine career.

Then, at age 43, he was nominated to the Supreme Court.

These are all facts, but there is more to know.

Thomas got those government jobs in no small part because he was a conservative. He may have gotten some of those jobs because he was conservative *and* black. It is true that all administrations, Republican and Democrat, have for decades been concerned with the diversity of their nominations for government jobs. Reagan and Bush chose well, because Thomas was a strong spokesperson for their views on civil rights and affirmative action.

Once he was nominated, everything seemed to be moving along well. The one sensitive part of the early hearing before the Senate Judiciary Committee was when he was asked if he had ever discussed the abortion issue with anyone, anytime. He said no, he could not remember ever doing so. After gently restating the question, as if in disbelief, committee members accepted his answer.

The mostly liberal senators did not accuse him of being incompetent (they could have—his leadership at the EEOC left a huge and growing backlog of unresolved cases) or mediocre (they could have—speeches he made and articles he wrote as an appeals court judge did not show him to be the smartest legal expert). Based on his record, the NAACP—the very group that Marshall had once represented—opposed his nomination.

But again, stick with the facts. What we do not know, and so it is beyond the realm of facts, is why the senators did not press those issues. People speculate that the issues were not pressed because Thomas was black. We will never know.

Most of the black political groups, such as the NAACP and the Southern Christian Leadership Conference (SCLC), were much slower than usual to endorse or oppose the nomination. There was actually debate over *whether he acted authentically black.* Simply put, most blacks are not as politically conservative as Clarence Thomas.

On the basis of the first hearings, which looked just at Thomas's record and the questions he answered, the committee voted seven to seven on his confirmation, and sent the nomination to the full Senate without recommendation. Those on the committee who voted against his nomination cited his overly conservative views and his weak qualifications. On the floor of the Senate, both supporters and opponents predicted he would be confirmed, perhaps by four or five votes.

But we have to back up a bit, to the week before that seven to seven vote. It was the week Anita Hill accused Thomas of sexual harassment, and the Senate Judiciary Committee conducted a special session of their confirmation hearings on the subject. The hearings were televised.

How did the charges of sexual harassment emerge? This is convoluted.

A friend of Anita Hill called another friend who did not want Thomas on the Supreme Court. The person the friend called in turn called a staff member of a Senate Judiciary

Committee member and said the committee might want to talk to Hill, suggesting that Thomas had sexually harassed Hill.

The staff member called Hill, but she would not talk about sexual harassment. A couple of days later, a staff member of another senator on the committee called Hill. She asked for time to decide whether to talk to the committee. She called back a couple of days later, and arranged an appointment to talk to staff members of the committee.

Anita Hill did not want to be involved in public hearings. She offered the name of a friend, a judge, as a reference so that committee members could be sure she was not just making up these charges a decade after the fact.

The committee staffers told Hill she could not tell her story to the committee unless the charges were revealed to the nominee and he was given a chance to respond. Hill agreed to the use of her name, and the FBI investigated and made a report on her allegations to the committee. Thomas was given a copy of the FBI report. Not all members of the committee read the report, apparently because the ranking Republican did not share the report with colleagues of his party.

Then the committee voted, seven to seven, on Thomas's nomination.

Three days before the full Senate was to vote on Thomas's nomination, someone leaked part of the FBI report to the news media. The next day the story was printed.

Thomas denied the charges. On the day of his scheduled confirmation, he asked for a delay in the Senate vote. At that point, it was not clear whether the nomination would pass.

During much of September, the FBI conducted an investigation of Anita Hill. Norman, Oklahoma, where Hill teaches, was full of FBI agents. They interviewed Hill's friends, neighbors, colleagues, and students. They found no evidence that compromised her character or her story.

The committee held four days of hearings, filled with several readings of Hill's account of the lewd and lascivious things Thomas allegedly said to her. Four people testified that Hill had told them of the events years before. Thomas supporters said that he could not have done such a thing. Thomas showed that he could be forceful and persuasive—he directly confronted the committee and told them the hearings were "a national disgrace. And from my standpoint as a black American, it is a high-tech lynching for uppity blacks who in any way deign to think for themselves." At the close of the hearings, committee chair Joseph Biden said that Judge Thomas must be given the benefit of the doubt if the committee could not agree upon the truth.

Two days after the hearings closed again, Thomas was confirmed by the full Senate, 52–48.

Clearly, the hearings were about more than a Supreme Court nomination. The Thomas hearings opened up the subject of race in American society. The episode shows that race is connected to everything else.

The episode was also about power. A year after the hearings, a record number of women were running for national elected office. Many of them cited the importance of gender issues, and specifically cited the way Anita Hill was treated by the all-white-male Senate Judiciary Committee. How could the committee just dismiss the charges? The critics charge that the committee would not have held the hearings had the FBI report not been leaked to the press. How could the committee be so cold and accusatory toward Hill? (Arlen Specter served as the Republicans' questioner of Hill on the committee, and he gave her a rough time.)

One reading of the episode is that it demonstrated a problem with male domination of power in politics and in the workplace. Apparently, sexual harassment is widespread, it goes unpunished, and our leaders are insensitive to it. The committee members did not seem to understand this. As one white woman said, "I just couldn't believe how stupid those senators were."

A second reading of the hearings asks us to see the stereotypes that cling to black men and women, and how those stereotypes played out in the hearings. What this means, of course, is that you are asked to see the hearings in the context of a racist society.

The hearings opened up to the wider world sensitive issues that are not generally discussed among black and white Americans. On one hand, there are stereotypes of black men and women, stereotypes that were conjured, even if remotely, in the hearings. Hill's account of Thomas's alleged misbehavior included his claims of his larger-than-normal penis, enjoyment of pornographic films, ability to sexually please women, and tasteless remarks at work (such as the one about the pubic hair on the Coke can). One black woman who was watching the hearings said, "Of all the issues they could criticize him on, why this one? Why this one?"

It's an ugly stereotype. It plays into roles that keep whites fearful and leery of black males, now and all the way back to slavery. Sex plus race is a story of power in America.

Here is how Rosemary L. Bray put it:[3]

> As difficult as the lives of black women often are, we know we are mobile in ways black men are not—and black men know that we know. They know that we are nearly as angered as they about their inability to protect us in the traditional and patriarchal way, even as some of us have moved beyond the need for such protection. . . . In our efforts to make a place for ourselves and our families in America, we have created a paradigm of sacrifice. . . . That sacrifice has been an unspoken promise to our people; it has made us partners with black men in a way white women and men cannot know. . . . There are those who believe the price of solidarity is silence. . . . Hill confronted and ultimately breached a series of taboos in the black community that have survived both slavery and the post-segregation life she and Clarence Thomas share. Anita Hill put her private business in the street, and she downgraded a black man to a room filled with white men who might alter his fate.

Llenda Jackson-Leslie focuses on, among other things, the dynamics between roles of black men and women. She argues they are in a tension that was drawn out in the hearings. She wrote:[4]

> Hill bore the brunt of intraracial hatred: the resentment of black men toward upwardly mobile black women; the contempt of black men who view all black women as bitches, skeezers, and hoes; the envy of black women who are less talented and less attractive. The campaign to undermine Anita Hill's credibility succeeded because of historical divisions within our community. Men against women; educated against uneducated; middle class professionals against working class; light skin against dark skin.

The roles were used in a racist context, she argues. But is the argument convincing? You judge. Thomas's strongest defender on the committee was Strom Thurmond. Thurmond has opposed civil rights legislation since World War II, and in 1948 received 39 electoral votes running for president on a segregationist ticket. How does Mr. Segregation come to defend Clarence Thomas? Jackson-Leslie applies her reasoning to show us how:[5]

> How do we resolve this paradox? First, the alleged harassment was against a black woman, in Thurmond's eyes, as in the distorted vision of other racists, no crime at all. Second, the equation of power must be considered, both as Hill's boss and Bush's manservant, Thomas had more power than Hill. In the mentality of a Strom Thurmond, Thomas had the same right to abuse Hill as the white master to abuse and debase his female slaves.

Is the connection to slavery so close? Is the analogy to servitude too immediate? Does this genuinely describe one of the dynamics of our society?

Everyone who doesn't think so is left with a burden: Can you explain why the hearings pushed that button?

That button gets pushed, in no small part, because of the complexity of identity. Remember the analogy of the circle— 20 different folks in a circle, all holding hands, all tied together. They are all part of one person's identity. The complicated reactions to the hearings begin to make sense if we grant the idea that those connections are, really, part of the identity of the people we hear.

You may not like them, but the connections are real.

A third reading of the episode overlaps the second but focuses on how we reason about issues like this. Should we begin our thinking with the category of race? What does racial thinking help us see, and how does it blind us?

Here are some things that racial thinking may help people see.

Did anyone in the country, one single person, believe George Bush when he said that Clarence Thomas was the best candidate for the vacant seat on the Supreme Court?

Assume, for a minute, that the answer is No.

Why would Bush make such a statement? Racial thinking has us analyze the dynamics between the group in power, Bush and his fellow white Republicans, and a group that will be active on this nomination, Democrats. Republican thinking could have been this: Black voters are an important part of the Democratic coalition, and black groups and Democrats would not be able to agree on a position on Thomas. Let the Democrats oppose Thomas! But don't kid yourself that the next nominee will be black. Who will be to blame if Thomas was denied a Supreme Court seat? Who will look racist? Will the opposition dare to assert that a black nominee is unqualified? Nonsense! They have the stereotype of black intelligence, too.

So we easily find cynicism if we start with racial thinking.

Racial thinking also helps us constantly make a connection between today's events and a racist past. The Civil Rights Act of 1964 and the Voting Rights Act of 1965 were not so long ago. Legal segregation ended about the same time. It is unrealistic to suppose that all the effects of practices outlawed in those years have vanished.

Attitudes and stereotypes from those days, and earlier, have certainly continued.

This all means that events that happen today need to be checked against a memory of a time when racism, a racism we now reject, was the law of the land.

Racial thinking helps in a third way, although the help is more partisan here. Racial thinking is a way of arguing, a way of teaching, and a way of vying for power. If we believe that the nation is racist, we may need to join a side. Are we for it or against it? Racial thinking is divisive and, skillfully wielded, has the ring of justice. So it may be useful in mobilizing people and winning political conflicts.

But there is a cost to racial reasoning, a big one.

Simply put, in the long run racial reasoning is not very bright. Few special talents are required. Like demagogues who preach nationalism and go to war to win power, racial reasoning is applied in utterly simplistic categories.

In the case of the Thomas nomination, the assumption that a black person is needed on the Court, and can represent blacks just by being there, is connected to other beliefs. Only certain black beliefs can represent black Americans. Many of his critics alleged that Thomas was not properly representing black ideas—he wasn't "authentically black." Cornell West points out that this misses an important point:[6]

> [B]lackness is a political and ethical construct. Appeals to black authenticity ignore this fact; such appeals hide and conceal the political and ethical dimensions of blackness. This is why claims to racial authenticity trump political and ethical argument—and why racial reasoning discourages moral reasoning. Every claim to racial authenticity presupposes elaborate conceptualizations of political and ethical relations of interests, individuals, and communities. Racial reasoning conceals these presuppositions.

It does not take a long look at those presuppositions to see both Hill and Thomas as two "conservative supporters of some of the most vicious policies to besiege black working and poor communities since Jim and Jane Crow segregation," according to West.[7] The hearings should have given rise to arguments about those policies, and not about who is, as West puts it, "on a pedestal or in the gutter."

The strange trail of racial thinking is taken to its limits in a *New York Times* piece by Derrick Bell.[8] He argued that what he heard and saw was so unreal, it must be part of some wider strategy that does make sense. Bell said he was "baffled" by Thomas's opposition to affirmative action, "cringed" at his support for capital punishment, "wondered" at his condemnation of people who receive welfare, and concluded that his antiabortion position "seemed to fly in the face of reality."

No sensible black man, Bell was saying, could believe these things.

"Then I realized," wrote Bell, "that Judge Thomas's seemingly ridiculous statements must be part of a carefully conceived conspiracy." That conspiracy amounts to this: His arguments and court decisions will convince everyone of America's rampant racism. "Militant arguments that blacks now have no alternative except disruptive protests and boycotts will be invulnerable to more moderate responses." "Within months" after Thomas takes office, Bell wrote, more blacks will come to this radical conclusion.

Bell claims that Thomas knows this and will deny it.
Maybe Bell was merely being ironic. Or, and this could be worse, maybe Bell was having a difficult time identifying Clarence Thomas. Like all of us, Thomas is his own collection of roles and traits. It may well be that Bell looked at Thomas on television and saw a black man, while Clarence Thomas may look in the mirror and see a conservative judge.

There is a flip side to Bell's argument, and a powerful one at that. He asks how Thomas can be considered a qualified candidate for the Court, let alone the most qualified candidate. He offers a set of rules for making sense of this.[9] He argues that blacks do not and will not have full equality in this country. Period. Their opinions matter little, particularly when it comes to their opinions about other blacks or what policy should be in areas such as affirmative action. The rule is, their opinions are discounted.

"The usual exception to this rule," writes Bell, "is the black person who publicly disparages or criticizes other blacks who are speaking or acting in ways that upset whites. Instantly, such statements are granted 'enhanced standing' even when the speaker has no special expertise or experience in the subject he or she is criticizing." The Thomas nomination, he says, is an "example of the awards awaiting blacks who gain enhanced standing."

Identities are far more complicated than race, but race makes it difficult to see those complications.

Rodney King and the L.A. Police

The Rodney King affair was surely more disruptive, at least in the streets, than the Thomas nomination. On Thomas's journey to the Supreme Court, no one died, and no one's store was burned down.

Again, we start with facts.[10]

Rodney King was driving his car on the night of March 3, 1991, too fast and too erratically, on a Los Angeles highway. The police tried to pull him over, but he refused to stop. A dangerous chase ensued, and several police cars finally stopped him. The police didn't like the way he was acting, and they started to beat him.

They beat him senseless.

While this was happening, a man on a nearby apartment balcony had a video camera he had just purchased. He looked out his window and saw he had a chance to take some exciting footage. For 81 seconds, he recorded several police officers clubbing and kicking Rodney King.

After the beating, the police put King into the back of a squad car. Instead of taking him directly to the hospital, where he needed to go, they drove around for nearly two hours, taking him to such places as a police station, where others could look at the results of their beating of King. Finally, he was taken to the hospital.

The man with the videotape told the police what he had on tape. Those he talked with did not care and dismissed him. He then told a television station what he had. They wanted the tape and played it on the news the following day.

The story became a national political issue. *Nightline* and major networks showed the tape, or parts of it, and people around the country and in Los Angeles wanted to know what would be done about it. The upheaval eventually cost the L.A. chief of police his job and led to charges filed in a state court against four of the police officers involved in the beating.

Defense attorneys for the four police officers argued that they could not get a fair trial in L.A. They argued that the media had prejudiced the case. They won a change of venue. The trial was held in Simi Valley. Simi Valley is a suburb that is mostly white, has many retired people, and is a place in which police are generally regarded as friendly.

The trial was long and involved and drew worldwide coverage. In the end, the four officers were acquitted of assault. Not guilty.

Los Angeles erupted in violence. Rioters killed 53 people and caused almost $1 billion of damage to property. The police and politicians were surprised by the violence and slow to respond.

For those following the trial through the media, it was difficult to understand the verdict. People watched the most brutal parts of the beating and found it hard to justify. Even the

President of the United States said he would have the Justice Department look into the situation.

The local U.S. Attorney General filed charges against the four officers, this time for violating the civil rights of Rodney King. This trial would be in federal court and in Los Angeles.

As the second trial was to begin, rumors were all over Los Angeles about a new paroxysm of violence. Gun sales reached all-time highs in this already heavily armed city. People in Los Angeles were afraid.

Nearly a year after the first trial, in April 1993, the second trial came to a close. Two of the officers were convicted, and the other two were acquitted. The police and politicians expected violence, and were prepared for it. It did not happen.

During the riots after the first trial, some black men on a street corner were stopping cars and hurting anyone who wasn't black. They pulled one truck driver from his vehicle and beat him severely. One assailant pounded in the skull of the truck driver with a concrete construction block. Almost miraculously, the driver survived. Videotapes again led to arrests, and the assailants were arrested and put on trial. The defendants were acquitted on the most serious charges, those of attempted murder and aggravated assault, but convicted on lesser charges. They are doing jail time. They were acquitted of the more serious charges because the defense attorney convinced the jury that their assault was not a case of one responsible person assaulting another. Their personal responsibility was diminished, went the argument, because they were angry and were acting as part of a mob.

Why was the Rodney King affair about race? Almost all the police involved in the beating, and all the officers charged with a crime, are white. The men who beat the truck driver are black. Rodney King is black.

The Los Angeles police force had a reputation for being one of the worst in the nation when it came to race relations. The charges against the department, before and after the King affair, included racist language, excessive force (especially against minorities), and an unwillingness to admit they have a problem. In an average year, about 200 civilians file claims against the police of excessive force, and 3 percent of the claims are sustained by the police investigators.

The difference in the Rodney King affair was that it had been videotaped.

Some more facts might be helpful. The Los Angeles police department polices one of the largest cities in the country, both in population and area. Los Angeles has more residents per police officer than any other large city in the country. Police in Los Angeles do not get out in the community much. They emphasize rapid and forceful response to emergency calls and quick investigation of major crimes. The statistics upon which individual officers are evaluated emphasize aggressive pursuit of lawbreakers and arrests.

With this system, they get more arrests per cop, but the citizens often do not see police as their friends.

A commission investigating the police department in the summer of 1991 found that about 5 percent of the police force believed in using force to discipline suspects, and another 11 percent had no opinion on the subject. These attitudes were widespread enough to allow excessive force, and the department leadership turned a blind eye to the problem. So said the commission.

What was so divisive about the King affair?

First, the videotape offered undeniable evidence of a severe beating. But why did it go that far? If you want to see members of a racist institution viciously beating a black man, the tape provided all the evidence you need. For people who shared those attitudes with 16 percent of the L.A. police force, maybe that wasn't compelling evidence. It wasn't in the first trial.

The original trial was the second very divisive part of the King affair. The results helped to touch off the violence that hurt so many people. Again, if you want to see a racist system at work, it didn't take much imagination. The trial was moved, and as a result the jury was all white. The white police accused of assaulting a black man were all acquitted. They claimed that they had to subdue a big, strong black man who acted as though he was wild on drugs, oblivious to pain. King did not testify at their trial. The police officers' defense attorneys took the jury through the videotape, frame by frame, to show how the officers feared this big, strong, crazy black man, and used reasonable force to subdue him. And the jury believed it.

If you don't want to see a racist system, a different reading of the trial is possible. The law governing the assault charges against the police did require some knowledge of the intent of the assaulters. The police made a good case, a case not refuted directly by King himself. Several police officers and experts who testified of violations of police procedure were not called in the first trial. Put differently, the prosecutors did not do a good job in the first trial. They thought the videotape spoke for itself, but it didn't.

A third divisive event in the King affair was the violence following the first trial. Was it a riot or a rebellion? Maxine Waters, a member of Congress, called it a justifiable rebellion. She said a racist system had become just too much for people to take. She didn't go into details about the extensive looting, also known as stealing, that was at the center of the violence.

The chief of police, Daryl Gates, called it a riot by lawless hoodlums. News media stories focused on black rioters attacking stores owned by Korean immigrants.

Both interpretations, the blacks rioting and the oppressed rebelling, fell into the trap of racial thinking. The people doing the looting and burning and hurting were black, and white, and brown, and yellow. Call it a diversity riot. The mishmash of people did not act as a unit. For every person willing to say this is a justifiable response by an oppressed race or class, you could find a thug out for a little fun and profit.[11]

The prevailing image of the King beating, the riot, and all three trials, however, was about race. The verdict against the men who nearly killed the truck driver was celebrated as a victory by their supporters. Most people who expressed an opinion about the verdict saw it as cynical, as going easy on thugs just to avoid the danger that they might riot again. It was seen as a black versus white issue.

Not, we should say, by everyone. The truck driver, Reginald Denny, said that he forgave his assaulters and did not want them or anyone else to be hurt more by this whole episode.

The Thomas/Hill affair and the Rodney King affair show that we are a society divided. As a nation, we easily slip into racial thinking.[12]

Racial Minorities as Other

So far, this chapter has mostly focused on divisions between black and white citizens. The focus has been deliberate because we believe that the black/white racial division is the most stark and consequential. But it is not the only one.

When the first European explorers and settlers came to North America, there were somewhere between three and eight million natives here.[13] In the early accounts of the natives that filtered back to Europe, tales of cannibalism and savagery were prominent. This probably had a lot to do with the way sixteenth- and seventeenth-century Europeans tended to reason about human societies, beginning with state-of-nature arguments. These arguments posited a presocial condition in which people lived without a state. The brutality and savagery of humans in this original condition led them to seek the protection of a government. These kinds of arguments helped to justify governments formed with the consent of the governed and laws made by elected representatives. They also contributed to the view that the natives in the New World were brutal, savage, and primitive. The early explorers' expectation that they would find India by a westward crossing of the Atlantic provided the name for these natives: Indians.

When different civilizations meet for the first time, there is often conflict and killing. Usually lots of people die. The most destructive force brought by the Europeans was disease.[14] The North American continent had no dense populations with sustained contact between them, and so few diseases developed to the extent they had in Europe and Asia. Native Americans fell prey to childhood diseases of Europe on a disastrous scale. It is likely that more than 90 percent of Native Americans died from such diseases. Some tribes lost all but a few percent of their members and simply ceased to exist. There are accounts of whites deliberately infecting native tribes, but that is a small part of the whole picture. The mere fact of contact was enough to kill all but a small number of the natives. (Ask yourself: How would it change our society if all but 19 million U.S. citizens died?)

A second reason for the clash between civilizations is that the natives and the Europeans had radically different ways of life. The Europeans recognized land ownership by individuals and organized states, while the natives lived in tribal ranges. The Europeans believed that their own ways were civilized (read: better), and that they had a duty to convert the natives to their religion. The Europeans believed in individual economic autonomy coupled with central authority, authority that could enforce norms through imprisonment and executions. The Europeans organized their economies around intensive cultivation and permanent settlements, which were peripheral to the natives. There was to be no blending of cultures between the two civilizations.

The clash took the form of a series of wars that lasted from the 1620s to 1890. With the exception of a few battles, the whites won all of the contests. The victories were total, and meant that the white way of organizing land, economies, states, and social norms prevailed. Where there were native survivors of the wars, they were usually moved to reservations. Reservations were lands that whites generally did not want because of the land's poor resources, and the natives were living at a subsistence level. A series of laws passed by the Congress pushed the natives away from traditional ways of life and into the white norms of land ownership and social organization. This approach to native tribes did not begin to change until the 1970s.

According to the 1990 census, Native Americans now constitute about .8 percent of the U.S. population, a bit under two million people. Those numbers are suspect, however. "Native American" is a self-described category in the census. The criteria for inclusion differ widely. For example, most of the Alaska tribes require members to have at least one-quarter native ancestry (at least one grandparent must be a full Indian). Some tribes grant membership to those with one-sixteenth or less ancestry. Native Americans may classify themselves as white on the census, and many do.

A racial classification of Native Americans is very misleading. Skin color varies widely among native populations, from considerably lighter than some European populations to a dark copper brown. Facial features, size, and tooth patterns also vary. Most of the variation stems from the fact that the migrations into the hemisphere, across the Aleutian land bridge, took place in several waves over thousands of years. The origins of native peoples, and their patterns of contact with each other, varied.

We may currently think of Native Americans as a race because, from the first contact with Europeans, they have always been the Other. Racial thinking classifies people into Us and people Not Like Us. It obscures the diversity among the Others, and the prevailing monochromatic view of Native Americans allows government to enact policies that ignore important differences. Some tribes focus on fishing, and some on agriculture. Some are large, and some are small. Some have comparatively more resources on their reservations, or are situated close to resources that enable them to develop their economy. Only recently has federal law begun to leave room for tribes to define themselves and choose their own methods of organization and paths of development.

Native Americans suffer the worst quality of life of any minority in the United States. The rate of unemployment on reservations is typically 50 percent or more, and over one-third in urban areas. (About 40 percent of Native Americans live on reservations, and about as many live in urban areas.) Their life expectancy is 10 years shorter than the national average, and almost 30 years shorter for some tribes. They are about three times as likely to die from accidents, including automobile accidents, from cirrhosis of the liver, and from diabetes. They are nearly six times as likely to die of tuberculosis, although relatively few people die from that. Death rates from heart disease and cancer are lower than the national averages, but probably because not enough of them live long enough to die from these illnesses.

In the last 30 years, Native Americans have become more assertive in local and national politics, with the aim of coping with specific problems and achieving greater control of their lives. One of the more potent symbols was the occupation of

Alcatraz Island, in San Francisco Bay, for a few months in 1969. Occupiers announced their attention to operate the island as a cultural center. Here is part of their proclamation:[15]

> We feel that this so-called Alcatraz Island is more than suitable for an Indian Reservation, as determined by the white man's own standards. By this we mean that this place resembles most Indian reservations in that:
>
> 1. It is isolated from modern facilities, and without adequate means of transportation.
> 2. It has no fresh running water.
> 3. It has inadequate sanitation facilities.
> 4. There are no oil or mineral rights.
> 5. There is no industry and so unemployment is very great.
> 6. There are no health care facilities.
> 7. The soil is rocky and nonproductive; and the land does not support game.
> 8. There are no education facilities.
> 9. The population has always exceeded the land base.
> 10. The population has always been held as prisoners and kept dependent upon others.
>
> Further, it would be fitting and symbolic that ships from all over the world, entering the Golden Gate, would first see Indian land, and thus be reminded of the true history of this nation.

Indians have also become more effective in using the court system and pressuring Congress to respond to their needs. Change comes slowly, and often opens up renewed conflict with surrounding communities. For example, a 1979 court decision that interpreted an 1856 treaty as requiring an equal division of fishing resources in Washington state pitted commercial and sport fishing organizations against the Indians. Prejudices run high in the state, fueled by questions of access to important economic resources.

This brief review of Native Americans in the United States suggests that an incredible amount of diversity is forgotten with a racial classification, and that racial thinking leads us to misunderstand rather than understand others. Clear thinking is necessary to develop a consensus on effective policies that deal with race. Our experience with affirmative action, as discussed in the next section, suggests that we have yet to reach a consensus on race.

Affirmative Action

Affirmative action is not a simple idea. In a basic sense, it means to make an extra effort to ensure that a class of people, such as a minority group, is protected and given a reasonable chance at a job or promotion. In practice, it means a procedure to see that such opportunity is created. Sometimes it means a quota. Affirmative action is supposed to change who gets what.

One important question is, Why do it?

One rationale was offered by Malcolm X. He wrote, "All of us, who might have probed space, or cured cancer, or built industries, were instead black victims of the white man's social system."[16]

The idea is that affirmative action is compensation for past injustices and their lingering effects. The beneficiary of the policy is a group.

Derrick Bell brings the point up to date. He argues that black Americans will never enjoy full equality. Never. True, the "No Negras Need Apply" signs are gone, but, he argues, the reality of exclusion is still there.

> Today, because bias is masked in official practices and "neutral" standards, we must wrestle with the question whether race or some individual failing has cost us the job, denied us the promotion, or prompted our being rejected as tenants for an apartment. Either conclusion breeds frustration and alienation—and a rage we dare not show to others or admit to ourselves.[17]

According to Bell, whites who oppose programs such as affirmative action or strong fair housing law enforcement believe in a racial equality that just does not exist. Bell implies that affirmative action programs are just the tip of the iceberg. We will not think clearly about such policies and make effective policies until we "reassess the worth of the racial assumptions on which, without careful thought, we have presumed too much and relied too long."[18]

A second rationale is that employment and things such as enrollment in college are important social resources. These must be distributed among various groups so that each can contribute something from that group, and so that our institutions *appear* to be fair to all. When applied to government employment, this argument is called representative bureaucracy.

It makes sense that white males may see an issue differently from black females. It also makes sense that a policy might be more acceptable to a group if it looked as if the organizations making the decisions or giving out the awards somehow understood or included the group.

A representative bureaucracy would be one that includes, in roughly the right proportions, men, women, black people, white people, yellow people, brown people, red people, people of all religious beliefs, atheists, physically handicapped people, you name it. The idea has an intuitive appeal, but this question must be considered: Does everyone, in each group, think and act the same? If we believe that, aren't we oversimplifying and stereotyping? On the other hand, isn't it awkward, and somehow very wrong, to walk into a big office and see people of only one color or sex?

A third rationale has to do with our imperfect methods of deciding who is the best person to hire, promote, or let into school. It also has to do with a compromise among conflicting values.

The conflicting values are hard to reconcile. In this country, we value individual rights, equal opportunity, and rewards according to merit. No person should be treated differently because of his or her appearance or beliefs. We believe also in equality. A hiring method that systematically excludes women or black citizens is not fair. We believe also in efficiency and effectiveness, which means that we want the most efficient and effective people to work in our organizations.

How do we reconcile these values when they come into conflict? That is where a frank appraisal of our imperfect hiring methods is useful.

The argument goes like this. There is no such thing as general superiority among applicants to a job. Different applicants bring different qualifications to a job. This means that a score of 96 on a test may not mean the person will be a lot better than someone who received a 95. A 96 may not even be significantly better than an 89.

Instead of splitting hairs looking for the absolute "best" applicants, it is better to separate people into these categories: qualified or not qualified.

Once this idea is accepted, people who hire have larger pools to choose from, and can select, among other things, a work force that is as diverse as the people served.

There are, of course, objections to the three arguments. You can say to the first that there *is* substantial equality across colors. You can say to the second that organizations should work solely on merit and leave representation to the politicians. You can say to the third that there is a best person to hire and that hiring less than the best will lead to mediocrity.

Long arguments are possible. Indeed, the history of the last 30 years is the record of these arguments.

Affirmative action is the law of the land.[19] Organizations must look at the sex, race, and other attributes of the people they hire, promote, and fire. We also know that these laws may not have made much of a difference in outcomes. Black and female applicants were making slow progress in employment before affirmative action, and the progress since has been slow. On the positive side, black professional and managerial employment has improved, mostly in areas of the economy covered by affirmative action. On the negative side, it may have gotten worse in areas not covered. The military sometimes seems to be the only organization that took affirmative action seriously. Colin Powell, the former chairman of the Joint Chiefs of Staff, is black, and there are people of color in leadership positions throughout the armed forces. Women can now be fighter pilots. But the military is the exception.

Affirmative action is divisive. In Birmingham, Alabama, the fire department was all white until 1968.[20] In 1983, a white and a black firefighter each took a test for promotion. The white firefighter ranked sixth of all test takers, the black firefighter ranked eighty-sixth. Under the department's affirmative action program, the black firefighter got the promotion.

The white firefighter joined a lawsuit alleging reverse discrimination. His point was clear: "I can understand that blacks had been historically discriminated against. I can also understand why people would want to be punitive in correcting it. Somebody needs to pay for this. But they want me to pay for it, and I didn't have anything to do with it. I was a kid when all of this [discrimination] went on."

The black firefighter did not accept that argument. He thought white firefighters were "still living off what their forefathers did." The customary privileges of whites were rooted in the denial of access to blacks, according to him.

The challenge to the affirmative action plan was unsuccessful in the fire department, but the politics of the challenge are still strong. In Birmingham, the elected Democratic officials are almost all black, and they support affirmative action. The elected Republicans are all white, and they oppose affirmative action.

Nathan Glazer gives us one way to understand the problem. He argues that, although we should not be satisfied with the condition of black Americans, government has no business determining who should get jobs, promotions, and seats in medical schools.[21] Government should, instead, help to create more jobs, and vigorously punish instances of discrimination. Glazer writes that, as a country, we believe in the interest of the individual. He opposes affirmative action because it is about group rights.

Finally, affirmative action, according to Glazer, is just too divisive. It gives an easy opponent to people who refuse to face moral arguments about the real condition of black Americans. Glazer reminds us that it was not popular opinion or the democratic demands of the citizenry that led to the extent of affirmative action we now have. "The people do not determine what is constitutional; the courts do."[22] As long as we are politically divided over affirmative action, he does not expect us to get very far with moral arguments about justice for black Americans.

Stephen Carter refines Glazer's argument to find a limited place for affirmative action.[23] Here is the condensed version. He points out that most benefits of affirmative action go to people who least need them. The talented black Americans are probably going to do well, with or without affirmative action. The people who really need it, and need it early, are those mired in poverty. More young minorities need to do well in school. That means preschool programs, and lots of them. Many more young minorities need to get into college-prep high schools. Once those hurdles are cleared, an easier path is open to college. If black students do well in college, more will go on to graduate school. He argues that by the time black graduates are entering professions, the need for affirmative action has disappeared.[24]

As an argument, it is pretty clear. Of course we agree that more is needed to give a good education to the neediest black children. There are those who differ on Carter's conclusion about affirmative action at the more advanced stages of education and employment, but people often disagree about such things.

Carter's book, *Reflections of an Affirmative Action Baby*, was a best-seller and generated a great deal of criticism because he said that the issue is really about identity.

Carter said he benefitted from affirmative action, but he also got labeled. He was in the running for a National Merit Scholarship. He thought he had earned it. But he got a call offering him a different scholarship—one for African-American students. He was labeled as one of the *best black students*.

Carter would like to get away from the "best black" syndrome. He does not deny that black students and black professionals face barriers to success, but the barriers should be the proper focus of policy. Racial preference policies see black Americans as a group, and so embody that piece of identity in government and social policy. Carter writes:[25]

> Supporters of preferences cite a whole catalogue of explanations for the inability of people of color to get along without them: institutional racism, inferior education, overt prejudice, the lingering effects of slavery and oppression, cultural bias in the criteria for admissions and employment. All of these arguments are most sincerely pressed, and some of them are true. But like the best black syndrome, they all entail the assumption that people

of color cannot at present compete on the same playing field with people who are white. I don't believe this for an instant; and after all these years, I still wish the National Merit Scholarship people had given me the chance to prove it.

So far, we have a clear disagreement. Stephen Carter believes equality of individual achievement is possible, and Derrick Bell does not.

Carter is criticized for being black and saying the things he does. There are those who question whether he is really black if he says those things. Clarence Thomas had the same problem.

Carter rejects the idea that "there is a correct and predictable way in which a person of color will differ in his or her analysis of an issue from a person who is white."[26] But that idea is powerful. It is used to stifle dissent from people like Carter.

Carter cites the case of Julius Lester, a professor at the University of Massachusetts. Lester had said that some of the things James Baldwin wrote were anti-Semitic. He had also said that Andrew Young, when he was the U.S. ambassador to the United Nations, was wrong to have met with the Palestine Liberation Organization, and should resign. For those acts, Lester was vilified and mocked by his colleagues, and the tenured professor was kicked out of his department. His colleagues said that "while professor Lester has the right to publicly characterize James Baldwin in any way that he might desire, the actual results can only be depicted as capricious, irresponsible and damaging in a most pernicious way."

The labels others put on us limit what we can do and say.

Shelby Steele is often grouped with Carter as a "black conservative," as if the label conveys that this person is different and has predictable opinions. But there is more to it than that.

Here is what Steele has to say about affirmative action: "Rather than ask it to ensure equal opportunity, we have demanded that it create parity between the races. But preferential treatment does not teach skills, or educate, or instill motivation. It only passes out entitlements by color." The entitlements do not solve the basic problem of justice. "Blacks cannot be repaid for the injustice done to the race," he writes, "but we can be corrupted by society's guilty gestures of repayment."[27]

OK, he really does not like affirmative action, but what does he propose in its place? How do we get real equal opportunity?

"I think we need," says Steele, "social policies that are committed to two goals: the educational and economic development of disadvantaged people, regardless of race, and the eradication from our society—through close monitoring and severe sanctions—of racial, ethnic, or gender discrimination. Preferences will not deliver us to either of these goals, since they tend to benefit those who are not disadvantaged."[28]

We need to do more, to put it in practical terms, to change the fact that more black American college-aged males are wards of the criminal justice system than are in college. That means keeping them out of jail and creating the conditions to get them into college, employed, or both.

It takes big government programs to do that, much more than we are doing now. Why does this sound conservative to Steele's critics?

Here is where we get back to identity.

Steele argues that there is a game about innocence on the question of race. If one can claim to be morally innocent, then one can claim to rightfully control power to fix the guilty party. I can be innocent only if you are guilty.

He applies this concept to the Reagan years, years when the Republicans claimed to support equal opportunity but oppose quotas, and years when most black Americans claimed that the Republicans didn't care about their needs or concerns. If whites claim to be innocent, blacks can bargain the terms of that innocence or directly challenge it, getting concessions along the way.

Reagan claimed innocence. He claimed power out of this innocence. His claim to be color-blind served to decrease white feelings of guilt, and so the people he appointed could effectively turn back gains made by the civil rights movement. But not everyone bought it. "His posture of innocence drew him into a partisanship that undermined the universality of his values. He couldn't sell these values to blacks because he made blacks into the bad guys and outsiders who justified his power. It was humiliating for a black person to like Reagan because Reagan's power was so clearly derived from a distribution of innocence that left blacks with less of it and the white man with more."[29]

Not very nice to the conservatives, coming from someone who is called conservative.

The criticism for Steele's argument stems from another source. When he talks about white and black identity, he argues that each group has to change in order to mend the problems of racism in America. But he devotes a majority of the book to black identity.

Like Carter, Steele acknowledges the daily slights and insults that black Americans encounter. If you doubt that is true, no matter what your color, ask the people on your campus, in your class, wherever. But he puts them in a different context.

He calls it racial vulnerability.

"Racial vulnerability is best thought of not so much as the world of our oppression as the woundedness we still carry as a result of it—our continuing openness to inferiority anxiety and to racial diminishment and shame."[30] It arms a person to look for insults and slights, ones that, Steele implies, might best be ignored. It allows someone to see an insult where none was offered, or, more important, to fail to confront evidence of pain and doubt that are internal. He says that racial vulnerability is the core of identity. It "acts as a cause that generates many effects—effects that shape black life in everything from politics to clothing styles, from the way we dance to the way we vote."

He goes on to claim that in pursuit of the American dream of a better life and the things that go with it, racial vulnerability forms an identity that is a "hegemonic censor that holds us back."

Steele does not deny that white racism exists. But he doesn't spend most of his book talking about it, either. Instead, he focuses on identity. That identity is threatened now: "(o)ur oppression has left us with a dangerously powerful memory of itself that can pull us into warlike defensiveness at a time when there is more opportunity for development than ever before."[31]

"The most dangerous threat to the black identity," Steele writes, *"is not the racism of white society (this actually confirms the black identity) but the black who insists on his or her own individuality."*[32]

Steele suggests that he is tired of being called an Oreo.

Is there a balance in the argument? Steele says that the realities of opportunities and racism exist, side by side. Any reader of his book should get one message: No more Reagans, no more exaggerated claims of innocence. The difficult message is the controversial one about identity. That is a question, for Steele, of how to teach the children and live today. That is for parents and leaders to do now. He says:

> Our leaders must take a risk. They must tell us the truth, tell us of the freedom and opportunity they have discovered in their own lives. They must tell us what they tell their own children when they go home at night: to study hard, pursue their dreams with discipline and effort, to be responsible for themselves, to have concern for others, to cherish their race and at the same time make their own lives as Americans.[33]

Steele's argument focuses on one of the core tensions of the problem of race in America. In one sense, he is talking about black Americans in a community, and how a community can provide identity. But he finds the identity too narrow. His ideas on what to do about race and racism center on individualism.

Where should the emphasis be? Here is a summary from Andrew Hacker:

> America is inherently a "white" country: in character, in structure, in culture. Needless to say, black Americans create lives of their own. Yet, as a people, they face boundaries and constrictions set by the white majority. America's version of *apartheid*, while lacking overt legal sanction, comes closest to the system even now being reformed in the land of its invention. . . . So the question for white Americans is essentially moral: is it right to impose on members of an entire race a lesser start in life, and then to expect from them a degree of resolution that has never been demanded from your own race?[34]

—10—

Multiculturalism

*Surprises were not to our taste. We preferred the drawl
of custom, the glancing acceptance of whatever was.
You can't get the best of us. Death itself was only mere
nickname or mock peeve, something we spoke of but
never believed.*

—Baron Wormser

*But to my surprise, when I sat down to write—in order
to discover, as E. M. Forster once said, what I really
think—I found that I agreed with all sides in the debate
at once.*

—Katha Pollitt

*It's culture defined in the most generous of old-
fashioned concepts: the humanities. If it's human, it's
yours. Take it. Share it. Mix it. Rock it.*

—Enrique Fernandez

In this chapter we take up the problem of multiculturalism
on campus. It is a problem that goes to the heart of higher
education. We ask you to consider what a well-educated person should learn, who should make that decision, and what
the role of higher education should be.

We begin with what has traditionally been regarded as the core of a liberal education—the canon. The debate about the canon—to oversimplify, Is the thought of Dead White Males an appropriate base of liberal education?—is reviewed. There are strong arguments on both sides.

The discussion broadens to consider the idea that the canon should be replaced by a multicultural curriculum. At that point, we ask what the role of higher education should be. The debate about multiculturalism is often centered around the themes of historical accuracy, political inclusion, and personal identity. The debate about multiculturalism on campus is also often about who has power and who wants power. It reveals how academics fight for control.

The chapter ends with a discussion of Afrocentrism and Eurocentrism and asks you to consider how best to learn about our country, a country that is made up of many cultures.

It is reasonable to expect that your professors should know at least two things. First, you expect them to know their fields of study. That would mean, for example, that they know what to teach in upper-division courses and graduate courses. They have expertise in their field. They should be readers and possibly authors of scholarly articles and books. Second, you expect professors to know what to teach incoming students. You expect that, with all of our education, professors should know what is necessary and important for all students to study and learn.

But it seems that the more professors know, the less sure they are.

A driving force in the debate is multiculturalism. It means, literally, consideration of many cultures. Multiculturalism, for our purposes, is more than merely adding a course in African history or Asian philosophy to an existing curriculum. Multiculturalism, as argued by many who favor it, is about beginning to understand the world from the perspectives of people from different backgrounds and anticipating the world as different people believe it is going to be. Multiculturalism is about a United States, and a world, that is more than and different from the sum of European thought.

Cultures have intermingled and changed. There are no "pure" cultures—we are increasingly affected by all of the countries in the world, just as we affect all of them. To begin to understand the culture we live in, it is important to understand the cultures that helped create it.

That is the short definition of *and argument for* multiculturalism. There are fights on campus over what it means. The fights on campus are often over the books you will read and what you will discuss in your classes. The fights are also about who has power on campus. Finally, the fights are over the very role of higher education. Multiculturalism, it turns out, is a direct line into the debates over what higher education is all about.

The Canon

Canon is a serious word. On campus, we have people teaching something call *The Canon.*

The word *canon* may sound religious, and a check of the dictionaries suggests why. An etymological dictionary says it came from the Greek word *kanna,* which meant "a rod, hence a rule." It worked its way to mean "a moral rule . . . esp. a code."[1] In Latin it meant "a reed . . . esp. a large tube," and finally became "English as canyon . . . a deep valley . . . a hollow."

The second edition of *Webster's Deluxe Unabridged Dictionary* offers 14 different definitions of the word *canon.* Clearly, the most used meanings have to do with laws or rules—church (especially Roman Catholic) laws in particular. The *Oxford English Dictionary* gives historical examples of usage, and the term refers to rules or orders with more than a hint of authority behind them. The authority was usually ecclesiastical.

There is a hint at the start of the debate about the canon. It is called that because, for most people, the word does sound religious. This is a debate about the soul of the university, and critics of the canon chose the name to imply that its defenders rely on tradition and power instead of reason.

What is curious is that the defenders of the canon have also come to use the word. Both sides take the definition seriously. On one side, we have a group of people who have taken it upon themselves to change knowledge they see steeped in power and authority. On the other side is a group of people who have decided that what they teach in higher education deserves the stamp of authority. We can guess that these people have more than a little love and respect for their canon. We can easily imagine that this group of people has invested its soul in the work.

There is a roughly agreed-upon list of books that make up the canon. The canon is, "say, Socrates to Wittgenstein in philosophy, and from Homer to James Joyce in literature, and is essential to the liberal education of young men and women in the United States that they should receive some exposure to at least some of the great works of the intellectual tradition."[2] We know that the canon always includes Plato and Shakespeare, and generally works by Aristotle, Augustine, Luther, Hobbes, Locke, Rousseau, Marx, and Freud.

The list is long and is aimed, according to defenders of the canon, at helping undergraduates "in Matthew Arnold's over quoted words, 'know the best that is known and thought in the world.'"[3]

The canon-believers argue that the canon is the backbone of our civilization. The works of the canon form the basis of what we believe and why we believe it. Don't misunderstand—the points of view within the canon are wildly different. Thomas Hobbes and Jean Jacques Rousseau paint two very different pictures of the world. What they demonstrate is that if you look carefully at a full list of the canon, you can find a counter-opinion for every opinion.

What is so important about the canon is that all of the points of view, all of the different opinions, are part of the same tradition. There are violent disagreements over what is right and what is wrong, but the disagreements take place within the tradition of Western thought. *The Republic* of Plato and *The Communist Manifesto* of Karl Marx are, for example, two parts of an ongoing debate. They are linked by thousands of years of intellectual history. Dialogues took place in the past. People used ideas and debated ideas, and *people thought*. For decades, knowledge of this tradition has formed the heart of what it meant to be well-educated; it formed the heart of the intellectual heritage of the Western world.

The attack on the canon came (and continues to come) from several different groups: 1960s-style radicals, feminists, Marxists, deconstructionists, gays and lesbians, people in ethnic studies, and different left-wing groups. Each group, for its own reasons, has done what it can to destroy the canon.

The deconstructionists offer a good example of criticism of the canon. Deconstruction is an approach to philosophy associated with Jacques Derrida and his followers. He argued that all texts, such as the books in the canon, are grounded in hierarchy and dualism. A true and a false, a real and an unreal, a legitimate power and illegitimate challengers are all part of a metaphysic embodied in a text. In this sense, each text constructs a reality. Derrida argued that the job of a philosopher is to reveal that underlying structure and to explain what got left out or silenced because of the constructed hierarchy and dualisms—in other words, to deconstruct it. The method is an assertion that prevailing standards of truth and reason are not objective, but are instead masks for power.

Irving Howe, in an article titled "The Value of the Canon," tried to list the arguments against the canon.[4] These, roughly, are the reasons why the critics dislike the canon.

- By requiring students to read what you call "classics" in introductory courses, you impose upon them a certain worldview—and that is an elitist act.
- Your list of classics includes only dead, white males, all tied in to notions and values of Western hegemony. Doesn't this narrow excessively the horizons of education?
- To isolate a group of texts as the canon is to establish a hierarchy of bias, in behalf of which there can be no certainty of judgment.
- The claim that there can be value-free teaching is a liberal deception or self-deception; so too the claim that there can be texts untouched by social and political bias. Politics or ideology is everywhere, and it's the better part of honesty to admit this.

- Wittingly or not, the traditional literary and intellectual canon was based on received elitist ideologies, the values of Western imperialism, racism, sexism, etc., and the teaching of the humanities was marked by corresponding biases. It is now necessary to enlarge the canon so that voices from Africa, Asia, and Latin America can be heard. This is especially important for minority students so that they may learn about their origins and thereby gain in self-esteem.

Quite a list. While it is not at all subtle and not quite complete, this list of complaints gives us more than a hint about what is going on.

It might be helpful to put the objections in different language. Basically, the arguments are these: To choose works of Dead White Males, who represent only the Western world, is elitist, sexist, and racist. To claim that teaching the list is apolitical is foolish—the list itself is a genuine demonstration of politics and power. It seems obvious that the elitist attitude that produced the list is a product of imperialism as it effectively disenfranchised people from the rest of the world. It follows that people who learn only what the Dead White Males produced have the most narrow of educations. There is a world of knowledge out there and it is wrong and foolish to focus on this relatively small and limited group of people.

Imagine if you were a believer in the canon. Imagine that you had been educated in these "great books," imagine that you genuinely loved these books and had made it your life's work to teach them. Imagine that they had an almost religious significance—the writings are the canon—and that they represented what you believed to be truth and beauty.

Now imagine how you would feel if different groups of people kept attacking you for loving and teaching those books. They say there are not many important differences between the things written by Dead White Males, but you have studied those differences for years. They called you all kinds of bad names (elitist, imperialist, oppressor, narrow, racist, sexist), accused you of deeply held biases, and tried to gain control of what you had been teaching. The words you hear would be fighting words, and the stakes of the fight would range from who had power in your department to what you may consider the continued existence of Western civilization. At every level, those attacking and those being attacked disagree.

The people who win get to choose what you read.

Two defenders of the canon—at least the two defenders who are most likely to be attacked—are the late Allan Bloom, who wrote *The Closing of the American Mind: How Higher Education Has Failed Democracy and Impoverished the Souls of Today's Students,* and William Bennett, the former Secretary of Education, who wrote the monograph *To Reclaim a Legacy: A Report on the Humanities in Higher Education.*[5] Their titles were pretty much to the point.

Both Bloom and Bennett firmly believe that the educational, intellectual, and cultural standards of the United States are in danger. They are convinced that the successful attacks on the canon mean that our civilization is in jeopardy. Bennett pleads for a curriculum that teaches "a common culture rooted in civilization's lasting vision, its highest shared ideals and aspirations, and its heritage." He argues for a central and shared vision that is beyond either the politics of the day or the politics of the academy. To teach anything less than a vision of a common culture is, for Bennett, cultural suicide.

Strong words are used on both sides of the debate.[6]

In an essay titled "Aiming a Canon at the Curriculum," Robert Scholes writes that

> where the Empire went, the cannon and the Canon went too. . . . I am opposed to the establishment of a canon in humanistic studies because I believe such a move to be fundamentally undemocratic: a usurpation of curricular power by the federal government. . . . William Bennett's cry for strong leadership from those on top, combined with the charge that the loss of our legacy is the fault of a "failure of nerve and faith" strongly suggests that the first move of an educational leader should be a purge of those lacking in nerve and faith.[7]

In that same essay, Scholes suggested that people who want to reclaim this legacy have something in common with Hitler.

This is not a polite academic discussion. In the end, it is a fight for power. The ultimate victory on campus is when one side purges the other side and makes the department safe for its friends.

Is One Side Right?

Let's go back to the criticism of the canon. It is not difficult to agree with many of the criticisms of the canon. Common sense, in this particular case, is useful. We will take up the points in order.

First, to make students read the "classics" is an elitist act. Is that true? Sure it is. To make anyone read anything is elitist, if that is the word you want to use. Any list of books to read, chosen by your professors, leaves out a world of books. What is meant by *elitist?* Critics of the canon use it to mean the defenders of oppressive power, while defenders of the canon mean a (too small) group that knows and can take part in a rich dialogue of ideas.

Second, the canon is a list of Dead White Males. We can easily check this point. If we find that only Dead White Males are on the list, then we know that the point is accurate. In the past, Dead White Males have made up the canon. We can ask a couple of questions about what that means. What are we to believe, for example, about every woman who lived and died? Did they not produce, think, contribute? What are we to think? What about the many female authors and artists who seem to take part in the traditions of Dead White Males—are they insufficiently different? We can also ask whether Dead White Males are limited in important ways. Are they, for instance, tools of oppression? People such as Henry David Thoreau, Mark Twain, and William Faulkner? Do we emphasize John Locke's justification for rule by a commercial and property-owning class, or his justification for government controlled by the governed? One interpretation emphasizes class oppression, the other liberation from class oppression.

Third, the list is clearly the result of a "hierarchy of bias," and we cannot be certain of the judgment behind the bias.

This is like the first point—any list is the result of bias. Any list comes from some group's or someone's judgment—maybe even the list of things you read in your science classes. The point is accurate. But what does the hierarchy represent: the small group of people who understand and take part in a dialogue about (among other things) freedom, or simply a small oppressive class?

Fourth, there is no such thing as value-free teaching. Politics and ideology are everywhere. Of course that is true. We may want to ask what pervasive politics and ideology have to do with teaching. Should we be surprised by this dynamic? Until recently, Live White Males were educated to teach Dead White Males. These were the men who controlled academic departments. They said, and probably believed, that what and how they taught was value-free. No one challenged them. It just happened that what they taught was written by Dead White Males. When they were challenged, they resented the "political" attacks on their "value-free" canon. Is that really surprising?

Finally, the canon not only leaves out women, it leaves out the rest of the world. For the most part, Yes it does. A great deal of literature in the last 20 years has been devoted to exploring ideas of women and the rest of the world.

Working through the criticisms suggests that they all hit their mark, but leave us with more questions than answers. Knowing about the canon and the criticisms is not a quick or simple exercise. What don't these questions and answers tell us?

Henry Louis Gates, Jr., is an interesting person to begin with. Gates is the head of African-American Studies at Harvard. His basic take on the canon is that it is a "nostalgic return" to that time "when men were men and men were white, when scholar–critics were white men and when women and people of color were voiceless, faceless servants and laborers, pouring tea and filling brandy snifters in the boardrooms of old boys' clubs."[8] You get the sense that Gates is not a fan of the canon.

Indeed, Gates helped edit an African-American canon *(The Norton Anthology of Afro-American Literature)* that, by definition, does not carry on the tradition of Dead White

Males. So why include Gates in this discussion? He is important because he reminds us of two things that we need to remember. "I agree with those conservatives," he writes, "who have raised the alarm about our students' ignorance of history."[9] He argues that we need to know not only the important historical and intellectual events of our past, but also the history of the very idea of the "canon" that involves both literary pedagogy as well as the very institutionalization of higher education. In other words, we have to know our own organizational past.

While recalling his educational coming of age, Gates gives us another lesson: There can be a genuine love for wonderful literature. Gates writes, "There's no point in avoiding the narcissism here: We are always transfixed by those passages that seem to read us."[10] People who spend their lives teaching literature love that literature. It seems foolish to assume that only white males can produce great literature, but it seems equally foolish to assume that blacks can love only something written by a black, that a woman can love only something written by a woman, and so on.

It may be helpful to understand arguments in a different context.

The Context of the Canon

At the risk of offending people, let's label the participants in the battle of the canon.[11] Conservatives, people like Bennett and Bloom, believe that some books are better, deeper, and more profound than others. A reasonable argument. They are appalled at what they perceive to be the poor education many college graduates now get.

Liberals, people who want to be in the middle and are always ready to figure out a plan to make everyone happy, argue that the canon should be revised. That seems reasonable. Most people agree that different books need to be added to the list. Conservatives argue that the list does change with time. They are right. For example, *Moby-Dick* was not considered a great book until the 1920s. Fine, say the liberals. We will add to the great books in order to include different kinds of greatness. The one thing that liberals agree on is that the change cannot be left to the conservatives, because if they would be willing to change things, the changes would be ever so slow.

It is the radicals who really attack the canon. They do not accept the language of the debate: They reject the idea of "greatness," "shared," "culture," and "lists." They see no great merit in complexity, seriousness, or ambiguity. To quote Katha Pollitt, they "think that one might as well spend one's college years 'deconstructing,' i.e., watching reruns of *Leave It to Beaver.*"[12]

If the deconstructing image is a little too much, the radicals suggest that we "scrap the one-list-for-everyone idea and let people connect with books that are written by people like themselves about people like themselves." This is the logical conclusion of what the radicals see as a way to help those with low self-esteem in a multifaceted, conflict-ridden society.

This may be an important insight into the debate. The critics of the canon emphasize two goals of higher education: to empower dispossessed people and to help build the self-esteem of traditionally undervalued people, such as women and minorities. To conservatives, this talk of self-esteem and empowerment is an excuse for sloppy thinking and mediocrity. They believe that the goals higher education should emphasize are excellence in understanding and using the ideas in the complicated history of the development of our institutions.

Katha Pollitt takes an interesting turn on the debate. She asks us to think about what everyone (with the possible exception of the deconstructionists) has in common. In other words, she advises us to ask not what books we should read, but ask why we read books. While she readily admits that we read to understand culture and history, to support our own positions, and to help our self-esteem, she argues that there are other reasons to read.

Pollitt believes that the canon debaters themselves read to acquire more reasons, to know things, to support their own positions, and to enhance their own self-esteem. She writes, "but what about reading for the aesthetic pleasures of language, form, image? What about reading to learn something new, to have a vicarious adventure, to follow the workings of an interesting if possibly skewed, narrow and ill-tempered, mind? What about reading for the story? For an expanded sense of sheer human variety?" There are, Pollitt argues, "a thousand reasons why a book might have a claim on our time and attention, other than its canonization."[13]

Pollitt also claims that the canon debaters all believe reading is medicinal. She suggests that the assumption underlying their arguments is that the chief end of reading is to produce the right kind of person in the right kind of society. Reading becomes the right medicine; it is used to cure us individually and to cure our problems collectively. The conservative list would produce conservatives, the liberal list would produce liberals, and a radical list would produce radicals. She puts it this way:

> The culture debaters turn out to share . . . the belief that there is a simple, one-to-one correlation between books and behavior. Read the conservatives' list and produce a nation of sexists and racists—or a nation of philosopher kings. Read the liberals' list and produce a nation of spineless relativists—or a nation of open-minded world citizens. Read the radicals' list, and produce a nation of psychobabblers and ancestor-worshippers—or a nation of stalwart proud-to-be-me pluralists.[14]

Pollitt's questions about why we read books, and what reading books can do for us, get us past seeing the canon as having religious significance or seeing it as a racist, sexist, imperialist remnant from pre-enlightened days. Yet it only partly gets at the question of what a person needs to know to be well-educated. There seems to be little discussion of that in the debate on the canon.

That may be the important question. What should a well-educated person know? What should you know?

For all of the debate about Western thought and men, what seems to be missing is any serious discussion about science. Science. The signature of our culture. The United States is an object-oriented society, and here we are on campus debating all of the issues except science. What can we make of that omission?

John Searle finds the absence of science in the debate curious. He writes, "No one seems to complain that the great ideas in physics, mathematics, chemistry, and biology, for example, also come in large part from dead white European males. . . . I have not heard any complaints from physics departments that the ideas of Newton, Einstein, Rutherford . . . etc. . . . were deficient because of the scientists' origin or gender."[15] Searle points out that in the past, many talented women have been discouraged from going into science. We know that continues to be true. We know that, because of continuing sexist attitudes, there are too few women who major in math and physics.

What do you make of no one talking about science? Is there really a physical world out there that we all agree on? Is it simple sexism and racism that have kept white men in charge of scientific knowledge? Is science the last hangout for the Western tradition, and is no one out there willing to attack it? Are the issues of race and sex not real in science? Is ethnicity invisible in science?

Searle offers a list of things a well-educated person should know. Science figures heavily in what you should know. Here is the list:[16]

You should know about your cultural tradition and how it got to be that way. Because our culture is derived mostly from European origins, the knowledge is going to include a lot about Europe, probably written by white males. It should also include all the parts of our society, including those that have not been treated as well as the white males.

You should know enough about science to be literate about the physical world. Something about relativity and quantum mechanics should be included, as should Darwinian evolution, genetics, and microbiology.

You should know how society works. This includes things such as interest rates, trade, and other aspects of getting and distributing goods and services. You should understand political economy.

You should be sufficiently fluent in at least one foreign language to understand its best literature and carry on a conversation. Searle claims "you can never understand one
language until you understand at least two."
You should understand the methods and content of philosophy well enough to be able to follow and construct logical
arguments.
Finally, you should be able to write and speak well. Without
mastery of the language, "you cannot think clearly."

That's quite a list. How does your education compare?
Think about why you like or dislike parts of the list or about
why you find important pieces missing. What you think says
something about Searle's view, and your view, of what it
means to be educated. The list says something else, too. The
debate over the canon is really not about you and your education. So many things on the list are simply not at the center of
the debate. The debate is about something else.

It is about who controls academic departments and professional associations. It is about who gets hired and fired at
universities.

But you are in the middle.

Politics and Academics

The fight for the content of the college curriculum might have
your best interests at heart. It is possible that, when it does its
job best, college is a place where you are forced to think
about who you are. If you are away from your family, neighbors, and long-time friends, college is the place where differences—color, race, religion, sexual orientation—are right in
your face. It is a chance to sort out who you are and what you
think about everybody else.

This implies something about the "proper" role of higher
education. Opinions about what college should be range from
a place for the impartial pursuit of truth, to a place to get
good job training, to a place to produce good citizens and,

therefore, a good society. Put differently, higher education can be a place of social stability or of social change.

In the first part of this chapter, we saw the arguments about the canon. The canon represents a kind of impartial but skewed search for truth and beauty. Its defenders see the canon as what the university has been and should continue to be about. We know that "disinterested" appreciation of greatness, that particular vision of rightness, is in retreat. The conservatives in the debate see the canon advancing backward about as fast as it can.

We saw the canon attacked in academic ways. We read that the "traditional curriculum . . . calls books by middle-class, white, male writers 'literature' . . . [it calls] white middle-class, patriarchal heterosexual family and its values . . . 'Introduction to Psychology' . . . [it calls the] values of white men and property and position 'Introduction to Ethics' . . . [and it] reduces the true majority of people in this society to 'women and minorities' and calls it 'political science.'"[17] And so on. We know that the critique goes through just about every traditional discipline—with the exception of math and science—and demands changes.

It is time to understand a different kind of critique of the traditional curriculum. The heart of the matter for the rest of the chapter is this: The attack on what was the traditional curriculum revolves around the issues of historical accuracy, political inclusion, and personal identity. If this attack is successful—and most likely, it will be—then the nature of what we learn and how we think about ourselves will change. The stakes are high.

The short explanation is this: People have not been taught about the contributions made by the various groups making up American culture. For simple historical accuracy, it is necessary to teach who contributed what. Second, it is time that each group has a say in the business of higher education. From the boardrooms of the regents' offices to faculty meetings to student senates, it seems right that every group has a voice, or is finding one. Finally, if education is to deal with self-esteem, it is important that the contributions of all cultures be acknowledged and taught.

Put simply, education is now firmly tied to political power and personal identity. It is neither disinterested nor connected to universal standards. The driving question of personal identity that we took up when you unpacked your stuff for college in Chapter 1 is now addressed in the curriculum—an all-inclusive curriculum that will include a history and an identity for every student.

That is, in truth, a harsh way to think about it. Here is a less harsh way: It seems only reasonable that the curriculum accurately reflect the contributions that created American culture. Not every important contribution came from heterosexual white men educated in the European tradition. Higher education should be a place where one can learn about the different contributions by different people and can identify with whomever she or he wishes.

Here is a Jewish male example from one of the authors of this book. As an undergraduate, he did not read about any Jews, nor did he read any Jewish writers. His public image of Jews was the television stereotype of New York City Jews. The New York Jewish stereotype was neither wholly attractive nor widely respected in Tulsa, Oklahoma. There was much to be embarrassed about. It was not until he had finished graduate school and was teaching at the University of Washington that a good friend suggested he read Hannah Arendt (not a very religious Jew).[18] All of a sudden, after he read her, an amazing number of things that he had thought about began to make some kind of sense. Many of his thoughts and feelings suddenly had a context and a history.

He was lucky. If you were of the same age and grew up being called nigra, negro, colored, black, Afro-American, and African-American, things were much harder. Despite the civil rights movement during the sixties, where would you learn about blacks? Not in public schools, not in college, not really in graduate schools. In terms of identity and formal learning, you grew up invisible.

Identity and formal education should and do have a relationship. Just what that relationship is and how it should be understood on campus are not easy issues. Part of the debate about multicultural education has become the debate over the relationship between personal identity and education.

—— 244 ——

Edward Said gives us a sense of how to begin to understand the issues.[19] Said has worked out the relationship of imperialism (and he means European imperialism) to culture. Basically, he argues that when the Europeans colonized different countries, the citizens of those countries were routinely treated as primitive and backward. The cultures were understood, in European terms, as undeveloped.

Out of the oppression came resistance. Native resistance. Out of the resistance came many nationalist and independence movements. That was a fact in India; North, South, and Central America; the Caribbean; Africa; and the Middle East. What is important for us to understand is that "at the heart of the imperial cultural enterprise . . . was a politics of identity." What the politics assumed—indeed, Said tells us that politics needed to assume—was that there were differences between native and imperialist cultures.

The dynamic of imperialism and the following nationalist movements that grew in resistance led to a "nationalist politics of identity."[20] It is a politics of separation. It is the effort to define the people of a nation in opposition to others.

That same dynamic seems to come into play with different populations in the United States. In a variety of ways, people who have been oppressed now seek an identity as well as political power. The way to hang on to identity may be to create a separate place, or to extend the nationalist metaphor, or to claim or reclaim a homeland.

At the University of Texas, for example, the Black Faculty Caucus made clear what they believed necessary for a genuinely (what they call "transformative") multicultural education. The first thing they want is for minority people to be a part of all levels of the chain of command. From the highest places of policy-making power to staff workers, the Caucus wants to change who makes decisions. They want a diversity of race, gender, and class at all levels of decision making.

In terms of curriculum, the Caucus's vision of multiculturalism means more than inclusion of different "nondominant" groups. "It requires that the curricula of the 'West,' as it is currently understood, be placed under scrutiny and transformed in order to fairly represent the variegated nature of American culture."[21] And just who will do the teaching? We know who won't: "Euro-Americans teaching the materials of people of color cannot make the University multicultural because multiculturalism demands empowered people of color as well as empowered areas of knowledge."[22]

The bottom line is this: "[M]ulticulturalism is not just about what constitutes culture, but how power is wielded between cultures and the ways in which cultures reflect racial diversity, the ways in which culture is organized by contemporary and historical politics."[23] Education, in this vision, is about politics, power, and change. It is about who gets jobs (people who are not Euro-Americans), it is about what jobs they get (positions at every level of power), and it is about what students are required to learn.

There is no messing around here—those in higher education need to understand that there will be new "empowered" areas of study, and these new areas can be taught only by "empowered" people of color. It is possible to have some of the old stuff taught, but it must be subjected to "critique and reformation." It is all right, for example, to teach state history at a state university, but that history has to reflect "the complexities of minority cultures' participation."

The university gets transformed. It also gets a new cast of characters. In this version, the university becomes a "center of multicultural learning." Anything less, argues the Black Faculty Caucus, simply "reproduces racism and racists."

Is the Black Faculty Caucus right? Shouldn't power be more evenly distributed? Shouldn't people learn an accurate history of Texas, or Alabama, or Florida—or anywhere else for that matter? Can a white heterosexual Baptist man truly understand and teach black lesbian poetry? Could a Hispanic woman teach Euro-American physics?

The above questions should be taken seriously. They suggest tough problems. Do you agree with all of those points? Any? And why? And what does it mean if you do? Does the thinking of the Black Faculty Caucus emerge from the idea that identity has come from oppression and is by its very being a narrow definition of identity? These are genuine questions. They are at the heart of much of what we on campus and we in the United States are going through.

Are you a racist (no matter your color) if you agree with the Black Faculty Caucus? Are you a racist (no matter your color) if you disagree with the Black Faculty Caucus? Think about what they are suggesting. It could be that they are exactly right. Maybe they're half right. Maybe not even that. What do you think?

Centrism: Euro and Afro

Afrocentrism is the most developed attack on the traditional Eurocentric curriculum. In this section, we will see what the Afrocentrist arguments are about and begin to think our way to a possible solution to the fights over what should be taught and why.

We can begin with a short reminder about Afrocentrism. Martin Bernal has written a two-volume work titled *Black Athena*.[24] He argues that the basis of Greek culture—and hence the basis of European and then American culture—comes from Egypt. Egypt, he argues, is African. It follows, in the most obvious of ways, that the basis of American culture is African. So what?

Identity is the point. For example, the idea of being called African-Americans rather than black Americans is a way of having a home continent instead of just a color. It also follows the tradition of other groups—Greek-Americans, Italian-Americans, and on and on.

We can see the search for identity clearly in the words of two Howard University students. "The African tradition is very spiritual, less oriented toward conquest. . . . African thought is not individualistic. . . . Our biggest problem as Africans is losing our identity. It's very hard to get it back. . . . Our (black) culture does not come from racist Greeks. Our ancestors were Africans. Yet we were brought here in chains, against our will. If someone takes you away from paradise, you can never get it back."[25]

Here is the claim. Africa, the mother continent, was a paradise. If you are an African-American, your ancestors, who lived in a nonindividualistic way, were brought in chains to the new world, a world built on individualism and competition. Your ancestors were slaves, and even after slavery, you were discriminated against. The very roots of your culture are not the roots of the culture you were born and raised in. What is clearly needed is a way to recapture the identity that was lost.

In the most ironic way imaginable, the way to regain both lost identity and lost pride is through Afrocentrism. The idea that Africa has been the unacknowledged source of European and American civilization is as interesting as it is strange.

The basic argument is that Africa—mostly Egypt—invented the basic principles of mathematics, science, art, music, and language. These principles, along with Egyptian gods, architecture, technologies, notions of justice, and the polis came to the Greeks from Egypt and the Phoenicians of Canaan. Martin Bernal, a man with remarkable skills, has laid out these claims using a wide range of linguistic and archaeological evidence.

If it is so, if European culture was built on African culture, what would that mean to African-Americans? At first glance, it would be extraordinary. It would certainly be a source of identity and pride. An African-American could claim the invention of the beginnings of virtually all of the important elements of American society. Black pride, indeed.

There is, of course, an other hand. It is American society, with its roots buried in ancient Greece, that Afrocentrists are fighting against. Put simply, what does it mean about Africa if Africans invented the critical parts of Greek culture? That culture led to where we are today, with racism, sexism, and so on. The problem, then, would have originally been African, not Greek. A genuine problem.

But, you might be thinking, that is just a game. Just like an academic to look for irony instead of seeing the bigger and more important point. You could be right. Let's rework the argument.

It is generally agreed that Egypt interacted with and had an influence on the Greeks. The archaeologists have found good evidence for all kinds of Mediterranean interaction. Also, there are clearly traces of Egyptian and Eastern languages found in early Greek writing.[26] The push Bernal and others are making is that the influence of Egypt should be recognized. He contends that it has not been acknowledged in the past because of the racist and anti-Semitic scholars of the last two centuries.

If we are going to do it right, argues Bernal, we must give credit to those who developed the roots of Greek civilization. Those roots, at least to him, came from Egypt. To take the next step, if you look at the map, it is easy to see that Egypt is African. Be accurate, Bernal says. Begin to understand that African civilization helped give birth to Western civilization.

Blacks have every right to this intellectual heritage.

The impulse is clear and justifiable. Everyone is better served with full and accurate information. To shut out the contributions of whole continents is in no one's interest. We can come back to the ideas of learning and identity: There are good and legitimate reasons, both academic and personal, to accurately retrace the sources of our society.

It is with the word *accurately* that the learning and the help can begin. It turns out that Bernal's research is deeply flawed. What he has written, according to the experts, ranges from being called interesting to being called a "painfully jumbled exposition of ideas," to being called "absolutely wrong."[27] For our purposes, one of the most pressing problems the scholars suggest is that Egypt was not African. Egypt, all those centuries before Christ, was more Middle Eastern than African. It was culturally distinct from most of Africa. Egyptians certainly consider themselves Middle Eastern today.

Do we want to know that? Do we want to say that Bernal reminds us of something important (of the multicultural forming of Greece) but has screwed up the message? The point is that Bernal has a powerful and powerfully flawed message. It is exactly the role of scholarship to figure out what is really the case. It is also the role of higher education to be accurate in what gets taught.

Accuracy cuts both ways. The attack on traditional curriculum has been brutal and, in many ways, needed. Whole groups of people and their contributions have been left out of academia. Racism and sexism and homophobia and religious bias do not make good scholarship. Scholarship, when any of those things are present, is merely political babble. It's mind poison. While there may not be any such thing as wholly impartial scholarship, there are some pretty basic rules about how to use facts and how to separate what you know from what you make up. There is something to be said about trying to be as clear-eyed and clear-headed as possible and trying to explain what you mean as clearly as you can.

If that is the case, it is important to at least suggest that what's good for traditional studies is good for emerging studies. We can continue to take Africa as an example. If we decide to learn more about Africa, we must face the fact that the slave trade was not as simple as the traditional studies have taught. What most of us know about the slave trade is that Africans were captured, chained, put on ships, and brought to the United States. An ugly story.

Nothing can change that story. It just happens that there is more to it than that. (By the way, slavery is not unique to Africans. The word *slave* comes from the Slav people of Eastern Europe. So many Slavs were enslaved by others, including Africans, that their very name became synonymous with the condition.) The slave trade began in the Middle East about 1,000 years before the European slave trade started. Indeed, Africans were still being sold into slavery as late as the 1960s. Some of our oil-rich allies (Saudi Arabia, for one) simply bought young Africans and owned them.[28] The Egyptians were involved in the slave trade, as were the Romans during the time of the Empire and the Muslims. We also need to know that Africans captured and sold other Africans into slavery.

Africans made good money selling other Africans into slavery.

Perhaps as few as 5 percent of the slaves taken to the Western Hemisphere were brought to what is now the United States. And it was Western values, enforced largely by British warships, that put a stop to the slave trade.

So what? Why spend a paragraph on slavery and the African involvement in slavery? Is it to excuse the slave owners in the United States? Not at all. Is it to make the United States seem better in comparison to others? Not really. Is it some kind of racist ploy to curse Africans for making money that way? No, it is not racist.

It is merely a way to suggest that one of the things higher education is about is accuracy. As we change what we study, as we rethink where we come from and what we are about, the bottom line is to remember that the rules, whatever they are, must be the same for everyone. If Bernal's gift to African-Americans was a sense of pride and identity, then that's wonderful. If Bernal was factually wrong and academically sloppy, then it is no gift to those who look to him for guidance. Given the history of the twentieth century, it is very hard to listen to arguments about any "race" being superior.

There is a relationship between academic arguments and what goes on in the rest of the world. What any of us think and write about can have an effect. No matter why we do the work, no matter how good our intentions, once the work is done it has a life of its own. Ideas have consequences.

Consider science education. The real topic is that we live in an age of sophisticated science and technology, and for decades, women and minorities have been much less likely than white males to pursue careers in science. In order to get more people interested in science, the key place to change education is in elementary schools. "We know that people who choose science careers usually become committed in early grades; we also know that minority children start behind whites in mastery of scientific concepts and mathematical skills as early as the fourth grade."[29] Ouch. Not a promising thing to happen.

What should we do? Should the history of science be changed so that people who are not white and male can be told that people like them contributed? There are many examples of such scientists. But a new history has to be accurate, especially if we want to train people to use their brains carefully and creatively. A new history, one without much regard for facts, was tried in Portland, Oregon.[30] The curriculum plan included claims that Africans, and more specifically, Egyptians, discovered quantum mechanics, the theory of biological evolution, and electric batteries, and mastered psychokinesis and extrasensory perception.

There might be a way to make the teaching of science more inclusive, without wacky claims. Bernard Ortiz de Montellano suggests that it takes several steps to make science more accessible.[31] First, he believes that minority children should be taught that "people like them" have done science in the past and are doing science in the present. Second, he argues that people in higher education need to become more interested in science education. From the people who teach science in schools to those who take science courses for nonscience majors, teaching has to be better. Finally, he says that people in higher education have to be interested enough to make sure that claims are carefully checked. The argument, then, is that what we produce—even if it is merely foolish claims—can have real effects. There is no doubt that in science, like in every other discipline, we need to learn the contributions of everyone. But to confuse science with pseudoscience, to mistake religion for science, to simply overstate what went on is not helpful. If the end is to make science equally accessible to everyone, the means shouldn't be silly claims and tall tales. The means should be good teaching—which, so far at least, seems beyond what we can do.

To repeat the point that was made before the discussion of science: The push for multiculturalism has been and continues to be strong. The role of higher education in somehow rolling politics, knowledge, and identity together into a legitimate whole is critical. If multiculturalism is our future, the real question becomes this: What do we do?

Plans

There are, as we have seen, a range of plans for developing multicultural education in colleges and universities. At one end of multicultural education (the minimalist end) is the mere adding of a book here and a book there. To circle back to the beginning of the chapter, it would be taking the canon and adding a book by a woman and a book by a person of color. The addition of a couple of books would keep the canon alive while acknowledging that important things have been said and done by people other than Dead White Males.

There is support for that kind of change. It is a conservative change, and conservatives argue that the canon should evolve in carefully considered ways.

At the other end of the scale are the suggestions made by the Black Faculty Caucus at the University of Texas. The university, in this plan, is actually centered on the idea of multiculturalism. New fields of study are "empowered"; old fields of study are rethought, critiqued, and changed; and all areas of decision making are opened to different populations (color, class, and gender). Finally, particular people would be needed to teach particular courses. New faculty would come with new fields of study.

From what the authors understand, few institutions of higher education are ready to reorganize themselves around the needs of multicultural education. This is not a right or wrong judgment, but simply an acknowledged fact that colleges and universities are slow-moving, conservative institutions that simply do not change very quickly. And the faculty may not like the ideas for other reasons. It may well be that higher education will move in the direction that the Black Faculty Caucus wants, but if so, the change will take an awfully long time.

Somewhere in the middle are different institutes and centers of study: women's studies, Asian-American studies, and the like. When first suggested, these programs were resisted by many academics. They have now become normal parts of many campuses, fighting for funds and faculty and students just like other programs. The faculty members produce scholarly work, teach courses (sometimes required) and promote the idea of multicultural education.

These centers and institutes have produced the kinds of scholarship that help others see and understand more about a particular group. It is exactly that single, narrow vision that makes the work useful. It is that same single, narrow vision that may ultimately limit how long these institutes last. If they are successful (what they have to say is accepted by society), then they may well be taken over by other parts of the campus community. Quite possibly, centers and institutes are necessary halfway houses for genuine multicultural education.

In general, we don't know of a campus that is not trying to figure out what to do with multicultural education. But we probably don't know specifically what the faculty is doing on your campus. At Stanford, they had a huge fight to figure out what to teach. It was a big news event starring Jesse Jackson. They changed the traditional curriculum. On one of the campuses where we teach, the faculty senate decided to require every student to take a designated course about diversity. In other schools, different departments want faculty in certain classes to teach at least one book about diversity. What we know is that, in general, the academic community has decided that something needs to be done and has not agreed on what that something should be.

One interesting program comes from the University of California, Berkeley. Since we saw in Chapter 8 how Berkeley handled—or is trying to handle—admissions, it seems only fair to see what the school is doing with diversity. It is a glimpse into one plan about the direction of multicultural education.

At Berkeley, all incoming students are required to take an American cultures course.[32] The course has two requirements. First, the course must deal with three of the following groups: African-Americans, Native Americans, Asian-Americans, Chicano- and Latino-Americans, and European-Americans. The second requirement is that the course cannot look at any single group in isolation. Each course must be comparative, each group must be studied in the context of American society.

The courses are offered by people all over campus. For example, there is a Music in American Culture class that compares music of Native Americans and Latinos and American forms of music such as jazz and rock. There are courses called Race and Gender in the Hollywood Film, Experiencing Education: Race and Ethnicity Inside Schools, and The American Languages. The linguistics department offers an American cultures course, and so do the physical education and comparative literature departments. Indeed, there are about 45 American cultures courses now offered, and the faculty hopes to have 120 courses by 1995.

There are two elements that make the Berkeley program worth our attention. The first is the mechanics of it. A very big problem was this: Who is qualified to teach a course that requires knowledge of three different cultures? We are simply not educating people in that kind of genuinely multicultural way. What to do?

Berkeley began to solve the problem by offering summer seminars for interested faculty. They are four-week seminars and the teachers are given a stipend ($6,000 in the first year). The seminars feature guest speakers as well as discussions that center on how the American identity is defined. The seminars generate proposals for courses in American cultures, and most of the courses have come from these seminars.

In other words, the faculty at Berkeley decided that the intellectual requirements to teach these kinds of courses were unusually difficult. They realized that they had the expertise on campus, but no single person had it. The seminars were a way to get people together to share knowledge and begin to develop the kinds of material needed to teach multicultural courses.

Beyond the mechanics of just who is capable of teaching these courses is the idea of *American cultures* itself. If the argument for multicultural education is that we have been, are, and are becoming more of a multicultural society, then it makes good sense to see how that has developed. In order to understand what multicultural means, teaching needs to be comparative. Different groups of people have to be put in the context of other groups of people. If ours is an evolving society of many cultures, then to focus on one group at a time is to miss the point of a multicultural society altogether.

Michael Rogin, a political scientist who teaches a class called Race, Ethnicity, and the Formation of American Identities, says, "The main thing you want to do in teaching is get students outside of their perspective, to get people to think in new ways about things they think they already understand."[33] To compare cultures—to see what each group contributes to a collective identity—cannot help but create an interesting context, a context in which new things are learned.

Different groups have always contributed to our culture. They contributed whether the contributions were acknowledged or not. It is not hard to predict that with this kind of multicultural education, we as a society will have a chance to become more open to how our national identity developed and continues to develop.

Berkeley may be on to something. In order to begin to fully understand how we evolved and how we are evolving, courses have to be comparative. Our culture develops at the intersections, and that is how we have to begin to learn.

Does Berkeley have the final answer? The faculty voted 227 to 194 to institute the program in 1989. That means that at least 194 faculty members didn't think the American Cultures program was even a good idea.

What should be clear is that multicultural education goes to the heart of what higher education is about. It has to do with what is important to teach and with academic and political power. It has to do with not only personal identity but also American identity. It asks not only what to teach but who can and will teach it.

It is also fair to ask if you can even talk about an "American identity" that is distinct from the different ethnic mixes in different parts of the country. What is true about the "American identity" in Colorado may not be true in Maine, and what is acceptable in Utah may not be in Mississippi. If our multicultural education reflects reality, there are many realities to reflect. Multicultural education is a tough topic, and all the more interesting and fun for it.

—11—

Multiculturalism II: The Wider World

No one quite knows what ethnicity means: that is why it's so useful a term.

—Irving Howe

It was as if the United States were two separate countries: A North in which low-wage labor came from a continuing stream of migrants, to some extent from the local countryside but more often from remote parts of Europe, and a South in which low-wage labor came from whites who felt rooted in a sympathetic culture and blacks who felt rooted because they feared, with considerable basis, that because of racial discrimination they could not get jobs or make a living anywhere else.

—Michael Barone

E pluribus unum.
—Inscription on the seal of the United States of America

I n this chapter, we discuss some of the social and political tensions that underlie multiculturalism.

—— 257 ——

The tension between individual rights and group rights—between individualism and group identity—is very strong in the United States. An underlying theme of American political and social history is the search for some kind of balance between individual and group identity. We ask you, for example, to consider how difficult it is for many of us to deal with ethnicity, groups, and individualism in one thought.

We will see how immigration, the Mother of our multiculturalism, has played a huge part in the development and growth of the United States.

It is important to consider the kind of social glue that holds our diverse society together. We ask whether the English language is an important social glue, or whether we should teach and make arrangements for a multilingual society.

Finally, we believe it is important to remember that there are many different kinds of cultures in the United States. We offer a short discussion about the deaf as an example of a distinct culture.

Rights

We have to return to individualism to understand the dynamics of multiculturalism in the United States.[1]

Our basic rules of politics, written into the Constitution, are about individualism. We can think of a constitution as *the rules of a society that govern circumstances where power is openly contested.* Our Constitution separates powers among different branches so that government power is limited. When we say *limited*, we mean that, compared to other forms of government, ours has a difficult time exercising power. Other sources of power operate relatively free of government control. The dynamic that drove on the framers of our Constitution was the power that full citizens wield in deciding to use their person and their property as they see fit.

Another important feature of our Constitution is *federalism*, the principle that some powers belong in a central government, and some belong in governments that are closer to where people live. Again, this feature is designed to limit the exercise of national government power. While federalism has eroded over the centuries, the dynamic of letting different spheres of power operate remains.

The Bill of Rights and other amendments to the Constitution add to the protection of individual rights.

The dynamics of individualism have evolved, and the changes are important for understanding multiculturalism today. What started out as mainly individual rights have evolved into something approaching group rights. The stronger the support for group rights, the stronger the base of multiculturalism in the rules of political power.

There is not much doubt that early interpretations of constitutional rights focused on property rights. For example, the debates over established churches (prohibited in the first amendment) centered on the government's power to levy taxes to support a church. It was about worship, to be sure, but the fight was over money and property, and who has the power to control them.

There is a simple reason why the rights referred to the property, and not just the person who could own property. Not all people could own property in all the states. Women, who could not vote, had limited political rights. Some people *were* property. The constitutional compromises over slavery focused the framers on the exercise of the rights, not just the abstract rights due to all individuals.

This point becomes clear when we remember that the Constitution really was a product of the ideas of the eighteenth century, the Enlightenment, and the colonists' experience under British rule. The Enlightenment brought together such ideas as the ability of men (they did mean men) to reason through their common problems, their ability to write out a set of rules that would govern their activities, and a basic respect for educated individuals doing what they please. Under the British, the colonists learned the importance of a limited national government. Together, these ideas produced a consensus that the national government really should not do very much. It would defend the shores, stop serious internal problems such as rebellions, print money, deliver the mail, protect patents, build some roads, pay its debts, and not much else. (See Article I, Section 8, of the Constitution.) Government didn't have to do much else, people reasoned at the time, because individuals (white male Christian individuals) could be left to their own devices to handle the business of running a society.

Some important changes happened in the nineteenth century. Populations increased, and more and more people worked for other people rather than holding their own property. What is a government to do when faced with a growing number of individuals who are not citizens? The issue was debated in the states, which set the qualifications for voting. Who should be allowed to vote? The issue can be understood as an early battle about multiculturalism, as many of the new people were immigrants. Generally, only free males were allowed to vote. The prospect of a large, politically disenfranchised working class was frightening. The prospect of a lot of Irish-American voters was also frightening. Rights subtly shifted from the property to the person, perhaps a person without much property.

The Civil War brought more important changes. During the Reconstruction, which lasted from the end of the war until 1876, the rights of former slaves rested in the person, not the property, and many of these former slaves voted.

In the last quarter of the century, the Fourteenth Amendment was interpreted by courts as protecting individuals who own property, including the legal individuals we call corporations. The amendment reads, in part:

> No State shall . . . deprive any person of life, liberty, or property, without due process of law; nor deny to any person within its jurisdiction the equal protection of the laws.

It is another example of an expanding pool of people with rights protected under the Constitution.

With the coming of women's suffrage in the early twentieth century, the pool of people with rights expanded even more. Although the right to vote resided in each person, some of whom were women, the Nineteenth Amendment was a significant change to legally recognize a group as having a right. The Fifteenth Amendment did so as well, but not very effectively after Reconstruction ended.

The New Deal, which occurred during the first two terms of Franklin Delano Roosevelt's presidency, roughly from 1933 to the beginning of World War II, added another dimension to group rights. The national consensus on the role of a national government shifted to include more management of the economy and help for needy people. Rural people, farmers, older people, students, and other groups were recognized as needing aid. Groups became more self-conscious and powerful in party politics. Labor unions, immigrants, and Jews, for example, provided solid blocks of votes.

The idea developed that groups had needs, groups suffered harms, and government had the role of offering solutions. The idea of a group right grew stronger. Since the New Deal, both Democratic and Republican administrations have organized their platforms around group needs and pressures.

The Civil Rights Act of 1964 is perhaps the strongest piece of legislation that tied group membership to specific rights. Women and minorities were singled out as having been harmed, and governments were enjoined from actions that hurt members of these groups. Subsequent legislation and court cases worked on the questions of how to define harms and the appropriate remedies to those harms. Affirmative action, which we discussed in Chapters 8 and 9, is one example of this dynamic.

The Republican administrations of the 1980s tried to reverse this trend toward group rights and rely more on individual or corporate definitions of harms and remedies. Although major legislation did not change in this direction, administrative and court decisions did. In Chapter 9, we discussed the Supreme Court nomination of Clarence Thomas. One of the important changes he enacted with the Equal Employment Opportunity Commission was to accept only individual claims of discrimination, instead of group-based claims. Presidents Reagan and Bush tended to appoint federal judges, including those on the Supreme Court, who saw issues in terms of individuals instead of groups.

It is fair to say that the trend to recognize group rights slowed or stopped during the 1980s.

While the two major language groups in Belgium and those of the French-speaking Canadians recognize group rights, our politics does not. It is important to remember that group rights were evolving as part of a political consensus, without a firm constitutional foundation. A shifting consensus, such as we saw in the 1980s, is able to change things without constitutional change.

In constitutional terms, we are weak at recognizing group rights. In our politics, group rights remain a source of conflict.

We remain the land of individualism. We value individual rights. That means protection for people; politically, those rights are protected more readily if they are seen as residing in each person rather than as part of a group. Problems begin when groups live differently than is conventionally acceptable for individuals. The individual rights may not address the group concerns. For example, every individual in the military is seen has having a full range of rights, but homosexuals do not have group rights that protect what is seen as unconventional behavior.

Cultural pluralism is, in our tradition, outside the law, and only recently have laws changed to specifically deal with issues of cultural pluralism. We are unsure how to deal with ethnicity, groups, and individualism in one thought.

Welcome to Our Shores

One way to sort out the multicultural scene is to remind ourselves that immigration has, at different times in U.S. history, been a main source of population growth. Through the nineteenth and twentieth centuries, more than 60 million people came to this country, about 20 million in the last three decades alone. All but about .8 percent of our population are directly descended from immigrants.

Immigration law has changed through our history. During the nineteenth century, when most immigrants came from Europe, the restrictions on immigration focused on health. If a person could not meet the requirements of the health inspection at the port of entry, they were told to leave. The exception to this pattern in that century was Chinese immigrants. Informal practices discouraged their coming at times and encouraged them at other times (such as during the 1849 California gold rush). In 1882, Chinese immigration was legally banned.

In 1924, the first comprehensive immigration law sought to freeze the racial and ethnic composition of the United States through the use of national quotas. Eighteen ninety was used as the base year for calculating the proper mix of peoples (Italians, Greeks, and Eastern European Jews arrived mostly after 1890) desired by the Congress. The law came at a time when the proportion of immigrants in the total population was actually decreasing. In 1900, about one-third of all citizens were foreign-born, and this dropped to about one-fourth by 1924. But the mix had changed. Italians, Poles, Jews, Greeks, and Mexicans had made up the bulk of immigrants after 1890, as Irish, German, and Scandinavian immigrants had done earlier.

The strongest support for immigration restrictions came from organized labor. The union leaders argued that the new immigrants depressed wages. It was true. Crucial support in Congress for the 1924 act materialized after a Massachusetts shoe manufacturer tried to break a strike by importing Chinese laborers.

The quota system of the 1924 law remained in effect until 1965. At times, certain national quotas were relaxed, such as for Cubans after their 1959 revolution or for Vietnamese after the war we fought there.

The 1965 immigration law dropped national quotas. The new criteria for immigration were uniting families and letting in people based on needs of the work force. If family members were already here, or if immigrant skills were needed, they could get in. Otherwise, the law was designed to keep people out.

That law didn't work very well. The technology of getting around the world, and of crossing borders, changed. No other major industrial country shares a 2,000-mile border with a developing country. Several million illegal immigrants (no one really knows how many) entered the country during the next two decades. The procedures of checking each immigrant for needed labor-force skills never worked. During these years, the bulk of immigrants came from South and Central America, and they spoke Spanish. Another large group has come from Southeast Asia.

Another important immigration law was passed in 1986. This one acknowledged the problem of illegal immigrants, and established a formula for legalizing those who could show that they had been in the country for four or more years. It set aside money for beefing up border patrols and allowed immigration officials to crack down on employers who hired illegal immigrants.

The law contained weak security rules for immigrants, and the simple identity cards needed to work in this country are easy to duplicate.

Why be concerned about immigration? Some argue that immigrants are an important engine of economic growth.[2] They are generally willing to take jobs for lower wages than current residents are willing to accept. Many start new businesses. Others argue that only skilled immigrants help the economy.[3] The unskilled may contribute little compared to the demands they make on public services.

The issue of illegal immigrants and non-English-speaking immigrants will be with us for decades. Immigration policy still hinges on family ties, so immigration is a function of individual actions rather than national policy. As we sort out who we are, and what that means for policy, we might remember that just about all of us and our not-too-distant ancestors are immigrants. One useful way to define multiculturalism is that process by which we have made a nation of immigrants.

Ethnicity

Ethnicity is consciousness of a shared background with other people, a background that can have elements of nationality, language, race, or place. Here we want to focus on the relationship between identity and ethnicity. If people see important things in common between themselves and others of a similar origin, they constitute an ethnic group. Conversely, a group of people may be called an ethnic group if others see important similarities in that group. This means that people identified as an ethnic group may not want to be lumped together, but are. It might also mean that an ethnic group wants to be recognized, but isn't. Ethnic groups, put differently, are partly formed by the exclusion on the part of others, and partly formed by inclusion around a common place, behavior, or idea.

In the United States, ethnicity is a focus for identity. Does that make us stronger and better able to live together, or does it make us weaker and less able to live together as a people?

One way to begin to see it is to focus on what happens when people marry across such groups.[4] People marry for all sorts of reasons. This is true for people of similar origins and people of different origins. Yet when people marry across groups, others tend to put special meanings on their reasons. Was it rebellion, kinkiness, or guilt that drove the person to the marriage? Of course, people marrying within groups marry for those reasons as well. When ethnicity is an issue for a community and for an individual, intermarriage is low. Where the trappings of ethnic communities are scarce—such as churches, community organizations, and such—intermarriage is higher. Strong ethnic communities discourage intermarriage.

Although ethnicity is an issue in the United States, it matters much more in the world beyond our borders. As we write in 1993 and 1994, most of the wars in the world are over matters of ethnic division. They seem unusually ugly because they are between citizens of the same country. Wars of neighbors. Today's newspaper describes six such conflicts, in Kashmir, Bosnia, Lebanon, Georgia, Somalia, and Sudan (others are happening in the world, but these ones made the paper today).

Historians show us why a focus on groups, ethnic and otherwise, will continually produce conflicts.[5] Historians have, at different times, presented the ideas that ethnic-group experiences in the United States have been inclusive and exclusive. The inclusive pattern suggests that America was a place of refuge from the stark groupings and hatreds of other countries. Here people could live together united by ideas instead of by blood. By accepting the values of individualism, equality, limited government, and voluntary associations for social ties, people from all sorts of groups could live together and prosper in peace. The inclusive interpretation of our ethnic history says that this is the core of our national identity.

The exclusive pattern suggests that there has always been resistance to immigration, hatred for those who were different, populist movements with heavy doses of nativism, and separation between groups. Our Civil War is a sign of our inability to settle a question peacefully of whether one group was inferior and subject to ownership.

Both patterns are present in our history. What do we want to emphasize, and why? It is not difficult to take any non-WASP group and show how racism, discrimination, and hatred have been expressed, sometimes to the extreme form of genocide. Similarly, it is not difficult to show systems of prejudice dismantled, and formerly hated groups accepted into the mainstream.

Right now, we are in another period of immigration of non-WASP people, another period of questioning what the country is about, and just what being an American means. Again, we look at the new and growing groups and ask, are we inclusive, or are we exclusive? On what terms are the new arrivals welcome, if at all?

The past pattern of welcome was uneven, but a theme does run through it. Groups that wished to preserve ethnic identity, however they understood it, did so on a *voluntary* basis. They had no formal legal status. Government stayed out of it, and the groups could form what associations they would, meet in their churches, marry within their groups, and live in their sections of cities. For some groups, the ties were and remain complicated and strong. For others, the ties are not much beyond treasured family recipes.

The emergence of the recognition of group rights, described in the previous section, clashed with the voluntariness of ethnic associations. The 1964 Civil Rights Act, for example, stated that no discrimination would be tolerated on the basis of race, color, national origin, religion, or sex.

To carry out the law, the state had a legal problem. It had to start keeping track of the groups people belonged to, and it became a matter of public policy. This was, in an important way, a government attack on the tradition of voluntary associations in ethnic ties. The advocates of affirmative action, for example, did not just attack prejudice. In real ways, they attacked communities. In many organizations, employment was organized around ethnic communities. The schools may have employed mostly Jews in administration, the police may have been mostly Irish, the sanitation workers Polish, and so on.

There is a powerful logic to keeping track of the numbers. For example, many of those voluntary associations of Poles or Czechs were also strong in labor unions. It meant that prized, high-paid trade apprenticeships could be acquired only by members of the dominant ethnic group. Should a government contract be given to a group that, by hiring its Polish-American relatives, excludes African-Americans from employment? No, according to the 1964 Civil Rights Act.

These new concerns with public policy signaled a change that many Americans have yet to accept. To the Polish-American student about to graduate from high school, knowing he will not get a union apprenticeship that he could have expected before affirmative action, it can be a source of bitterness. But wasn't his group's lock on the jobs a privilege enjoyed at the expense of others?

There is a wider version to the conflict. Ronald Takaki argues that the emphasis on an inclusive interpretation of our history, voluntary associations, and a deemphasis on affirmative action relies on a strong faith in the power of law and tolerance that we might not live up to: "a vision of a good society in which men and women are judged on the basis of their abilities rather than their color, race, or ethnic origin."[6]

Takaki relies on the exclusive interpretation of our history to suggest that we still have a long way to go toward peace between different ethnic groups. Again, it is not hard to show that in the past awful things were done to any number of non-WASP groups. The patterns have not disappeared. The racial inequality and employment stratification may now be indirect and without the force of law, but it is still powerful. It's not just a problem of prejudice where we can enforce the law against specific instances of discrimination. It is institutional and structural; it is where the groups that acquire the best educations and the best positions in organizations are able to preserve these privileges for their members. Whether it is the children of certain groups who live in the richer parts of town getting better schools, children of alumni getting into the leading universities, or graduates of certain schools getting into the leading businesses, the patterns of social rewards remain fairly steady.

The exclusive pattern is a strong argument for affirmative action. Affirmative action is a recognition of a group right, a group harm, and a policy for a group-based remedy.

Without a national consensus on group rights, group harms, and group remedies, we will witness more conflicts over ethnicity.

Social Glue

How does ethnicity figure into the binding of a nation? What is the social glue that holds people together and enables them to act and live in peace?

In Chapter 10, we looked at different interpretations of the canon taught in our colleges and universities. The arguments are about education, in large part, because the debaters believe that education is at the center of transmitting a culture. It is no surprise that professors regard their work as vitally important. But their arguments are part of a debate that is going on beyond the university. It is found in political parties as well.

Among the functions political parties are supposed to perform, in addition to contesting elections, is the mobilization of support for their program. It is a truism of American politics that most people don't care about most things most of the time. Political parties assemble platforms and run campaigns to get more people interested in more things, at least at election time. The two parties have taken sides in the multiculturalism debate. While each party contains many conflicting opinions, the broad outlines of their platforms are clear.

The Republicans have put themselves where most white Americans say they stand on questions such as affirmative action and other equality issues. They are for the principle of equal opportunity but are against using governmental power to regulate whom one may hire, promote, or fire. They argue that merit should determine access to college and jobs, and that membership in a group should have little to do with it. They want to spread the message that hard work and determination are the road to success, and they don't want government to change the structure of incentives for success offered by markets. The more conservative members of the party use the term "culture wars" to refer to the multiculturalism debate—they oppose the recognition of gay and lesbian rights and group rights in general, and believe that immigrants should work hard to learn English and assimilate.

The Democrats have adopted a platform that fails to win a majority of white voters, but does bring in enough voters from other groups to dominate Congress and occasionally win the presidency. Their picture of equality includes support for affirmative action, although that support is weaker now than it was a decade ago. They also talk about merit, but emphasize the need to open opportunities for groups that receive fewer of the awards in the economy. Democrats tend to be more confident about managing parts of the economy than are Republicans and are less willing to trust markets to guide society. They deliberately take the other side of the "culture wars" debate and accuse the Republicans of unfairness and worse. Black voters are essential to Democratic national success, and the Democrats endorse protection for gays, lesbians, and other minorities.

The parties are a place where the conflict over multiculturalism can take place under relatively controlled conditions. They channel opinion and conflict. That is their purpose. That is what they do. They are an example of an institution that works as social glue, binding us together despite important differences in views. Over the years, they have had mixed success.

A wider picture of social glue is provided by Arthur M. Schlesinger, Jr.[7] He approvingly quotes Hector St. John de Crèvecoeur, who wrote in the eighteenth century:

What then is the American, this new man? He is an American, who leaving behind him all his ancient prejudices and manners, receives new ones from the new mode of life he has embraced, the new government he obeys, and the new rank he holds. The American is a new man, who acts upon new principles. . . . Here individuals of all nations are melted into a new race of men.[8]

Schlesinger does not deny that ethnic groups are important parts of American history, but he rejects placing them at the center of our self-understanding. What "has thus far managed to keep American society whole" is the theory that we are one people who share an identity *apart* from our ethnic origins.

He argues that the contributions of ethnic groups, minorities, and women to the development of our culture are necessary parts of an accurate history. Yet we are a Eurocentric nation. English is the language of the United States, notwithstanding bilingual people and communities (such as parts of Miami and Los Angeles) in which other languages are the medium of business and society. English came from Europe, as did the core ideas of our political culture. An accurate history shows how that tradition has been modified by people from all over the world. It shows how some groups were well served—and others poorly served—by the tradition. But to teach children an Afrocentric education exclusively, for example, is to poorly equip them for a successful life in this society. It also would mean that society loses supportive citizens.

Schlesinger sees a movement within the United States to reject that common identity. Instead of a message of assimilation, "ethnic ideologues"[9] want us to think about group rights more than individual rights, group identity instead of individual identity, and ethnic curricula in the schools instead of a common education, and to think of minorities as victims of a democratic tradition that has left them out.

He asks important questions. For example, should ethnic groups aim to assimilate into the mainstream culture while preserving their own traditions? Would that not put the American dream of prosperity and independence closer to their grasp? Does an emphasis on group rights alienate a good deal of the citizenry, possibly resulting in the divisiveness we saw over those issues in the 1970s and 1980s? Does a bilingual education enable students from non-English-speaking homes to do well in high school, get into the college of their choice, and succeed in society? Has our democratic politics become more open to minorities and women?

For Schlesinger, and for us, these questions matter. Is he right? Is this common culture the social glue that binds us together? Does a common education help build that common national identity?

Underlying his argument is a commitment to core values. He makes a strong argument for historical accuracy, and he offers the judgment that our core values have served us well. Compared to our society, none of the other societies of the world have better managed to combine people of many different origins into a peaceful whole. As we write, Europe is home to more than one war over ethnic identities, in former Yugoslavia and in parts of the former Soviet Union. Do those people think Europe is one culture? The Czech Republic and Slovakia recently divorced peacefully. Has Spain successfully combined the different groups that live there? Is Israel doing well at getting people to live together in peace? Have Nigeria, Uganda, and Morocco found a unifying theme to keep their societies at peace? In African politics, it is the relatively homogeneous countries that have the brighter development prospects.[10]

It is comparisons like these that lead Schlesinger to conclude that our society is basically healthy and that the movement against a common identity will fail. It is likely, he says, that the movement is led by elites in various groups, and that the message will not appeal to the masses of those groups. He writes, "Americanization has not lost its charms." It is important to remember, he tells us, that a culture is never fixed or final. With each wave of immigrants and each admission of more groups into the mainstream, the culture is remade. We should expect this to continue, and it is part of the strength of our society.

Culture and Wealth

In Chapter 4, we discussed class divisions in the United States. In this section, we look at a relationship between culture and class.

Nearly a century ago, Max Weber wrote *The Protestant Ethic and the Spirit of Capitalism.*[11] He held that the values contained in some religions, notably Protestant Christianity, were instrumental in the making of capitalism. Some values are better than others, goes the argument, for encouraging people to work hard, save, invest, and look for commercial success.

The argument is expanded by Lawrence Harrison in his book *Who Prospers? How Cultural Values Shape Economic and Political Success.*[12] Briefly put, there are some cultural values that pay off in capitalism.

Culture is a broad concept, and when Harrison uses it he means the values, attitudes, and institutions that affect people's group behavior and a nation's political, economic, and social behavior. He compares how immigrants and new values affected growth and development in Spain, Brazil, Taiwan, Korea, and Japan. He compares the United States experience of Chinese, Japanese, Korean, and Mexican immigrants, and black Americans.

Here are the parts of culture that Harrison argues are at the center of success in capitalism. To understand these points is to understand which cultures will do well in the United States. First, the radius of trust, or how widely a person identifies with other people in the society, is important to social equity and progress. If the radius is small, say, confined to the family, political elites will not share rewards widely, and opportunities are limited. A wide radius means that power can be more easily shared among in-groups and out-groups, philanthropy is greater, and commercial dishonesty is lower.

Second, the rigor of the ethical system contains a sense of social justice and fairness. An ethic that contains a strong sense of social justice, for example, will more likely support an independent judiciary and more substantive legal justice. This results in more calculable results of buying and selling property, something capitalists need.

Third, the exercise of authority can be more or less democratic, more or less hierarchical. The less democratic and more hierarchical variants tend to be poor at achieving legal justice, less likely to contain abuses of power; they suppress the risk-taking and innovation that capitalism depends upon for growth.

Fourth, attitudes about work, innovation, savings, and profit can vary. Do the values of immigrants promote education, encourage savings and hard work, and view the world as a place where rationality pays off and wealth can be accumulated? Do officials who make public policy have similar values? Cultures where these values are strong also value investment and new economic ventures.

So far, it all sounds very plausible. It is when we get to policy questions that the trouble begins. As we will see, Harrison's statements thrust him into the politics of multiculturalism.

This summary does not do justice to the substance of Harrison's argument. It only reports the conclusions.

The advocates of multicultural education emphasize that cultures are not superior or inferior, just different. Some of the arguments we looked at in Chapter 10 did argue that, for instance, African culture is superior to European culture, but this seems to be a view held by only a small number of people. Harrison does claim that cultures can be distinguished by their relative abilities to enhance and develop the capacities of their members. Because his book is about economic and political rewards, he focuses on those attributes of culture that, he argues, have a role in who gets more income and who gets more power.[13]

In his summary of the development problems of Brazil, he notes that the traditional Iberian worldview, with its support for social inequity, indifference to others outside a close-knit family, poor work ethic, and loose ethics of those in authority, is largely to blame. The Spanish economic boom of the last quarter-century is attributed mainly to Spain's opening itself to values of the West and to markets. Iberian culture would not impede progress if it were open to more progressive values.[14]

In his summary of the development success of Japan and other East Asian countries, again cultural values and opening to progressive world forces figure heavily. The Japanese values regarding responsibility to a wide radius of people, work, family, education, self-discipline, and even child-rearing practices contributed to Japan's rapid economic growth.

The same concepts for studying culture and economic and political success are then turned on the United States, and

Harrison finds that the immigrant groups who most rapidly adopt the values that succeed in a liberal culture reap the social rewards. They get the higher incomes, the education, and the political clout.

Near the end of his book, Harrison turns his analysis to black Americans. This is his summary:

> [W]hile racism still exists . . . in my view it is no longer the principal obstacle to progress for people in black ghettos. The just-cited statistic of two-thirds of America's blacks having moved into the mainstream is one compelling evidence of that assertion. I believe that the principal obstacle today is culture: a set of values and attitudes, strongly influenced by the slavery experience, perpetuated by the isolation enforced, historically, by the Jim Crow laws and, today, by the ghetto. Accordingly, antipoverty policies and programs must emphasize access to the mainstream.[15]

What do these policies look like? In the case of affirmative action, he believes it should have a time limit, such as the year 2000. Other programs would include "Head Start/supervised play/day-care activities as early as possible; busing to schools where the student body composition includes significant numbers from the cultural mainstream—white and black—along the lines of magnet school programs; summer work and summer camp programs, perhaps combining the two; the use of university students as tutors of ghetto children; courses that better prepare high school youngsters for effective child rearing."[16]

That list of programs sounds expensive, but if we accept the argument, a lot of work needs to be done. If we think of it as an identity issue, two kinds of changes are involved. The poor, in particular poor urban blacks, have some changing to do in the group, in their culture. The changes add up to a greater emphasis on individualism. The wider society has responsibilities, too. The programs Harrison lists will take many billions of tax dollars.

There are issues that need sorting out. One is the idea that a culture is broken, and needs to be fixed through programs like this. If "broken" sounds too strong, how about this: The proposed programs are aimed at enabling more group members to succeed in the nation's economic and political institutions. A second issue is how a book like Harrison's is read. We can report conclusions, as we have done here, but that gives, perhaps, the least important parts of the argument. You should make up your mind based on the substance, not whether or not you like the conclusions. But what happens to such an argument in practice? As with Shelby Steele and Stephen Carter, described in Chapter 9, people who oppose programs such as affirmative action pick out sentences and cite them as more evidence for the case against. What gets left out of the discussion is that these three authors emphasize the dire need for a substantial increase in what we call the welfare state—many more and perhaps greatly expanded programs aimed at the most needy.

Is the price of our multicultural society, given the history of the United States, expensive government programs for groups that have less?[17]

English Only

Earlier in this chapter, we discussed the idea of social glue. It is possible that a common national identity serves that purpose. Ask yourself this question: Is a common language an essential part of that national identity?

To put this in context, remember that most immigrants to the United States did not speak English. That was true for the Germans, the Scandinavians, the Italians, as well as the Hmong and the Guatemalans. Just about everyone who comes to this country does learn to speak English. The rate of learning seems to depend on the number and dispersion of immigrants. If you recently moved from Cuba and stay in Miami, you can get by just fine with Spanish. People you meet in stores, churches, nightclubs, and restaurants may all speak Spanish. If you come from Cuba and move to anywhere in Minnesota, you are likely to pick up English very fast.

There is the surrounding culture watching this process, too. If they see you living together with similar people, all speaking Spanish, having your own stores, movies, churches, nightclubs, and restaurants, they may see you as Other.

It is not a new phenomenon. Theodore Roosevelt, commenting on the need for immigrants to rapidly assimilate, once said, "A hyphenated American is no American at all."[18] For Roosevelt, Italian-Americans should become just plain Americans. The same with German-Americans. Everyone should speak English.

The English-only movement in the United States is real. It started in the 1980s as part of the reaction to group rights, described in the first part of this chapter. In policy terms, English-only means that government documents such as ballots should be in one language. It means that government should not cater to those who speak another language; if new citizens want to be part of the country, they should learn the language.

Is it important, for example, if ballots in East Los Angeles are printed in Spanish and English?

In large part, the argument is an extension of our earlier point about social glue. Cultural pluralism notwithstanding, there are degrees of "otherness" that a nation can tolerate. We do not know where the line is, but if a group becomes too unlike the rest of the population, the nation may not hold together. That's the fear.

What does it mean to not hold together? French-speaking citizens of Quebec have almost opted out of Canada twice. Secession. You are likely to see it come close to happening again in Canada. It happened in January of 1993 to the former Czechoslovakia. The largely Czech parliament simply decided it would do better without the Slovakians. Now they are separate countries.

We fought a civil war over secession. Lots of countries do.

On a lesser, more common scale, strong divisions within a nation lead to political problems. Policy is difficult to make. National purposes get stalled. Energies go toward quieting those conflicts instead of toward prospering in the world economy.

Do different languages lead to conflict? We can return to the problem in the United States.

The argument came up, in large part, because of bilingualism in education. In 1968, the Bilingual Education Act, also known as Title VII of the Elementary and Secondary Education Act (ESEA), became law. The law was a shift to recognizing the needs of non-English-speaking students, but it was not clear whether Congress actually required school districts to offer bilingual education. In 1974, the Supreme Court decided that was the purpose of the law. The national government had never done that before. Tax dollars are spent on bilingual education.

Yet once a law is passed about bilingual education, the difficulties of implementation emerge. First, can we find enough teachers who are sufficiently fluent in both languages (assuming we only have two languages to deal with) *and* qualified to teach the necessary subjects? Will students in bilingual classes catch up with or fall further behind the English-speaking students? Does a bilingual education speed or slow the learning of English?

These problems were fairly serious in the early years. That is to be expected. School districts were doing something they had not done before.

The political reaction to bilingual education has been divisive. Why can't children who live in Spanish-speaking neighborhoods also learn in the language of their communities? Advocates of bilingualism see an attack on communities. On the other side, descendants of other groups, who immigrated earlier and assimilated rapidly, see the current groups receiving different treatment. My tax dollars, they say, are going to help them do something my people did on their own.

Do people who speak languages other than English have a right to bilingual education? In the Los Angeles school district, significant groups of students speaking more than 40 different languages attend school. Do all of these groups have a right to this service?

Under Title VII of ESEA, the school districts must serve bilingual students in order to get federal dollars. While they do their best, many would like to see those resources go to other kinds of education.

There are wider issues that help us understand the English-only idea.

Language divisions can be class divisions. In Miami, two black women applied for minimum-wage jobs with a cleaning service. They were denied the jobs because they could not speak Spanish. Many of the clients of the cleaning service speak Spanish. The women complained to Dade County's Fair Housing and Employment Board. They had a point: This is our home, other people come in with a different language, and now just to survive in our own town we have to learn another language? The board found that the women were unfairly denied the jobs.

Another example touches a source of fear for many citizens who see the non-English-speakers as Other, and perhaps dangerous.[19] In Long Beach, California, about one-fourth of the population of 429,000 is Hispanic. About one-eighth is of Asian origin, largely Cambodian. About 4,000 Hispanic kids belong to gangs. About 800 Cambodian immigrant kids belong to gangs. Another 4,000 kids are in black, white, and other gangs. They wear the clothes, they put up the graffiti, and many of them carry guns.

It was not unusual, at the height of the gang violence, to have a drive-by shooting every week in Long Beach.

To outsiders, these people look very Other. The resentment toward them supports the English-only movement. The politics of language get mixed up with class, with ethnicity, and with how people live.

We have millions of immigrants in this country, and there are concentrations of them and their descendants. This means that they will not stop speaking their own languages, and their children will probably learn both languages.

To remind us of an earlier conflict, we had many German-speaking communities in this country. Most of them quit speaking German shortly after we entered World War I. The politics of language do not take place in a vacuum.

Language is a tough issue. For first-generation Americans, their native language is often the one in which they think. Their native language is part of their identity. For their children, that language is also part of their identity. It is part of their cultural context.

But these people live in the wider society. The surrounding communities, and their fears, help to define the new immigrants. Jobs, government, and education are all involved. The way people fit into the society is, in large part, set by the language they speak.

There is no national consensus on bilingualism or multi-culturalism. As a nation, we have yet to figure out how protection of individual rights and the realities of groups fit together.

Identity

Multiculturalism does not revolve solely around ethnicity, color, and language. The key ingredient in the recognition of the many cultures among us is that the members of different groups feel different. They see the world differently; their experience is different.

There is a man for whom the key event in life was his great difficulty learning to read.

Had he been born 50 years later, his teachers would have understood that he had a learning disability, and perhaps he would have gotten some help. But he was born 50 years too soon.

This man is bright enough. He has made a good living; he might even be considered wealthy. He has figured out how to adapt and prosper in a society that reads. But he was not treated well in school. The rewards and status that educated friends and family received were never to be his, and he resented it. It has been a source of great bitterness.

Those with learning disabilities frequently feel different from everyone else. What if you cannot concentrate for more than 20 minutes, or you just cannot sit still, or if numbers are never in the correct order for you? If you can't learn like other people, how do you respond? Are there other people with similar difficulties?

If they find each other and share those experiences, is that part of multiculturalism? At the least, it is part of the diversity of our culture.

Consider a different disability: severe deafness.[20] About 250,000 people in the United States have been deaf since birth.

About one out of every 1,000 children worldwide is born deaf or becomes so before the onset of language. Severe deafness can be a very serious disability, as Oliver Sacks explains:

> The prelingually deaf, unable to hear their parents, risk being severely retarded, if not permanently defective, in their grasp of language unless early and effective measures are taken. And to be defective in language, for a human being, is one of the most desperate of calamities, for it is only through language that we enter fully into our human estate and culture, communicate freely with our fellows, acquire and share information.[21]

Are the deaf a different culture instead of a group of people with a disability? Is it useful to think of them as a group instead of as individuals? Will we see things we can't otherwise see?

Martha's Vineyard in Massachusetts was settled, in part, by deaf immigrants. A genetic basis for deafness was passed on to children, so that at one time as many as 25 percent of the population of the town was deaf. The whole town learned sign language. Sacks reports that the deaf were not regarded as incapable and certainly not as handicapped.[22]

The same conclusion can be drawn from a visit to Gallaudet University in Washington, D.C., the only liberal arts college for the deaf. Sacks tells about his first visit:

> I had never before seen an entire community of the deaf, nor had I quite realized (even though I knew this theoretically) that Sign might indeed be a complete language—a language equally suitable for making love or speeches, for flirtations or mathematics. I had to see philosophy and chemistry classes in Sign. . . . I had to see the wonderful social scene in the student bar, with hands flying in all directions as a hundred separate conversations proceeded.[23]

In 1988, students at Gallaudet University launched a protest of the appointment of a nondeaf president. The students complained that, of the top three candidates for the job, two deaf candidates were passed over. They shut down the campus and presented their demands: first, that a deaf president be appointed immediately; second, that the chair of the board, who had been on the board for seven years without learning much sign language, resign; third, that the governing board of the university have 51 percent deaf membership, compared to the current 14 percent; fourth, that there be no reprisals against the students for this uprising.

Eventually, the students won all their demands with the exception of the third. But that is not, perhaps, the point. When people act together to decide what kind of world they want to live in, they are doing politics. Here was a group of people, deaf people, asserting themselves at their school, changing the administration, marching on the Capitol building, closing deaf schools around the country, coming together for politics. They defined themselves as a group. It was a way of saying, Here is a big part of our identity.

During the demonstrations at Gallaudet, a picketer held a sign that read *Laurent Clerc Wants Deaf Prez. He is not here but his spirit is here. Support us.*[24]

Virtually no one outside the deaf community knows who Laurent Clerc was. Virtually all deaf people know. In 1817, he helped found the Hartford Asylum, a pioneering school for the deaf. He is responsible for sign language as the language of deaf schools in the United States, and he is perhaps more responsible than anyone else for the spreading of schools for the deaf around the country.

Deaf communities will usually find a focus in the local school for the deaf. Laurent Clerc is at the heart of deaf communities.

Here is a people, partly formed by the exclusion on the part of Others and partly formed by inclusion around a common place, with their own language, a common history, doing politics.

Subcultures are about identity.

Conclusion

Multiculturalism is a fact of life in the United States. It is part of our identity as a nation. Even the earliest humans on the continent immigrated by crossing the Bering strait.

Is multiculturalism a divisive force, or is it something that has made us a stronger nation? For our common life as a nation, is it a good fact of life, or a bad fact of life?

The examples and issues in this chapter suggest that multiculturalism is not one thing, that it is never settled. It evolves as our experiences as Americans evolve. Populations and communities change, groups that used to be excluded from the best rewards of society begin to be included. Groups that did not assert themselves begin to assert themselves. Groups that were never politically active become politically active.

The United States has a history of repression and a history of finding ways for people from all over the world, people who see differences among themselves, to live together in peace and prosperity. There is an ongoing desire for more peace and prosperity than we have and for wanting more of it for groups that have been excluded. That dynamic has been working here since the founding, and it is a healthy dynamic when we see it today. The issues of multiculturalism range from the politics of immigration and bilingualism to how families work out the marriage of a couple from different cultures.

However we work out the issues in multiculturalism, what remains will have to be a distinct American identity, consistent with principles that have taken us this far. One would hope that the next working consensus about multiculturalism will revolve around freedom and democracy, toleration and respect, optimism about a shared future, and a place where more people can pursue what they want in life.

—12—

Politically Correct

Defending the Constitution is something of value, but so is achieving a sense of community. Somehow, we must do both.

—Charles V. Willie

It is our personal responsibility to define what we will and will not tolerate.

—Camille Paglia

There is a controversy called *politically correct,* or **PC**. It is about the politics of language, and in this politics there is a way to be right and a way to be wrong. To read media stories about **PC** is to see a serious fight between people who want to change an oppressive society and people who defend traditional values. A president of the United States included an attack on **PC** in a speech he made on a college campus. What is at stake, to hear combatants tell it, is the kind of society we will live in.

This chapter looks at the **PC** controversy. We argue that it is a complicated affair, exaggerated by the media, deadly serious on some college campuses, and a sign of more important issues about education and politics. The fight is about language, what it contains, and who gets to control it. The fight is about how college campuses deal with the concept of diversity and make policies about it. It is also about the push and pull that is part of the nation's long history of working out how we construct a society that draws from many cultures.

First, we look at what is considered politically correct. The next section explores the aims and techniques of the PC movement. The PC controversy is important because it is an attempt to change the way we see fundamental values in the United States.

The next topic is the politics of language. We argue that language is important and that politically, language is about identity. We follow with a section that suggests control of language is a sword that cuts two ways, and we need to say what we think.

We move back to college campuses to explore the relationship between PC and standards of free speech. We discuss the First Amendment to the Constitution and academic freedom.

A Guide to Correctness

It is not hard to portray the advocates of change as a little silly. Drawing evidence from academic conferences, memos, campus demonstrations, and student orientation guides, critics of PC claim that they are defending us from a new thought police (as suggested on the cover of the December 24, 1990, *Newsweek)* that want to make us talk a new way.

You have probably heard examples like these: One college guide to appropriate speech suggests that we not call people *disabled* but instead refer to them as *differently abled,* and that people without disabilities be referred to as *temporarily abled.* One such list says that among the commonly practiced forms of oppression are *ableism,* which is discrimination against the differently abled by the temporarily abled, and *lookism,* the belief that appearance is an indicator of the person's value, which applies standards of attractiveness and beauty by making generalizations about those who fit and those who do not. One administrator suggested banning phrases such as "calling a spade a spade," "a chink in the armor," and "a nip in the air" because, used in a different way, those words can express prejudice.

Some students and administrators have complained of feeling vulnerable to charges of racism when they voice their opinion that affirmative action programs or parts of women's studies programs or ethnic studies programs are somehow wrong. One university administrator read a memo from a faculty committee member that included a statement of her "deep regard for the individual and my desire to protect the freedoms of all members of society." The administrator circled the word "individual" and returned the memo with this advice: "This is a RED FLAG phrase today, which is considered by many to be RACIST. Arguments that champion the individual over the group ultimately privilege the 'individuals' who belong to the largest or dominant group." A group of students in a Stanford University demonstration chanted, "Hey, hey, ho, ho, Western culture's gotta go." The SAT test of 1991 mentions Zora Neale Hurston, Ralph Ellison, Maya Angelou, and Jackie Robinson (twice), but not Albert Einstein or Saul Bellow.

Many examples can seem silly, but we shouldn't judge the PC movement solely by them. We should also look at the consequences of the work of various groups and people on campus who are, in some way, trying to change what others do and think. Take a look at your own campus: Is there someone in charge of multicultural affairs, or a coordinator of sexual harassment complaints, or an officer for multicultural education, or something like that? Do their duties include the generation and promulgation of rules about speech? Have they done so? It's a simple matter to check. At the University of Michigan, there was a speech code, but part of it was deemed an unlawful restraint of speech in a court of law. At Smith College, such a code is advisory and handed out to incoming students.

Progress

The people who want to change the language and society have not set out to cause confusion. They want to make the world better in a particular way. The way one teacher of English (and a member of a campus diversity committee) put it was this: "You have to give people who feel that they cannot speak up, that they cannot be open, that they will be judged on the campus, some sort of voice. . . . [I]t's empowering diverse groups."[1]

By "empowering" groups, she meant changing society so that the have-nots have more. They can have more power, more of the material goods this society has to offer, and more of the symbolic rewards such as status. The argument is about creating more equality of outcomes in the United States and in the world beyond our borders. The path to equality is blocked, goes the argument, until we can remove the institutional, linguistic, and ideological barriers that some groups use to keep advantages over others. Put differently, women don't get what they should because of sexism, nonwhite people don't get what they should because of racism, and so on for all the have-nots. The categories mentioned earlier—ableism, lookism, and more—are extensions of the idea that the path to equality lies in empowerment of disenfranchised groups.

The fact is, very few people come out and say that blacks should not be offered a college education, that women should be in the home and not the university, or that gays and lesbians should leave school. The inequality addressed by the PC movement is about deeply embedded prejudices, prejudices that might not require many prejudiced people in order to operate. Policies that seem neutral on the surface, such as the idea of equal opportunity, may rest on many social structures and practices that unevenly distribute rewards. Generations of exclusion of women and minorities, for example, might mean that the encouragement to enter a given profession, the connections with alumni that increase chances of admission to high-powered colleges and to professional schools, the money that makes it easier to gain access to institutions, the old-boys' networks of recommendations within a profession, and the role models that show young people what is possible, are available much more to the dominant groups than to the traditionally excluded groups.

The desire for greater equality means specific actions when we apply it to institutions. It means that we ask, Who should be a member of the institution? In the case of a university, who should be the students, the faculty? Who should occupy the key decision-making roles, or be the vice presidents? Or the department chairs? Are there enough women, blacks, Hispanics, and so on?

It means more than just numbers. It also means that the campus environment should feel like home, a welcoming place. Women won't feel comfortable in an environment hostile to women, racial minorities won't be at ease in a racist environment, people with a different sexual orientation won't feel welcome on a homophobic campus. None of this will change, goes the argument, until there are programs to solve these issues.

According to the PC movement, the programs needed to achieve this social progress on campus are special studies programs (women's studies, ethnic studies, gay and lesbian studies, centers for multicultural education, and the like), student orientation sessions that contain material about diversity, faculty sensitivity training on diversity (sometimes on a complaint basis and sometimes campus-wide), and the inclusion of more multicultural themes in the college curriculum, especially the required curriculum. The programs also include policies about appropriate behavior (equal employment opportunity, affirmative action, and discipline programs concerning issues such as sexual harassment) and, occasionally, appropriate speech. Some of the programs are extensions of federal law, and some are home-grown. The Americans with Disabilities Act of 1990, for example, makes it public policy to literally reconstruct the social environment and rebuild those structures that had, by design or inadvertently, ignored the needs of people with disabilities (such as curbs without ramps, buildings without elevators, and rest rooms with too-narrow stalls).

Other activities are incorporated into the network of programs. For example, student and faculty groups may organize around a theme that focuses on empowerment of some group. They may try to start a campus boycott of fruits or vegetables from growers who refuse to bargain with migrant farm workers. They may join international boycotts of countries with undesirable policies on race or other issues. Is there a chapter of

STAAR (Students Taking Action Against Racism) on your campus? They are an example of students working for social change.

There it is. The story behind PC is an assertion that this needs to be a better society, that it will be better when groups with less have more—more power, goods, and status—and the way to change is through programs and political action. The university is just one institution in our society where this vision of equality has taken form.

We have been over this before. In the chapters on class, racism, and multiculturalism, we saw that there were different interpretations of why social rewards are distributed as they are. The more traditional liberals, now called conservatives, the people who value individualism, liberty, and nongovernmental ways to cope with change, do not like the idea of using programs to promote equality. One person's view of empowerment is another person's view of a narrow interest group using power to seize special benefits for members of their group. Opposition to affirmative action usually hinges on an assertion that only individual qualifications should matter. Opposition to multicultural and multilingual education focuses on the idea that official recognition of group behavior and rights amounts to government and institutional support for the things that separate us as citizens, rather than the things that we share as a nation.

It might be helpful to see this as a contest over the idea of how to make progress: Should we focus more on equality or on liberty? There will be times when the two conflict. The comparison is an old one.

We have seen in earlier chapters that people disagree over how we should distribute opportunities and rewards in our society. There is a mainstream culture right now that adheres to the value that markets should be the way we settle most of these issues. The main attribute of a market is that agreements between people (about where to work, about how to spend your money, about where to go to school) are made voluntarily. Your life is a contest, played with many other people, about how well you take opportunities and win rewards. People who are best at performing—and this includes working hard—tend to win more than people who aren't so good at performing. According to this idea, any imposition of rules other than market decisions takes away voluntary choice, punishes excellence, and diminishes liberty. Advocates of markets and liberty point out that this approach to social organization delivers the most individual liberty *and* the greatest possible social wealth.

Let's say you agree with the basic premises but you point out that not all people carry equal burdens in this contest of life. If your father went to Stanford and your mother went to Mills, we would expect you to value education highly and to go to a good university. That would be a head start in life compared to the person whose parents stopped going to school in the tenth grade. Or what if your parents were white? And what if the schools in the white section of your segregated town were much better than those in the black section of town (although both were in the same school district)? And what if the jobs available to teenagers were mostly in the white section of town? We could go on with many examples of ways in which decisions made by previous generations make for an uneven contest between today's citizens.

One of the central ideas behind the preference for markets is that through choice, we get a free and fair contest. People deserve what they get because the market hands out rewards based on things we all could do if we chose right and worked hard. But the objections based on uneven burdens cast doubt on that claim to fairness.

People in the PC movement who want to change the way we think and act usually value liberty, but they see a greater need to pursue equality. What separates the PC movement and its critics is not acceptance or rejection of the value of liberty. What separates them is a disagreement on the use of coercion to win the benefits of liberty.

That sounds like a contradiction. Here is the argument:[2]

The advocates of equality reject the premise that liberty means the absence of restraint. Instead, they believe that liberty is enhanced by laws that coerce us into proper behavior. It is possible to make someone act free.

Supporters of this idea believe that human nature is malleable and bound for improvement, yet they see corruption and repression in our society. These social ills are brought about by social relationships based on domination and the arbitrary exercise of power. The social improvement programs in the PC movement seek to change who is in charge and who wields power, with the prospect of changing the way different groups act toward one another. Power should be exercised, through law, to remake our behavior.

A community with more equality, goes the argument, will leave everyone better off because more people can then decide for themselves how they shall live. More equality would mean that more people have the ability to exercise their liberties. We might decide, for example, that no one should be allowed to live in substandard housing, and we will subsidize those who cannot afford standard housing. We will then take taxes from everyone (who then lose the liberty to decide what to do with that part of their income) and purchase the goods to fulfill this public interest. Or we might decide that racist speech creates conditions under which no one should have to live, and so we outlaw it. Those who want to make racist comments are limited, but others, presumably more numerous or more deserving, are more free.

This perspective relies on a vigorous concept of law. Advocates of these changes do not see law as a neutral set of rules within which all compete for their individual interests. It is purposeful. The vision of a more equal society, complete with newly empowered groups and a different set of values, is the meaning of law. Toward that end, some coercion of individuals is justified.

That's what is behind the PC movement.

This means that if we share the goals of the movement, if we want a more equal society, and we want to empower the groups without power, and we want to change who gets wealth and who has status, we have to seize power. At the national level, that means winning elective office, passing laws, and enforcing them. In universities, it means getting people appointed to key positions, placing sympathetic people or committees into decision processes, and contesting issues about the curriculum. The changes won't happen without offices of multiculturalism, coordinators for sexual harassment policies, diversity committees that review curriculum changes, or task forces to define just what needs to be done to promote diversity on campus.

The strong proponents of equality know this. So do the defenders of a different vision, the more traditional values. That's why they fight.

Language and Politics

It might seem to many people that supporters of the political correctness movement have a language disorder. They parse words with fine distinctions that most people don't care about. Why would anyone care if you said "people of color" instead of "colored people?" Yet you know the differences are powerful and important. The politics of language is important. The PC movement is a strong political move on our language. They are after the way people talk. The truth is that, used well, it can be very smart politics. If you capture the way people speak and the way they use language, then the chances are good that you will eventually point people in the direction you want them to go. The power to define is the power to rule.

For example, one of the first things that the women's movement did was attack the terms *he* and *him*. Not long ago, everyone who chaired something was called a chairman. How foolish it was to say "Madame Chairman." Now it sounds silly to our ears, but for decades that was what people said. We were told by the women's movement to get it right—is it a Madame or a chairman? Feminists told everybody that language should make sense—so now the chair of an organization is called a chairperson or, simply, a chair.

Those kinds of changes seeped through our language and into our brains. They allowed us to better understand equality in a way that we could not have when we used the old language. There is a quiet limitation on women if the good titles are always expressed in masculine terms.

One of the authors of this book used to drive a philosophy professor to school. It was at Berkeley during the time of upheaval, and the professor believed himself to be a trouble-making Marxist. During a drive, he complained about the women in his classes. "They resent me saying, 'the nature of man,'" he would say. "They don't like it when I talk about the 'history of mankind,'" he would complain.

Maybe the words he used, came the reply, did seem to exclude fully half of the population. Why did he keep doing it? "Because," he said, "it's the tradition."

Language is a political barrier for traditional radical Marxists, too. Widespread change may not be possible without changes in language.

The politically correct people want a sweeping change in how we look at the world, how we name it, and how we think about it. The PCers are hard listeners. They are going to hear slights and do their best to level us, take away our differences, and give us a neutral (neutered?) vocabulary. It is incorrect, we are told, to use the word *jungle*. The correct term is *rain forest*.

But each of us has a sense of the qualities and traits that help make us who we are. Our English, more than most languages, is vague and full of phrases that make no sense unless you have grown up in the United States. It is clearly necessary and important to do our best to say what we mean. To use the word *man* when you mean *people* or *woman* is a bad idea. The listener may well get a very different message from the one you intend. Who owns language? Who gets to decide what we can and can't say?

The messages we get about what we can and can't say can be subtle. For example, during the writing of this book, on three separate occasions colleagues saw one of the authors running a chapter or so off a central printer. They asked about the subject. When they were told, they said, "you're kidding." They all said it. When asked what they meant by that, they suggested that diversity is a topic that only some people are interested in—meaning, not white males.

George Bush, while he was president, did not like some people deciding what others couldn't say. He went to one of the country's great universities and charged that PC "declares certain topics off-limits, certain expressions off-limits, even certain gestures off-limits." He compared PC to an "inquisition" and praised the "freedom to speak one's mind."[3] Miles Harvey, a person well to the left of Bush, wrote that what the president said made him "furious." He was furious for two reasons.

The first reason was that Bush, no great advocate of free speech when he did not like what was being said, portrayed himself as a pious defender of free speech. The second reason was even worse: Miles Harvey found that he "could not deny that George Bush was right." The example Harvey provides is instructive.

Several months earlier, Harvey was at a meeting of graduate students who taught undergraduate writing courses. They were there to discuss pedagogy. The talk eventually got around to sexism and a female colleague told the group that she had established a writing rule for her classes.

The rule was this: Men were not allowed to write about rape in their short stories or poems. She reasoned that if men wrote about rape they would only be indulging in their own sexual fantasies and that exploring those fantasies was a bad exercise in imagination—she believed that the exploration was somehow akin to the act itself. Harvey writes:

> While I otherwise greatly respected my associate, her logic here reminded me of Jesse Helms' contention that exhibiting Robert Mapplethorpe's homoerotic photographs would somehow pose a threat to the American family. I was shocked when others at the meeting voiced their approval of my co-worker's approach. They constituted only a vocal minority, perhaps, but a very disturbing one.[4]

The division over who gets to use certain words, or what those words mean, makes many of us uncertain. It would be nice if the society had an agreed-upon list of words that you don't call anyone: Don't call people chinks, chicks, gooks, faggots, niggers, honkeys, kikes, or polacks. Simple. To be truthful, we do have a list like that. Polite and respectful people don't talk like that. If your parents didn't teach you that, they were wrong and didn't know about the list.

But it's not that simple. Standards of polite behavior vary, and people violate the standards on purpose to make a point. If your mother used to say, "colored people," and you said, "Which color, Mom?," did she tell you? The language can change over time. In different periods, the right word to use was negro, black, Afro-American, black (again), and now

African-American. What should you say? Spike Lee can call people nigger, but if you're not African-American, you had better not. In universities, most people nowadays say Native American, but almost all of the Native Americans we know call themselves Indians.

Different people see different things in the words. A former copy editor read an early draft of a chapter for this book, and objected to the phrase "blonde down the hall from Florida." The editor thought that would conjure up images of dumb blondes. Bad form. She suggested that we replace it with "redhead down the hall from Alabama."

The example suggests this is not about what dictionaries say a word means or what we want to say by using a word. An important part of the PC controversy is about who gets to define identity.

Not long ago, in a class taught by one of the authors of this book, he was talking about what people wanted to be called. It became very clear very quickly that each of us wanted and needed to be careful. One woman said she was white. The fact was that she had a great tan and was not white at all. Another woman—whose skin was about the same color as the white woman—did not say that she was white. And, for certain, she did not want to be called African-American. She was from Cape Verde, and Cape Verdeans once took Africans as slaves. She wanted to be called a Cape Verdean.

The man from Jamaica thought of himself as brown, and the biracial woman considered herself either biracial or black. She hated the term *mulatto*. The man from the Orient (he did not mind being called oriental) said he did not care what he was called. He paused, had a second thought, and then said that he really did not like being called a gook or a chink. When asked why he did not want to be called white although he had about the palest skin in the class, he said he knew that, and then didn't answer the question.

It was an interesting discussion. The white people didn't think about color. The actual color that people were did not have much to do with what they wanted to be called. People of the same color sometimes wanted to be called different things. The underlying point of the discussion was that no one wanted to call anyone else the wrong thing. The problem was that there were so few clues about what the right thing would be.

The politically correct people—underneath their sometimes remarkably silly language—are right to remind us that we should be careful about what we call others. Those who resist PC also seem to have a point when they make fun of the excessive self-righteousness of vocabulary politics.

Not all on the political left are happy with political correctness. Barbara Ehrenreich, in an article titled "The Challenge for the Left,"[5] argues the following three points. First, she writes that there is a very big problem with administration enforced rules about offensive speech: Rules don't work. The second problem is that "there is tendency to confuse verbal purification with real social change." She says, "Verbal uplift is not the revolution." The third problem is that the PC environment is so off-putting that many former radicals want nothing to do with radical politics any more.

Miles Harvey writes that "during my two years at graduate school, I perceived a kind of general free-speech funk, a faint but undeniable stench of intolerance in the hallowed halls."[6] What Miles argues is that unless we can seriously say what we mean, we will never solve our problems.

In "Race, Class and Candor," Salim Muwakkil argues that the PC people just plain miss the boat.[7] Muwakkil argues that the left, and particularly the PCers, simply focus on the wrong issues. He strongly suggests that the left turn its attention to reality—to the context of the lives of too many Americans. No one should have been surprised at what happened after the trial of Rodney King. We saw him being beaten a thousand times, and then we saw those who beat him be found not guilty.

Were the riots a result of the verdict? Of course the two were connected. Were there riots because we don't quite know what to call people? I don't think so. Were there riots because the living conditions of the poor are awful and seem hopeless? Could be closer to the truth. This left-leaning critique of the PC movement is straightforward enough: Get real.

Is there a way out of the dilemma? Probably not. It is wrong to hurt people's feelings, but it is just as wrong not to laugh at foolishness when it comes up.[8]

Say What You Mean

Ellen Goodman reported that the American Society of Newspaper Editors did a survey of attitudes toward the First Amendment.[9] That amendment seems to guarantee freedom of expression, but only from control by the state. She writes that "the greatest inhibitor of free expression wasn't the fear of the state or even the boss, but the fear that we might offend someone else. The people polled worried most that 'saying what's on your mind may harm or damage other people' and that 'speaking your mind may hurt the feelings of those you care for.'"

There are ways in which the sentiment is wonderful. It seems to suggest that at least a surface of civility has settled over much of the adult population. We may be spared the rude language of racism and sexism and all the rest. How can that be bad?

It isn't bad, but it is far from the whole story. The problem is that the things we fear talking about are often the very things we need to discuss. The fact is that we have centuries-old problems that revolve around race, religion, class, gender, and sexuality. To be ever so civil, and to ignore the fact of our biases, is to ensure that the misunderstandings and prejudices will continue.

Goodman's point can be put in the form of this question: What good is the freedom of speech if we decide not to use it?

Honest people, in public debate, say silly things. They also say offensive and rude and dumb things. David Duke has not cornered the market on offensive and rude, try as he may. But the First Amendment does not protect just the bright, sensitive, and politically correct people; it also protects David Duke.

To make matters even worse, when David Duke speaks his mind and 39 percent of a state votes for him, then it is probably in everyone's best interest to understand just what is going on.

In his own skewed way, Duke is politically correct. Most of the time, he is able to mask his racism and bigotry in code words. Isn't it a gigantic irony to have politically correct language used in the service of evil ideas?

Goodman writes: "While children learn in grade school to read and write, they often unlearn how to speak their minds. . . . So for the 200th anniversary party, celebrate free speech the old-fashioned way. Mix together civility and candor. Say what you think."

Back to College

This country has a short answer to controversies about language and politics. That answer is the First Amendment to the Constitution. After the first clause about religion (mentioned in Chapter 3) the amendment is clear about speech:

> *Congress shall make no law respecting an establishment of religion, or prohibiting the free exercise thereof; or abridging the freedom of speech, or of the press.*

Other amendments to the Constitution extend the prohibition on limiting speech to state and local governments. How clear does this need to be? Don't make laws limiting speech. With few exceptions, employers can't limit your speech, either.

On university campuses, there is one additional short answer to the PC controversy. It is called academic freedom. That means that your professors can write, teach, and research what they want to, without limits by the university. The rule that protects an individual professor's academic freedom is called tenure—this is the original justification of the tenure system. While you can find individual professors who are willing to limit speech, we don't know of a single university in the land that says it opposes academic freedom.

The First Amendment and academic freedom seem brutally clear on PC. A rule that limits speech (professors' speech, anyway) on a campus violates academic freedom and probably is against the law as well. Teaching and writing can be offensive, but they are protected.

Who could be against the Constitution? Who could say that all professors should be muzzled on certain subjects?

These protections of freedoms are the most basic rules of public interest we have—they limit power so we can be free.

But recall the discussion of sexual harassment in Chapter 5. The limits of sexual harassment policies turn out to be the First Amendment and academic freedom. People who want to extend harassment policies to prohibitions of "hostile environments" *are* willing to limit the First Amendment and academic freedom. There is no way to accomplish those ends without clear conflicts with rules about freedom of expression.

The argument deserves more than a comparison with, and dismissal by, the Constitution. We can start with academic freedom. The idea of academic freedom did not become popular until the Enlightenment, really the eighteenth century, when people in universities claimed that they had built a method—the scientific method—that allowed them to find truth. Their findings were not about one side or another of a conflict, went the argument—they were above conflicts. They were about truth. Truth. Universities did not change overnight, and until the early nineteenth century, professors had to worry about charges of heresy. With the advent of secular universities, professors were allowed to say things that offended ecclesiastical hierarchies. The actual practice of academic freedom is barely 150 years old.

The First Amendment has a more definite starting date, but it did not vigorously protect freedom of expression until this century. The sources of the amendment are similar to those of academic freedom. The period that produced our Constitution was the Enlightenment, and one of the chief concerns of the authors of the First Amendment was the dangerous combination of ecclesiastic and secular authorities. In this case, too, the current understanding of freedom is relatively new.

To someone who wants to extend sexual harassment policy into the realm of PC and limit speech as well as actions, the First Amendment and academic freedom may be suspect. The goals of greater equality and empowerment are directed against what is seen as the dominant group's hold on power in traditional hierarchies, such as universities. The rights that were protected were not, until very recently, the rights of women and minorities and other dependent groups. The rights protected white heterosexual males, who often said awful things about women, minorities, homosexuals, and so on.

The argument goes further. Social norms silence groups that don't have power. Women and others who did not wield power could not find a voice to express themselves. Because they did not have positions in recognized public institutions, their attempts at speech in other places (such as within the family) did not receive protection.

In sum, if we want equality, the First Amendment and academic freedom may not look like the best rules to live by. They can look like a shield for traditional power and privilege.

This interpretation of the PC controversy does not have an ending. It is something you should think about. This book has so far been a tour through many different accounts of groups that want more equality, more empowerment, more recognition of their contributions to diversity. The First Amendment and academic freedom are brief, fairly clear, and seemingly not universally accepted. A genuine dilemma.

Blame

Who do we blame? We are near the end of the book, and we still have not discussed who is responsible for the problems we have seen. By now, we should know there is no single answer; indeed, we should be aware of anyone who claims to know the answer. Still, it makes some sense to review quickly what is out there.

Conventional wisdom indicates this: White males are to be blamed for many of the problems we have discussed in this book. Historically, the equation is easy to see: White males have been in positions of power, and with that power a racist, sexist (and on and on) society has developed. Even the literature that has traditionally been judged as great and has been the foundation of our higher learning is now seen by some as biased. We know that literature was written by Dead White Males.

We have seen that the judgment of the work of white males, certainly in social and political terms, has been harsh.

— 299 —

The men in charge—from the workplace to the White House—have been judged as oppressive.

Things are beginning to change. White men are no longer the standard by which everything is judged. Because of affirmative action, white men, all things being equal, will not automatically be chosen for a job. There is nothing about white males on politically correct lists. Indeed, PC assumes that white males are the enemy. There is no question that white males are on the defensive. And, many would argue, none too soon.

But we also discussed stereotypes. We know that any group stereotype, in any particular case, is wrong. That includes good and bad stereotypes. Every person in every group is not identical. We saw that there has been legislation to help groups of people. There are, we know, positive and negative aspects of those laws and rulings. But what has never been at issue is the question of individual identity: Each of us is unique. No matter what color we are, what sex we are, what religion we are, what political correctness tells us, each of us is unique.

That makes everything more complicated. Although it can be easily documented that white males have had power in the United States, it is foolish to make the judgment that all white males are oppressors. To presume to know what a person believes or how a person will act because of color or sexual organs is nothing more than another form of bigotry.

If this book were a book of prophesy, one of the visions of the future might be this: The attack against white males—especially young white males—will lead to ugly racial and gender confrontations.

In truth, young adults (of all colors, of either sex) have almost no power. Like others, young white males are trying to figure out who they are, what they are good at, and what the world will be like after they graduate. They do not have the power to rule. They do not have the time to be oppressors. They do not seem to have the inclination to do all of the evil things they are accused of doing. It may not be wise to believe that they should be punished for the sins of their fathers.

Young white males—just like all other young people—are struggling to make sense of a world they did not create, a world that seems to be out of control. Young, all things being equal, white males are getting ready to enter a job market in which they are on the bottom of the list, a job market in which they will be asked to atone for wrongs they did not commit.

A sure way to ensure gender and race conflict is to make young white males the enemy. They will, understandably, become angry and resentful. They will, not surprisingly, become very unsympathetic to issues they would ordinarily support.

We are not suggesting that you take a young white male to lunch or that all young white males are perfectly reasonable and good-hearted people. We are not even suggesting that we forget who has been in power and where that has gotten us. What we are suggesting is that it is very foolish to create enemies out of potential friends.

Exploring Differences

This book has looked at diversity from many angles. The diversity of our society, and of the individuals in it, is broad and deep. We are getting to know more about it all the time.

We can end where we began, with the circle of identity. There you are, a circle of 20 beings, each of the 20 representing a different part of what you are. There is the sex part, the religion part, class, where you came from, who you are attracted to, age, cultural background, and a lot more. Everyone else is like that, too. None of us is one thing.

We can expect that this brings us a world full of different kinds of aesthetics: different kinds of beauties, reasons to work and live, different desires and dreams. It's a world that works only when the differences can be explored and appreciated. The world is much more diverse than we have discussed in this book. There are different kinds of organizations and different kinds of buildings and different kinds of living arrangements and different kinds of art and cars and pets and food and on and on. For each of us, there can be a world to live in, a best dream of a way to live, a rightfittingness to daily life that we often want to share with others.

It takes about one entire lifetime to figure that out and then to do it; maybe longer than that for slow learners. The process barely begins by college. There are other things to work out, which is where the topics in the book come in. You have to get through these topics before you get to others.

You may not know many new things even now, even after you have read the entire book. Your opinions about the book, about the topics, don't really matter. What matters is that you think about them. What matters is that you take care in how you think about others. What matters are your considered opinions.

There is a moral to the book. It is this: Look closer, think harder.

— Appendix —

Excerpts from the Civil Rights Act of 1964

Public Law 88–352   *July 2, 1964 (H.R. 7152)*

An Act

To enforce the constitutional right to vote, to confer jurisdiction upon the district courts of the United States to provide injunctive relief against discrimination in public accommodations, to authorize the Attorney General to institute suits to protect constitutional rights in public facilities and public education, to extend the Commission on Civil Rights, to prevent discrimination in federally assisted programs, to establish a Commission on Equal Employment Opportunity, and for other purposes.

Be it enacted by the Senate and House of Representatives of the United States of America in Congress assembled, that this Act may be cited as the "Civil Rights Act of 1964".

Title I—Voting Rights

Sec. 101. Section 2004 of the Revised Statutes (42 U.S.C.1971), . . . is further amended as follows: . . .

"(2) No person acting under color of law shall—

"(A) in determining whether any individual is qualified under State law or laws to vote in any Federal election, apply any standard, practice or procedure different from the standards, practices, or procedures applied under such law or laws to other individuals within the same county, parish, or similar political subdivision who have been found by State officials to be qualified to vote; . . .
"(C) employ any literacy test as a qualification for voting in any Federal election. . . .

Title II—Injunctive Relief Against Discrimination in Places of Public Accommodation

Sec. 201. (a) All persons shall be entitled to the full and equal enjoyment of the goods, services, facilities, privileges, advantages, and accommodations of any place of public accommodation, as defined in this section, without discrimination or segregation on the ground of race, color, religion, or national origin. . . .

Sec. 202. All persons shall be entitled to be free, at any establishment or place, from discrimination or segregation of any kind on the ground of race, color, religion, or national origin, if such discrimination or segregation is or purports to be required by any law, statute, ordinance, regulation, rule, or order of a State or any agency or political subdivision thereof. . . .

Sec. 204. (a) Whenever any person has engaged or there are reasonable grounds to believe that any person is about to engage in any act or practice prohibited . . . a civil action for preventive relief, including an application for a permanent or temporary injunction, restraining order, or other order, may be instituted by the person aggrieved and, upon timely application, the court may, in its discretion, permit the Attorney General to intervene in such civil action if he certifies that the case is of general public importance. Upon application by the complainant and in such circumstances as the court may deem just, the court may appoint an attorney for such complainant and may authorize the commencement of the civil action without the payment of fees, costs, or security. . . .

Sec. 206. (a) Whenever the Attorney General has reasonable cause to believe that any person or group of persons is engaged in a pattern or practice of resistance to the full enjoyment of any of the rights secured by this title, and that the pattern or practice is of such a nature and is intended to deny the full exercise of the rights herein described, the Attorney General may bring a civil action in the appropriate district court of the United States. . . .

Title III—Desegregation of Public Facilities

Sec. 301. (a) Whenever the Attorney General receives a complaint in writing signed by an individual to the effect that he is being deprived of or threatened with the loss of his right to the equal protection of the laws, on account of his race, color, religion, or national origin, by being denied equal utilization of any public facility which is owned, operated, or managed by or on behalf of any State or subdivision thereof, . . . the Attorney General is authorized to institute for in the name of the United States a civil action in any appropriate district court of the United States against such parties and for such relief as may be appropriate. . . .

Title IV—Desegregation of Public Education

. . . Sec. 407. (a) Whenever the Attorney General receives a complaint in writing—

(1) signed by a parent or group of parents to the effect that his or their minor children, as members of a class of persons similarly situated, are being deprived by a school board of the equal protection of the laws, or

(2) signed by an individual, or his parent, to the effect that he has been denied admission to or not permitted to continue in attendance at a public college by reason of race, color, religion, or national origin,

and the Attorney General believes the complaint is meritorious and certifies that the signer or signers of such complaint are unable, in his judgment, to initiate and maintain appropriate legal proceedings for relief, and that the institution of an action will materially further the orderly achievement of desegregation in public education, the Attorney General is authorized, after giving notice of such complaint to the appropriate school board or college authority and after certifying that he is satisfied that such board or college authority has had a reasonable time to adjust the conditions alleged in such complaint, to institute for or in the name of the United States a civil action in any appropriate district court of the United States against such parties and for such relief as may be appropriate. . . .

Title V—Commission on Civil Rights[1]

. . . Sec. 504. (a) Section 104(a) of the Civil Rights Act of 1957 . . . is further amended to read as follows:

"DUTIES OF THE COMMISSION

"Sec. 104. (a) The Commission shall—

"(1) investigate allegations in writing under oath or affirmation that certain citizens of the United States are being deprived of their right to vote and have that vote counted by reason of their color, race, religion, or national origin; which writing, under oath or affirmation, shall set forth the facts upon which such belief or beliefs are based;

"(2) study and collect information concerning legal developments constituting a denial of equal protection of laws under the Constitution because of race, color, religion or national origin or in the administration of justice;

"(3) appraise the laws and policies of the Federal Government with respect to denials of equal protection of the laws under the Constitution because of race, color, religion or national origin or in the administration of justice;

"(4) serve as a national clearinghouse for information in respect to denials of equal protection of the laws because of race, color, religion or national origin, including but not limited to the fields of voting, education, housing, employment, the use of public facilities, and transportation, or in the administration of justice;

"(5) investigate allegations . . . that citizens of the United States are unlawfully being accorded or denied the right to vote, or to have their votes properly counted. . . .

"(6) Nothing in this or any other Act shall be construed as authorizing the Commission . . . to inquire into or investigate any membership practices or internal operations of any fraternal organization, any college or university fraternity or sorority, any private club or any religious organization."

Sec. 506. Section 105 (f) and section 105 (g) of the Civil Rights Act of 1957 . . . are amended to read as follows: . . .

"(f) The Commission . . . may . . . hold such hearings and act at such times as the Commission . . . may deem advisable. Subpoenas for the attendance and testimony of witnesses or the production of written or other matter may be issued. . . .

"(g) In case of contumacy or refusal to obey a subpena [sic], any district court of the United States . . . within the jurisdiction of which the inquiry is carried on . . . shall have jurisdiction to issue to such person an order requiring such person to appear before the Commission . . . there to produce pertinent, relevant and nonprivileged testimony . . . any failure to obey such order of the court may be punished by said court as a contempt thereof. . . ."

"(i) The Commission shall have the power to make such rules and regulations as are necessary to carry out the purposes of this Act."

Title VI—Nondiscrimination in Federally Assisted Programs

Sec. 601. No person in the United States shall, on the ground of race, color, or national origin, be excluded from participation in, be denied the benefits of, or be subjected to discrimination under any program or activity receiving Federal financial assistance.

Sec. 602. Each Federal department and agency which is empowered to extend Federal financial assistance to any program or activity, by way of grant, loan, or contract other than a contract of insurance or guaranty, is authorized and directed to effectuate the provisions of Section 601 with respect to such program or activity by issuing rules, regulation, or orders of general applicability which shall be consistent with achievement of the objectives of the statute authorizing the financial assistance in connection with which the action is taken. . . .

Title VII—Equal Employment Opportunity

DEFINITIONS

Sec. 701. For the purposes of this title—

(a) The term "person" includes one or more individuals, labor unions, partnerships, associations, corporations, legal representatives, mutual companies, joint-stock companies, trusts, unincorporated organizations, trustees, trustees in bankruptcy, or receivers.

(b) The term "employer" means a person engaged in an industry affecting commerce who has twenty-five or more employees for each working day in each of twenty or more calendar weeks in the current or preceding calendar year. . . .

DISCRIMINATION BECAUSE OF RACE, COLOR, RELIGION, SEX, OR NATIONAL ORIGIN

Sec. 703. (a) It shall be an unlawful employment practice for an employer—

  (1) to fail or refuse to hire or to discharge any individual, or otherwise to discriminate against any individual with respect to his compensation, terms, conditions, or privileges of employment, because of such individual's race, color, religion, sex, or national origin; or
  (2) to limit, segregate, or classify his employees in any way which would deprive or tend to deprive any individual of employment opportunities or otherwise adversely affect his status as an employee, because of such individual's race, color, religion, sex, or national origin. . . .

(c) It shall be an unlawful employment practice for a labor organization—

  (1) to exclude or to expel from its membership, or otherwise to discriminate against, any individual because of his race, color, religion, sex, or national origin;
  (2) to limit, segregate, or classify its membership . . . .

(e) Notwithstanding any other provision of this title,

  (1) it shall not be an unlawful employment practice for an employer to hire and employ employees, . . . for a labor organization to classify its membership or to classify . . . on the basis of his religion, sex, or national origin in those certain instances where religion, sex, or national origin is a bona fide occupational qualifica-

tion reasonably necessary to the normal operation of that particular business or enterprise, and

(2) it shall not be an unlawful employment practice for a school, college, university or other educational institution or institution of learning to hire and employ employees of a particular religion if such school, college, university, or other educational institution or institution of learning is, in whole or in substantial part, owned, supported, controlled, or managed by a particular religion or by a particular religious corporation, association, or society. . . .

(j) Nothing contained in this title shall be interpreted to require any employer, employment agency, labor organization, or joint labor-management committee subject to this title to grant preferential treatment to any individual or to any group because of the race, color, religion, sex, or national origin of such individual or group on account of an imbalance which may exist with respect to the total number of percentage of persons of any race, color, religion, sex, or national origin employed by any employer, referred or classified for employment by any employment agency or labor organization. . . .

OTHER UNLAWFUL EMPLOYMENT PRACTICES

Sec. 704. (a) It shall be an unlawful employment practice . . . to discriminate against any member thereof or applicant for membership, because he has opposed any practice made an unlawful employment practice by this title, or because he has made a charge, testified, assisted, or participated in any manner in an investigation, proceeding, or hearing under this title.

(b) It shall be an unlawful employment practice for an employer, labor organization, or employment agency to print or publish or cause to be printed or published any notice or advertisement relating to employment by such an employer or membership in or any classification or referral for employment by such a labor organization or relating to any classification or referral for employment by such an employment agency, indicating any preference, limitation, specification, or discrimination, based on race, color, religion, sex, or national origin, except that such a notice or advertisement may indicate a preference, limitation, specification, or discrimination based on religion, sex, or national origin when religion, sex, or national origin is a bona fide occupational qualification for employment.

EQUAL EMPLOYMENT OPPORTUNITY COMMISSION

Sec. 705. (a) There is hereby created a Commission to be known as the equal Employment Opportunity Commission. . . .

(d) The Commission shall at the close of each fiscal year report to the Congress and to the President concerning the action it has taken; . . .

(g) The Commission shall have power—

(1) to cooperate with and, with their consent, utilize regional, State, local, and other agencies, both public and private, and individuals;

(2) to pay to witnesses whose depositions are taken who are summoned before the Commission . . . ;

(3) to furnish to persons subject to this title such technical assistance as they may request to further their compliance with this title or an order issued thereunder;

(4) upon the request of (i) any employer, whose employees or some of them, or (ii) any labor organization, whose members or some of them, refuse or threaten to refuse to cooperate in effectuating the provisions of this title, to assist in such effectuation by conciliation or such other remedial action as is provided by this title;

(5) to make such technical studies as are appropriate to effectuate the purposes and policies of this title and to make the results of such studies available to the public;

(6) to refer matters to the Attorney General with recommendations for intervention. . . .

PREVENTION OF UNLAWFUL EMPLOYMENT PRACTICES

Sec. 706. (a) Whenever it is charged in writing under oath by a person claiming to be aggrieved, or a written charge has been filed by a member of the Commission where he has rea-

sonable cause to believe a violation of this title has occurred
. . . . If the Commission shall determine, after such investigation, that there is reasonable cause to believe that the charge is true, the Commission shall endeavor to eliminate any such alleged unlawful employment practice by informal methods of conference, conciliation, and persuasion. . . .

(f) Each United States district court and each United States court of a place subject to the jurisdiction of the United States shall have jurisdiction of actions brought under this title. . . .

Sec. 707. (a) Whenever the Attorney General has reasonable cause to believe that any person or group of persons is engaged in a pattern or practice of resistance to the full enjoyment of any of the rights secured by this title, and that the pattern or practice is of such a nature and is intended to deny the full exercise of the rights herein described, the Attorney General may bring a civil action in the appropriate district court of the United States. . . .

INVESTIGATORY POWERS

Sec. 710. (a) For the purposes of investigation of a charge filed under the authority contained in section 706, the Commission shall have authority to examine witnesses under oath and to require the production of documentary evidence relevant or material to the charge under investigation. . . .

VETERANS' PREFERENCE

Sec. 712. Nothing contained in this title shall be construed to repeal or modify any Federal, State, territorial, or local law creating special rights or preference for veterans.

RULES AND REGULATIONS

Sec. 713. (a) The Commission shall have authority from time to time to issue, amend, or rescind suitable procedural regulations to carry out the provisions of this title. Regulations issued under this section shall be in conformity with the standards and limitations of the Administrative Procedure Act. . . .

Notes

CHAPTER 1

1. For an overview of the educational system at this level, see Ernest L. Boyer, *High School: A Report on Secondary Education in America* (New York: Harper & Row, 1983); and Jonathan Kozol, *The Night Is Dark and I Am Far from Home* (New York: Touchstone Books, 1990), revised edition.
2. The study is by A. B. Hollingshead, *Elmtown's Youth* (New York: John Wiley and Sons, 1949), and is quoted in Joel Spring, *American Education: An Introduction to Social and Political Aspects*, Fifth edition (New York: Longman, 1991), p. 89.
3. This information is also found in Spring, ibid., p. 90, and comes from Jeanne Ballantine, *The Sociology of Education* (Englewood Cliffs, NJ: Prentice-Hall, 1983). The questions of gender and race are the subjects of Chapters 5 and 7.
4. David Karen, "Access to Higher Education in the United States, 1900 to the Present," in Kevin J. Dougherty and Floyd M. Hammack, *Education & Society, A Reader* (San Diego: Harcourt Brace Jovanovich, Publishers, 1990), p. 269. Karen argues that things are getting better for all groups that have been denied access. How much better is certainly a genuine question.
5. Ibid., p. 272.
6. Peter W. Cookson, Jr., and Caroline Hodges Persell, *Preparing for Power: America's Elite Boarding Schools* (New York: Basic Books, Inc., Publishers, 1985).
7. Ibid.
8. Calvin Sims, "Late Bloomers Come to Campus," *The New York Times Education Life* (Aug. 4, 1991): 16–17.
9. The numbers are from "Fact File: State-by-State Enrollment by Racial and Ethnic Group, Fall 1991," *The Chronicle of Higher*

Education (Jan. 20, 1993): A31; "Earned Degrees Conferred by U.S. Institutions, 1990–1991," *The Chronicle of Higher Education* (June 2, 1993): A25; "Alcohol Abuse by Students Is Found Most Severe on Campuses in Northeast," *The Chronicle of Higher Education* (May 26, 1993): A26; Mary Crystal Cage, "Graduation Rates of American Indians and Blacks Improve, Lag Behind Others," *The Chronicle of Higher Education* (May 26, 1993): A29; Johnnella Butler and Betty Schmitz, "Ethnic Studies, Women's Studies, and Multiculturalism," *Change* (Jan./Feb. 1992): 37–41.

10. This point, and the argument that follows, is from Helen Lefkowitz Horowitz, *Campus Life: Undergraduate Cultures from the End of the Eighteenth Century to the Present* (New York: Alfred A. Knopf, 1987).
11. Ibid., pp. 3–4.
12. See the summary of findings in Robbie J. Steward, Joyce A. Davidson, and Sherry A. Borgers, "Racial Majority vs. Minority Status: A Study of Interactional Styles of Successful White Students on a Predominantly White University Campus," *Journal of College Student Development* 34 (July 1993): 295–298.
13. William Golding, *Lord of the Flies* (New York: Putnam, 1956).

CHAPTER 2

1. Location can consist of ideas and history, as well as physical location. For a short guide to seeing these aspects of location on college campuses, see Ernest L. Boyer, *College: The Undergraduate Experience in America* (New York: Harper & Row, Publishers, 1987), pp. 286–297.
2. For a remarkable sense of the Puritans, see Perry Miller, *Errand Into the Wilderness* (New York: Harper Torchbooks, 1964).
3. Many groups have tried to make new communities. Some of them are described in John Humphrey Noyes, *Strange Cults and Utopias of Nineteenth Century America* (New York: Dover Publishing, 1966); Arthur Bestor, *Backwoods Utopias* (Philadelphia: University of Pennsylvania Press, 1970); Rosabeth Moss Kanter, *Commitment and Community* (Cambridge: Harvard University Press, 1972). One recent example was the Branch Davidians, the followers of David Koresh.
4. For a description of relationships in this fragile college community, see Michael Moffett, *Coming of Age in New Jersey: College and American Culture* (New Brunswick: Rutgers University Press, 1989).

5. Paul F. Grendler, "The University of Padua 1405–1600: A Success Story," in *History of Higher Education Annual* 10 (1990): 7.
6. Ibid., p. 12.
7. Frederick Rudolph, *The American College and University: A History* (New York: Vintage Books, 1962), p. 92.
8. Ibid., p. 93.
9. Ibid., p. 94.
10. Ibid., p. 97.
11. Ibid., p. 98.

CHAPTER 3

1. For an excellent introduction to the context of religion in America, see James Reichley, *Religion in American Public Life* (Washington, DC: The Brookings Institution, 1984).
2. Ernest L. Boyer, *College: The Undergraduate Experience in America* (New York: Harper & Row, 1987), pp. 187–188.
3. Frederick Rudolph, *The American College and University: A History* (New York: Vintage Books, 1962), p. 6.
4. *Ibid.*, p. 68.
5. Page Smith, *Killing the Spirit: Higher Education in America* (New York: Penguin Books, 1990), p. 100.
6. Rudolph, op. cit., p. 76.
7. Ibid., p. 78.
8. William F. Buckley, Jr., *God and Man at Yale: The Superstitions of Academic Freedom* (Chicago: Regnery Gateway, 1977).
9. Smith, op. cit., p. 101.
10. Ibid., p. 103.
11. Ibid., p. 107.
12. For a good description of American restlessness, see Alexis de Tocqueville, *Democracy in America*.
13. B. Edward McClellan, "Moral Education and Public Schooling," found in Elizabeth Steiner, Robert Arnove, and B. Edward McClennan, *Education and American Culture* (New York: Macmillan Publishing Co., 1980), p. 214.
14. Ibid., p. 215.
15. Ibid., p. 216.
16. Ibid., p. 217.
17. Ibid., p. 218.
18. Neil G. McCluskey, "America and the Catholic School," in Steiner et al., p. 224.
19. The case is *Lemon v. Kurtzman*, 403 U.S. 642 (1971).

20. Cornell M. Hamm, "Providing Content to Moral Education," in Henry Ehlers, *Crucial Issues in Education*, Seventh edition (New York: CBS College Publishing, 1981), p. 253.
21. Milton Rokeach, "Toward a Clarification of Our Values," found in Ehlers, ibid., p. 249.

CHAPTER 4

1. The Copley Plaza and the Mary Beth Whitehead examples come from Benjamin DeMott, *The Imperial Middle: Why Americans Can't Think Straight About Class* (New York: Morrow, 1990).
2. The literature on classes overlaps with many other areas in American life. See, for example, Thomas Byrne Edsall and Mary D. Edsall, *Chain Reaction: The Impact of Race, Rights, and Taxes on American Politics* (New York: W. W. Norton and Company, 1992); Kevin Phillips, *Boiling Point: Democrats, Republicans, and the Decline of Middle-Class Prosperity* (New York: Random House, 1993); Susan Moller Okin, *Justice, Gender, and the Family* (New York: Basic Books, 1989); and sources in the other notes to this chapter.
3. The numbers come from Andrew Hacker, "Class Dismissed," *The New York Review of Books* XXXVIII, no. 5 (March 7, 1991): 44–46.
4. There are, of course, exceptions on every campus.
5. Thanks to Johnstone Campbell for the idea.
6. Robert Paul Wolff, *The Ideal of the University* (New York: Transaction Publications, 1992).
7. Jonathan Kozol, *The Night Is Dark and I Am Far from Home*, Revised edition (New York: Touchstone Books, 1990), p. 27.
8. Samuel Bowles, "Unequal Education and the Reproduction of the Social Division of Labor," in Elizabeth Steiner, Robert Arnove, B. Edward McClellan, *Education and American Culture* (New York: Macmillan Publishing Co., 1980), p. 125.
9. John I. Goodlad, *A Place Called School* (New York: McGraw-Hill, 1984).
10. Joel Spring, *American Education: An Introduction to Social and Political Aspects*, Fifth edition (White Plains, NY: Longman, 1991), p. 6.
11. Ibid., p. 12.
12. Ibid., p. 19.
13. Ernest L. Boyer, *College: The Undergraduate Experience in America* (New York: Harper & Row, Publishers, 1987), pp. 12–13.

14. The structure of school material is found in William H. Behn et al., "School is Bad; Work is Worse," in Martin Carnoy and Henry Levin, *The Limits of Educational Reform* (New York: David McKay Company, Inc., 1976); and the quotes about the structure of classes are found in Jean Anyon, "Social Class and the Hidden Curriculum of Work," in Kevin J. Dougherty and Floyd M. Hammack, *Education & Society, A Reader* (New York: Harcourt Brace Jovanovich, Publishers, 1990), pp. 426–428.
15. Anyon, op. cit.
16. Ibid.
17. Marcus Mabry, "The Ghetto Preppies," Newsweek (Nov. 4, 1991): 44–48.
18. William Domhoff, *The Bohemian Grove and Other Retreats* (New York: Harper & Row, 1984). and Lewis H. Lapham, *Money and Class in America: Notes and Observations on Our Civil Religion* (New York: Weidenfeld & Nicolson, 1988).
19. See Isabel V. Sawhill, "Poverty in the U.S.: Why Is It So Persistent?" *Journal of Economic Literature* XXVI (Sept. 1988): 1073–1119.
20. Christopher Jencks and Paul E. Peterson, *The Urban Underclass* (Washington, DC: Brookings Institution, 1991), p. v.
21. Ernest L. Boyer, *High School: A Report on Secondary Education in America* (New York: Harper & Row, 1983), pp. 225–226.

CHAPTER 5

1. Marion Lowe, "Social Bodies: The Interaction of Culture and Women's Biology," in Ruth Hubbard, Mary Sue Henifin, and Barbara Fried, eds., *Biological Women: The Conventional Myth* (Rochester, VT: Schenckman Books, 1982).
2. Ibid., p. 91.
3. Molly Ivins, *Molly Ivins Can't Say That, Can She?* (New York: Random House, 1991), p. xiv.
4. Lowe, op. cit., p. 92.
5. Ibid., p. 95.
6. Ibid., p. 96.
7. "Women Running Faster," *Springfield Union Times* (Jan. 4, 1992). The information is from Brian Whipp and Susan Ward in an article in *Nature*. The critique is in "Missing the Mark," in the Jan. 20, 1992, edition of *Sports Illustrated*.
8. Lowe, op. cit.

9. Lowe, op. cit., p. 99.
10. See Doreen Kimura, "Sex Differences in the Brain," *Scientific American* 267, no. 3 (Sept. 1992): 119–125.
11. For example, see Nancy Chodorow, *The Reproduction of Mothering* (Berkeley, CA: Stanford University Press, 1978). Much of the following comes from Charmian Sperling.
12. For example, see Carol Gilligan, *In a Different Voice* (Cambridge, MA: Harvard University Press, 1982).
13. Ibid.
14. See Carol Gilligan, Nona P. Lyons, and Trudy J. Hanmer, eds., *Making Connections: The Relational Worlds of Adolescent Girls at Emma Willard School* (Cambridge, MA: Harvard University Press, 1990).
15. See R. Derry, "Model Reasoning in Organizations: A Study of Men and Women Managers," Ph.D. dissertation, University of Massachusetts, 1987.
16. Connie Counts, "Towards A Relational Managerial Model for Schools: A Study of Women and Men as Superintendents and Principals," Ph.D. dissertation, Harvard Graduate School of Education, 1987.
17. Gary Powell, *Women and Men in Management* (Newbury Park, CA: Sage Publications, 1988).
18. Frederick Rudolph, *The American College and University* (New York: Vintage Books, 1962), pp. 310–311.
19. Ibid., p. 322.
20. See either Rudolph, op. cit., or Page Smith, *Killing the Spirit* (New York: Penguin Books, 1990).
21. Smith, op. cit., pp. 93–94.
22. Ibid., p. 93.
23. Ibid., p. 98.
24. Roberta Hall, "The Classroom Climate: A Chilly One For Women?," Project on the Status and Education of Women, Association of American Colleges, 1982, p. 4.
25. Also cited in Hall, ibid.
26. An unidentified woman cited in Hall, ibid.
27. See Nancy Tuana, *Women and the History of Philosophy* (New York: Paragon House, 1992); Susan Moller Okin, *Women in Western Political Thought* (Princeton: Princeton University Press, 1979); Mary Lyndon Shanley and Carole Pateman, eds., *Feminist Interpretations and Political Theory* (University Park: The Pennsylvania State University Press, 1991); and Mary Briody Mahowald, ed., *Philosophy of Woman: An Anthology of Classic*

and Current Concepts, Second edition (Indianapolis: Hackett Publishing Company, 1983).

28. Margaret Wilkerson, "How Equal is Equal Education: Race, Class, and Gender," in Carol Lasser, *Educating Men and Women Together* (Urbana: University of Illinois Press, 1987), p. 136.

29. Angela Simeone, *Academic Women: Working Towards Equality* (South Hadley, MA: Bergin & Garvey Publishers, Inc., 1986), p. 23.

30. Hall, op. cit., p. 3.

31. Ibid., pp. 8, 9.

32. Ibid., p. 8.

33. The case is *Harris v. Forklift Systems, Inc.,* no. 92–1168. It is briefly summarized in Linda Greenhouse, "Court, 9–0, Makes Sexual Harassment Easier to Prove," *New York Times* (Nov. 10, 1993): A1, A15.

34. See, for example, Richard Bernstein, "Guilty If Charged," *The New York Review of Books* XLI, nos. 1 and 2 (Jan. 13, 1994): 11–14.

35. An anonymous professor quoted in Billie Wright Dziech and Linda Weiner, *The Lecherous Professor: Sexual Harassment on Campus,* Second edition (Urbana: University of Illinois Press, 1990), p. 42.

36. Ibid., p. 15.

37. Ibid., p. 92.

38. Ibid., p. 119.

CHAPTER 6

1. The U.S. Bureau of the Census publishes figures on wages and salaries in the report *Money Income of Household, Families, and Persons in the United States.* Susan Faludi summarizes the generally negative side of the statistics in Chapter Thirteen of her book *Backlash: The Undeclared War Against American Women* (New York: Crown Publishers, 1991). Extended discussions of income issues are found in Thomas Byrne Edsall and Mary D. Edsall, *Chain Reaction: The Impact of Race, Rights, and Taxes on American Politics* (New York: W. W. Norton and Company, 1992), Chapters 9 and 11.

2. Rosabeth Moss Kanter, *Men and Women of the Corporation,* (New York: Basic Books, 1979).

3. A good summary of changes in the workplace and the law is found in Dorothy McBride Stetson, *Women's Rights in the*

U.S.A.: Policy Debates and Gender Roles (Pacific Grove, CA: Brooks/Cole Publishing Company, 1991), Chapters 7 and 10. See also Susan Bluck Mezey, *In Pursuit of Equality: Women, Public Policy, and the Federal Courts* (New York: St. Martin's Press, 1992), Chapters 2–5.

4. This section is based on Eric Schmitt, "Pentagon Plans To Allow Combat Flights by Women," *New York Times* (April 28, 1993): 1; and John H. Cushman, Jr., "Top Admiral Backs Full Combat Roles for Women in Navy," *New York Times* (April 5, 1993): 1.

5. See "Indecent Exposure," Time (May 3, 1993): 20–21; and "Rhino Spunk," *New Republic* (May 31, 1993): 12.

6. Mezey, op. cit., Chapter 5; Stetson, op. cit., pp. 161–168.

7. One of many examples of this is found in Don Carter, "Ferries Act to Curb Race and Sex Harassment," *Seattle Post-Intelligencer* (May 9, 1991): B2.

8. The point is taken from Ralph Hummel, *The Bureaucratic Experience* (New York: St. Martin's Press, 1982), Second edition, Chapter 3.

9. Patterson and Peter Kim, "TV Evangelists Rank Lower than Hookers," *Seattle Times* (Aug. 5, 1991): E1.

10. This section relies on the following: Mary Roth Walsh, ed., *The Psychology of Women: Ongoing Debates* (New Haven: Yale University Press, 1987), Chapter 8; Rita L. Atkinson et al., *Introduction to Psychology*, Eighth edition (New York: Harcourt, Brace, Jovanovich, 1983), pp. 88–96, 299–307.

11. See Jacquelynne S. Eccles and Janis E. Jacobs, "Social Forces Shape Math Attitudes and Performance," in Walsh, op. cit., pp. 341–354.

12. This section relies on Stetson, op. cit., Chapter 8.

13. The question is considered by Steven G. Smith, *Gender Thinking* (Philadelphia: Temple University Press, 1992). For analytical approaches to the issue in the history of political thought, see Mary Lyndon Shanley and Carole Pateman, *Feminist Interpretations and Political Theory* (University Park: The Pennsylvania State University Press, 1991).

14. This section is based on Stetson, op. cit., Chapter 4.

15. It was not until 1971 that Congress repealed the Comstock Act of 1873, also known as the Act for the Suppression of Trade in and Circulation of Obscene Literature and Articles of Immoral Use. The main obscene articles the law controlled were contraceptives. Roe vs. Wade, the case in which the Court found that the zone of privacy included abortions in the first trimester of pregnancy (and to some extent, into the second trimester), was decided in 1973.

16. Two good sources to begin a study of gender in Western philosophy and political thought are Susan Moller Okin, *Women in Western Political Thought* (Princeton: Princeton University Press, 1979); and Nancy Tuana, *Women and the History of Philosophy* (New York: Paragon House, 1992).
17. Mary Wollstonecraft, *A Vindication of the Rights of Woman* (London, 1792).
18. This section is based on Deborah Tannen, "There Is No Neutrality for Women," *Seattle Post-Intelligencer* (June 20, 1993): E1.
19. Elizabeth Fox-Genovese, *Feminism Without Illusions: A Critique of Individualism* (Chapel Hill and London: University of North Carolina Press, 1991).
20. Ibid., pp. 25, 32, 174.
21. Ibid., p. 179.
22. Ibid., p. 234.
23. Ibid., p. 229.
24. Ibid., pp. 238, 241.
25. Deborah Tannen, *You Just Don't Understand: Men and Women in Conversation* (New York: Wm. Morrow and Company, 1990), pp. 43–44.
26. Ibid.
27. The standard work on rape in history is Susan Brownmiller, *Against Our Will* (New York: Random House, 1975).
28. See Stetson, op. cit., p. 348.
29. Diana E. H. Russell, *Sexual Exploitation: Rape, Child Sexual Abuse, and Sexual Harassment* (Beverly Hills: Sage, 1984).
30. Stetson, op. cit., p. 219.
31. See, for example, "Increase in Reports of Sexual Assaults Strains Campus Disciplinary Systems," *The Chronicle of Higher Education* (May 15, 1991): A29–30.
32. Ibid., p. A30.
33. Excerpted from Camille Paglia, *Sex, Art, and American Culture: Essays* (New York: Vintage Books, 1992). pp. 57, 59.
34. Brownmiller, op. cit., p. 15.
35. How is rape seen on your campus? If a man and a woman are at a party, maybe even have had a drink, and end up alone in a room, she says no, and he overpowers her, did a "real rape" occur? Does a women get to say no to an armed intruder and have legal protection, but not have the same legal protection if she says no to a date? Should we presume that a woman should have tried harder to avoid being alone with a man who, it turns out, was not trustworthy? You can check the rules in your state. Are you in one of the states that considers it assault and pursues

rapes committed by spouses or acquaintances? What constitutes evidence of rape—does a woman have to physically resist, or be beaten up, be threatened with a weapon, or show some other example of coercion to show that she was assaulted? Are questions about a victim's sexual history permitted in the investigation and trial? What is the penalty for rape in your state?

36. Religious orders vary tremendously. The example is taken from the Sisters of the Holy Cross. The sisters are highly educated and are based in South Bend, Indiana, the home of their university, St. Mary's.

CHAPTER 7

1. For readings about the Greek context of our thought, see Orlando Patterson, *Freedom, Volume I: Freedom in the Making of Western Culture* (New York: Basic Books, 1991).

2. Michael Moffatt, *Coming of Age in New Jersey* (New Brunswick: Rutgers University Press, 1989).

3. See note 31 of this chapter for a good recent summary of issues. See also John C. Gonsiorek and James D. Weinrich, *Homosexuality: Research Implications for Public Policy* (Newbury Park: Sage Publications, 1992).

4. We don't have a section on pornography in the book. Most feminists regard pornography as part of an ideology of male dominance and violence in which women are commodities controlled by men. This position raises many issues about the appropriate moral and legal response to pornography. The range of ideas on pornography are represented in the following: Andrea Dworkin, *Pornography: Men Possessing Women* (New York: Perigree Books, 1981); Elizabeth Fox-Genovese, *Feminism Without Illusions* (Chapel Hill and London: University of North Carolina Press, 1991), Chapter 4; and Camille Paglia, *Sex, Art, and American Culture* (New York: Random House, 1992), pp. 249–298.

5. This history comes from Lillian Faderman, *Odd Girls and Twilight Lovers: A History of Lesbian Life in Twentieth-Century America* (New York: Penguin Books, 1991), p. 24. It is suggested reading.

6. Ibid., p. 40.

7. Ibid., p. 49.

8. Ibid., p. 63.

9. Ibid., p. 68.

10. Ibid., p. 99.

11. Ibid., p. 109.
12. Ibid., p. 126.
13. Ibid., p. 135.
14. Ibid., p. 157.
15. Sara Lucia Hoagland in the introduction to Julia Penelope, *Call Me Lesbian* (Freedom, CA: The Crossing Press, 1992), p. XV.
16. Penelope, ibid., pp. 5–7.
17. Ibid., p. 42.
18. Ibid., pp. 52–59. There is a footnote of interest on page 59 of Penelope's book: "Many mothers expect privileges and certain behaviors from others. I meet them everywhere I go. They expect strangers to smile approvingly at them; they expect others to allow them to cut into long lines; they expect others to put up with their childrens' screeches and squalls in restaurants, theaters, and other public places. I don't know why. There're already too many people in the world. Once, I boarded a plane, expecting my reserved seat to be available. Instead, there sat a breeder with her baby spread out in what was supposed to have been my seat! As I approached and began checking the numbers of the seats to be sure I hadn't made a mistake, she smiled at me confidently. I asked, 'Who do you think you are? Do you think that, because you are a breeder, you have the right to take over my seat?' The stewardess came rushing down the aisle, saying, 'Oh, I'm so sorry. I thought it would be alright.' Why would someone assume that I wouldn't mind having my seat taken away from me?"
19. Ibid., p. 50.
20. The survey we rely on in this section is in Jeffrey Schmalz, "Poll Finds an Even Split on Homosexuality's Cause," *New York Times* (March 5, 1993): C19.
21. Richard A. Isay, Being *Homosexual: Gay Men and Their Development* (New York: Avon Books, 1989), p. 3.
22. Joseph Nicolosi, *Reparative Therapy of Male Homosexuality* (Northvale, NJ: Jason Aronson, 1991).
23. David Gelman, "Born or Bred?," *Newsweek* (Feb. 24, 1992): 53.
24. Quoted in Isay, op. cit., p. 4.
25. Gelman, op. cit., p. 53.
26. Isay., op. cit., p. 6.
27. For a good, brief history see Isay, op. cit., pp. 1–15.
28. Ibid., p. 17.
29. Ibid., p. 18.
30. Cited by Isay, ibid., p. 12.
31. See Chandler Burr, "Homosexuality and Biology," *The Atlantic Monthly* 271, no. 3 (March 1993): 47–65. The quote is from page

65. Also see the exchange in "Is Homosexuality Biologically Influenced?", *Scientific American* 270, no. 5 (May 1994): 43–55.
32. Simon LeVay, "A Difference in Hypothalamic Structure Between Heterosexual and Homosexual Men," *Science* 253 (Aug. 30, 1991): 1034–1037.
33. Gelman, op. cit., pp. 47, 52.
34. Isay, op. cit., p. 20.
35. Ibid., p. 21.
36. See, for example, Eric Schmitt, "Compromise on Military Gay Ban Gaining Support Among Senators," *New York Times* (May 12, 1993): A1, A8; Eric Schmitt, "Gay Shipmates? Senators Listen As Sailors Talk," *New York Times* (May 11, 1993): A1, A9; and "Overlooked No More: Focus Is on Lesbians on Gay Ban," *New York Times* (May 4, 1993): A13.
37. Quoted from "On Our Backs," by Loraine Hutchins and Lani Kaahumanu, eds., *Bi Any Other Name: Bisexual People Speak Out* (Boston: Alyson Publications, Inc., 1991), p. 221. What follows is a definition of bisexual using gender-free pronouns: "A bisexual person is one who recognizes our capacity for being sexually intimate with males and females, whether or not it is acted upon. A bisexual person may, in action, have only same-sex or other-sex partners, or may never have a partner—and yet that person is bisexual if s/he senses that the possibility for sexual relations with either of the two major sexes is there. (Unless, of course, s/he rejects that label for herself.)" An important distinction to remember: The word bisexual does not imply any particular sort of lifestyle. "[B]isexual usually also implies that relations with gender minorities are possible. Can be used as either an adjective or a noun" (p. 106).
38. Thomas Geller, ed., *Bisexuality: A Reader and Sourcebook* (Hadley, MA: Times Change Press, 1990), pp. 31, 52.
39. Camille Paglia, *Sex, Art, and American Culture: Essays* (New York: Vintage Books, 1992), pp. 277–278.
40. Ibid., p. 67.
41. Ibid., p. 77.
42. The phenomenon of intersexuality is discussed by Anne Fausto-Sterling, "How Many Sexes Are There?," *New York Times* (March 12, 1993): A15; and in her book *Myths of Gender: Biological Theories about Women and Men* (New York: Basic Books, 1987).
43. The following material is from Anne Fausto-Sterling, "Why Do We Know So Little About Human Sex?," *Discover* 13, no. 6 (June 1992): 28–31.
44. Ibid., p. 30.

CHAPTER 8

1. These points are found in Boyce Rensberger, "Racial Odyssey," *Science Digest* (Jan/Feb 1981).
2. See the debate published in *Scientific American* 266, no. 4 (April 1992), Allan Wilson and Rebecca L. Cann, "The Recent African Genesis of Humans," pp. 68–73; and Alan G. Thorne and Milford H. Wolpoff, "The Multiregional Evolution of Humans," pp. 76–83.
3. Rensberger, op. cit., p. 50.
4. Ibid., p. 51.
5. Ibid., p. 50.
6. Ibid., p. 53.
7. Robert S. Cahill, "Plain and Fancy Racism in North America," a public lecture given at Ohio University, Lancaster, Jan. 15, 1990.
8. Ibid., p. 5.
9. Ibid., p. 7.
10. Ibid., p. 10.
11. Marcia G. Synnott, "The Admission and Assimilation of Minority Students at Harvard, Yale, and Princeton, 1900–1970." The reprint of the article is found in *The Social History of American Education*, edited by B. Edward McClellan and William J. Reese (Champaign: University of Illinois Press, 1988).
12. Ibid., p. 325.
13. Dinesh D'Souza, *Illiberal Education: The Politics of Race and Sex on Campus* (New York: The Free Press, 1991). It should be noted that D'Souza was known by some of his classmates as "Distort D'Newza" when he was the editor of the right-wing paper *The Dartmouth Review*. In one article he wrote a parody of a supposed incoming affirmative action candidate: "Now we be comin' to Darmut to be up over our 'fros in studies, but we still be not graduatin' Phi Beta Kappa." One suspects that what looks funny to D'Souza looks a lot like plain racism to Cahill.
14. We take up the question of affirmative action in the world beyond campus in the next chapter.
15. Ibid., p. 24.
16. Ibid., p. 25.
17. Troy Duster, "They're Taking Over! and Other Myths about Race on Campus," *Mother Jones* (Sept./Oct. 1991): 30.
18. Jane Meredith Adams, "Berkeley Reflects Diversity," *Boston Sunday Globe* (Oct. 13, 1991): A23.
19. D'Souza, op.cit., p. 31.
20. Ibid., p. 36.

21. Adams, op. cit., p. A21.
22. Ibid., p. 23.
23. D'Souza, op. cit., p. 57.
24. Duster, op. cit., p. 31.
25. Ibid., pp. 33–34.
26. Ibid., p. 33.
27. Ibid., p. 31.
28. National Institute Against Prejudice and Violence, *Ethnoviolence on Campus: The UMBC Study*, report no. 2, (Baltimore, MD: The Institute, 1987). There are no reliable data regularly collected on racial violence on college campuses. Even the recently required reporting of crime on college campuses is not at all uniform, and racial violence is not a required category of reporting. See Douglas Legerman, "Colleges Report 7,500 Violent Crimes on Their Campuses in First Annual Statements Required Under Federal Law," *The Chronicle of Higher Education* (Jan. 20, 1993): A32.
29. See the discussion in E. Gareth Hoachlander and Cynthia L. Brown, "Asians in Higher Education: Conflicts Over Admissions," in *Thought and Action*, pp. 5–20.
30. Stephan G. Graubard, "Why Do Asians Win Those Prizes," *New York Times* (Jan. 29, 1988): A35.
31. Robert B. Oxnam, "Why Asians Succeed Here?" *New York Times Magazine* (Nov. 30, 1986): 70.
32. Malcolm W. Browne, "A Look at Success of Young Asians," *New York Times* (March 26, 1986): A31.
33. The following analysis comes from Stephen Steinberg, *The Ethnic Myth: Race, Ethnicity and Class In America* (Boston: Beacon Press, 1989).
34. Ibid., p. 272.
35. Ibid., p. 272–273. Especially see the chart at the top of page 273.
36. "Fraternity's 'Old South' Parade Riles Students at Auburn U.," *The Chronicle of Higher Education* (May 6, 1992): A32.
37. Mary Crystal Cage, "On Campuses Across the Country. . .," *The Chronicle of Higher Education* (May 13, 1992): A33; Joye Mercer, "Students in Atlanta Angered. . .," ibid.; Jack McCurdy, "Colleges in Los Angeles Area Mobilize. . .," ibid., p. A34.
38. "U.S. Sets Rules for College Aid to Minorities," *Chicago Tribune* (Dec. 5, 1991): 12; Scott Jaschik, "Winthrop College to Alter Program for Black Students," *The Chronicle of Higher Education* (March 18, 1992): A26.
39. Michele N-K Collison, "Young People Found Pessimistic About Relations Between the Races," *The Chronicle of Higher Education* (March 25, 1992): 1.

40. See Nicholas Lemann, "Black Nationalism on Campus," *The Atlantic* 271, no. 1 (Jan. 1993): 31–47.

CHAPTER 9

1. Martin Luther King, Jr., wrote a history of the Montgomery bus boycott. See his *Stride Toward Freedom: The Montgomery Story* (New York: Harper and Row, 1958). King's book is a good place to start reading about the civil rights movement. See also his *Why We Can't Wait* (New York: Penguin Books, 1964). An excellent recent biography of King is by Taylor Branch, *Parting the Waters* (New York: Simon and Schuster, 1988). This section also relies on histories of the civil rights movement. See Harvard Sitkoff, *The Struggle for Black Equality* (New York: Hill and Wang, 1981); and Steven Lawson, *Running for Freedom: Civil Rights and Black Politics in America, 1941–1988* (Philadelphia: Temple University Press, 1990).
2. This section relies on chronologies contained in Robert Chrisman and Robert L. Allen, *Court of Appeal: The Black Community Speaks Out on the Racial and Sexual Politics of Clarence Thomas vs. Anita Hill* (New York: Ballantine Books, 1992); and Toni Morrison, ed., *Race-ing Justice, En-gendering Power: Essays on Anita Hill, Clarence Thomas, and the Construction of Social Reality* (New York: Pantheon Books, 1992).
3. Rosemary L. Bray, "Taking Sides Against Ourselves," in Robert Chrisman and Robert L. Allen, op. cit., pp. 48–49.
4. Llenda Jackson-Leslie, "Tom, Buck, and Sambo or How Clarence Thomas Got to the Supreme Court," in Robert Chrisman and Robert L. Allen, op. cit., p. 107.
5. Ibid., p. 108.
6. Cornell West, *Race Matters* (Boston: Beacon Press, 1993), p. 26.
7. Ibid., p. 29.
8. Derrick Bell, "A Radical Double Agent," in Robert Chrisman and Robert L. Allen, op. cit., pp. 36–37.
9. Derrick Bell, *Faces at the Bottom of the Well: The Permanence of Racism* (New York: Basic Books, 1992), pp. 111–115.
10. See "Looking Past the Verdict," *Newsweek* (April 26, 1993): 20–28; "Independent Panel Sharply Criticizes Los Angeles Police Department," *New York Times* (July 10, 1991): A1, A11. Sgt. Stacy Coon wrote a book, with Robert Dietz, telling his side of the story. It is called *Presumed Guilty: The Tragedy of the Rodney King Affair* (Washington, DC: Regnery Gateway, 1992). Several

claims Coon makes, such as the claim that the beating followed Los Angeles police rules, were effectively attacked in the second trial. But it makes interesting reading for understanding the first verdict. If you take a cop's point of view, one that is aware of the problems police face when they go out to do their job, it becomes clear that Rodney King was going to get a beating, and a legal one at that. The big question was whether the police went too far with the beating. The first jury did not think so. The second jury did. Coon and Officer Lawrence Powell were sentenced to two and one half years in prison for their roles in the beating.

11. Cornell West, op. cit., p. 1, put it this way. The riots were "neither a race riot nor a class rebellion. [It was] . . . a multiracial, trans-class, and largely male display of justified social rage. . . . [It] signified the sense of powerlessness in American society. Glib attempts to reduce its meaning to the pathologies of the black underclass, the criminal actions of hoodlums, or the political revolt of the oppressed urban masses miss the mark. . . . What we witnessed in Los Angeles was the consequence of a lethal linkage of economic decline, cultural decay, and political lethargy in American life. Race was the visible catalyst, not the underlying cause."

12. For an account of how racial thinking extends to nearly all important political issues, see Thomas Byrne Edsall with Mary D. Edsall, *Chain Reaction: The Impact of Race, Rights, and Taxes on American Politics* (New York: W. W. Norton and Co., 1992).

13. This section is based on Vincent N. Parrillo, *Strangers To These Shores* (New York: Macmillan Publishing Company, 1994), Fourth edition, Chapter 7; Dee Brown, *Bury My Heart At Wounded Knee* (New York: Bantam Books, 1972); and one of the authors' experience working with Native American tribes.

14. The section on disease is based on William H. McNeill, *Plagues and Peoples* (Garden City, New York: Anchor Press/Doubleday, 1976).

15. Parrillo, op. cit., p. 256.

16. Malcolm X, *The Autobiography of Malcolm X* (New York: Grove Publishers, 1964), p. 91.

17. Derrick Bell, *Faces at the Bottom of the Well: The Permanence of Racism* (New York: Basic Books, 1992), p. 6.

18. Ibid., p. 14.

19. Affirmative action became law through a variety of sources: the Equal Pay Act of 1963, Title VII of the Civil Rights Act of 1964, court cases interpreting Title VII such as *Griggs v. Duke Power*

Company (401 U.S.424, 1971) and *United Steelworkers of America v. Weber* (443 U.S. 193, 1979), the Equal Employment Opportunity Act of 1972, the Rehabilitation Act of 1973, the federal government's Uniform Guidelines on Employee Selection Procedures of 1978, and presidential executive orders 11246 (1965) and 11375 (1967).

20. Thomas Byrne Edsall with Mary D. Edsall, op. cit., pp. 125–126.
21. Nathan Glazer, *Affirmative Discrimination: Ethnic Inequality and Public Policy* (Cambridge: Harvard University Press, 1987).
22. Ibid., p. 209.
23. Stephan L. Carter, *Reflections of an Affirmative Action Baby* (New York: Basic Books, 1991).
24. Ibid., pp. 88–89.
25. Ibid., p. 69.
26. Ibid., p. 45.
27. Shelby Steele, *The Content of Our Character: A New Vision of Race in America* (New York: St. Martin's Press), pp. 121, 119.
28. Ibid., p. 124.
29. Ibid., p. 10.
30. Ibid., p. 57.
31. Ibid., p. 151.
32. Ibid., p. 72.
33. Ibid., p. 174.
34. Andrew Hacker, *Two Nations: Black and White, Separate, Hostile, Unequal* (New York: Ballantine Books, 1992), pp. 4, 219.

CHAPTER 10

1. Eric Partridge, *Origins: A Short Etymological Dictionary of Modern English* (New York: Greenwich House, 1983), p. 75.
2. John Searle, "The Storm over the University," *New York Review of Books* (Dec. 6, 1990), reprinted in Paul Berman, ed., *Debating P.C.* (New York: Laurel Trade Paperback, 1992), p. 88. A thorough discussion of issues surrounding the canon is in Paul Lauter, *Canons and Contexts* (New York: Oxford University Press, 1991).
3. Ibid., p. 88.
4. Irving Howe, "The Value of the Canon," *The New Republic* (Feb. 18, 1991): 40–47.
5. Allan Bloom, *The Closing of the American Mind: How Higher Education Has Failed Democracy and Impoverished the Souls of*

Today's Students (New York: Simon and Schuster, 1987); and William Bennett, *To Reclaim a Legacy: A Report on the Humanities in Higher Education* (Washington, DC: National Endowment for the Humanities, 1984). Bloom and Bennet are often called, perhaps ungraciously, the "Killer B's."

6. See the article by Searle, op. cit., and the response in letters to the Editor of the *New York Review of Books* (Feb. 14, 1991): 48–50, for examples of the level of discussion and adjectives used.

7. In Roger Kimball, *Tenured Radicals: How Politics Has Corrupted Our Higher Education* (New York: Harper and Row, 1990), pp. 5–6. Some of the attacks on the canon are quite remarkable. Kimball gives an account of a speech he attended. "Barbara Johnson wrote that a particular paper was a masterful demonstration of 'the fact' that gynophobia [i.e., the fear of women] is structured like 'a language' and, conversely, that 'language is structured like gynophobia.'. . . Women themselves conspire in perpetuating this unhappy situation, she told us, for 'the collective linguistic psyche exists in symbiotic relation to the fallen woman.' We also learned, by a similarly elusive logic, that the 'literary canon is a defense against its own femininity,' a defense 'against the woman within.' What any of this could possibly mean was never revealed, but no one seemed to mind: it all sounded so exquisitely chic."

8. Henry Louis Gates, Jr., "Whose Canon Is It, Anyway," (*New York Times Book Review*, Feb. 26, 1989), in Berman, pp. 190–191.

9. Ibid., p. 195.

10. Ibid., p. 194.

11. The argument comes from Katha Pollitt, "Why Do We Read?" *The Nation* (Sept. 23, 1991). The following is taken from Pollitt unless otherwise noted.

12. Ibid., p. 204.

13. Ibid., p. 205.

14. Ibid., p. 210.

15. Searle, op. cit., p. 97.

16. John Searle, "The Storm Over the University," *New York Review of Books* (Dec. 6, 1990): 42.

17. Paula Rothenberg, "Critics of Attempts to Democratize the Curriculum Are Waging a Campaign to Misrepresent the Work of Responsible Professors," *The Chronicle of Higher Education* (April 10, 1991), reprinted in Berman, op. cit., pp. 265–266.

18. The friend was Bob Waterman and the book was *The Human Condition*.

19. Edward W. Said, "The Politics of Knowledge," *Raritan*, Summer 1991, in Berman, op. cit., p. 177.
20. Ibid., p. 177. Said writes, "What I am talking about therefore is the opposite of separatism, and also the reverse of exclusivism. . . . Worldliness is therefore the restoration to such works and interpretations of their place in the global setting, a restoration that can only be accomplished by an appreciation not of only some tiny, defensively constituted corner of the world, but of the large many-windowed house of human culture as a whole. . . . One of the great pleasures for those who read and study literature is the discovery of longstanding norms in which all cultures known to men concur: such things as style and performance, the existence of good as well as lesser writers, and the exercise of preference . . . so many combatants have ears of tin, and are unable to distinguish between good writing and politically correct attitudes, as if a fifth-rate pamphlet and a great novel have more or less the same significance." Ibid., pp. 185, 188.
21. Ted Gordon and Wahneema Lubiano, "The Statement of the Black Faculty Caucus," *Daily Texan* (May 3, 1990), in Berman, op. cit., p. 251.
22. Ibid., p. 253.
23. Ibid., p. 255.
24. Martin Bernal, *Black Athena, Volume I: The Afroasiatic Roots of Classical Civilization* (New Brunswick, NJ: Rutgers University Press, 1987).
25. Quoted in Dinesh D'Souza, *Illiberal Education: The Politics of Race and Sex on Campus* (New York: The Free Press, 1991), pp. 114–115.
26. Emily Vermeule, "The World Turned Upside Down," a review of *Black Athena: The Afroasiatic Roots of Classical Civilization, Volume II, The Archaeological and Documentary Evidence,* by Martin Bernal, *New York Review of Books* (March 26, 1992): 40.
27. Ibid., p. 23.
28. D'Souza, op. cit., p. 118. It is said that boys were sold for $240 and girls were sold for $160.
29. Bernard Ortiz de Montellano, "Avoiding Egyptocentric Pseudoscience: Colleges Must Help Set Standards for Schools," *The Chronicle of Higher Education* (March 25, 1992): B1.
30. Ibid.
31. Ibid.
32. Denise K. Magner, "Faculty Members at Berkeley Offer Courses to Satisfy Controversial 'Diversity Requirement,'" *The Chronicle of Higher Education* (March 11, 1992): A1.
33. Ibid., p. A16.

CHAPTER 11

1. This section borrows from Alfred H. Kelley and Winfred A. Harbison, *The American Constitution: Its Origins and Development* (New York: W. W. Norton and Company, Inc., 1970) Fourth edition, Chapter 6; and David Schuman and Dick W. Olufs III, *Public Administration in the United States* (Lexington, MA: D. C. Heath and Company, 1993) Second edition, Chapter 2.

2. See Julian L. Simon, *The Economic Consequences of Immigration* (Cambridge: Basil Blackwell, 1989); and "Who Controls the Borders? An Immigration Debate," *National Review* (Feb. 1, 1993): 27–34.

3. See Michael E. Porter, *The Competitive Advantage of Nations* (New York: Free Press, 1990).

4. See Paul R. Spickard, *Mixed Blood: Intermarriage and Ethnic Identity in Twentieth Century America* (Madison: University of Wisconsin Press, 1989).

5. This section is based on Nathan Glazer, *Affirmative Discrimination: Ethnic Inequality and Public Policy* (Cambridge: Harvard University Press, 1987), Chapter 1.

6. Ronald Takaki, ed., *From Different Shores: Perspectives on Race and Ethnicity in America* (New York: Oxford University Press, 1987), p. 26.

7. Arthur M. Schlesinger, Jr., *The Disuniting of America: Reflections on a Multicultural Society* (New York: W. W. Norton and Company, 1992).

8. Ibid., p. 12.

9. Ibid., p. 130.

10. See, for example, Donald L. Sparks and December Green, *Namibia: The Nation After Independence* (Boulder, CO: Westview Press, 1992).

11. Max Weber, *The Protestant Ethic and the Spirit of Capitalism* (New York: Scribner, 1950).

12. Lawrence Harrison, *Who Prospers? How Cultural Values Shape Economic and Political Success* (New York: Basic Books, 1992).

13. Ibid., p. 215.

14. Ibid., pp. 39, 52, 70, 76.

15. Ibid., p. 192.

16. Ibid., p. 212.

17. You might want to compare, for example, Harrison's book with Gerald David Jaynes and Robin M. Williams, Jr., eds., *A Common Destiny: Blacks and American Society* (Washington, DC: National Academy Press, 1989).

18. The quote is from James Crawford, *Hold Your Tongue: Bilingualism and the Politics of "English Only"* (Reading, MA: Addison-Wesley Publishing Company, 1992), p. 57.This section relies heavily on Crawford, and also on Schlesinger, op. cit.; and Harrison, op. cit.
19. The example is from Seth Mydans, "As Cultures Meet, Gang War Paralyzes a City in California," *New York Times* (May 6, 1991): A1.
20. This section is based on Oliver Sacks, *Seeing Voices: A Journey Into the World of the Deaf* (Berkeley: University of California Press, 1989).
21. Ibid., p. 8.
22. Ibid., p. 33. For the story of the Martha's Vineyard deaf community, see Nora Ellen Groce, *Everybody Here Spoke Sign Language: Hereditary Deafness on Martha's Vineyard* (Cambridge, MA: Harvard University Press, 1985).
23. Ibid., p. 127.
24. Ibid., p. 135.

CHAPTER 12

1. Barbara Temple-Thurston, in a roundtable discussion published in *Prism*, a newsletter published by Pacific Lutheran University's Division of Humanities, Spring 1993, Volume VI, nos. 1 and 2.
2. The argument is based on Quentin Skinner's "Two Views on the Maintenance of Liberty," appearing in Philip Petit, ed., *Contemporary Political Theory* (New York: Macmillan Publishing Company, 1991), pp. 35–58.An earlier version of the argument appeared as "Machiavelli on the Maintenance of Liberty," *Politics* 18 (1983): 3–13.
3. Miles Harvey, "Politically Correct Is Politically Suspect: What the Left Leaves Out of the PC Debate," *In These Times* (Dec. 25, 1991–Jan. 14, 1992).
4. Ibid.
5. Barbara Ehrenreich, "The Challenge For The Left," *Democratic Left* (July/Aug. 1991).
6. Harvey, op. cit.
7. Salim Muwakkil, "Race, Class and Candor," *In These Times* (July 22–28, 1991).
8. For an example of someone who makes good fun of silly language, see John Leo, "The New Verbal Order," *U.S. News & World Report* (July 22, 1991).
9. Ellen Goodman, "Civility Is Necessary, but a Little Candor Is Needed, Too," *Springfield Union* (Dec. 13, 1991).

Bibliography

Adams, Jane Meredith, "Berkeley Reflects Diversity," *Boston Sunday Globe* (October 13, 1991): A23.

Anyon, Jean, "Social Class and the Hidden Curriculum of Work," in Kevin J. Dougherty and Floyd M. Hammack, *Education & Society, A Reader* (New York: Harcourt Brace Jovanovich, Publishers, 1990), pp. 426–428.

Ballantine, Jeanne, *The Sociology of Education* (Englewood Cliffs, NJ: Prentice-Hall, 1983).

Bell, Derrick, *Faces at the Bottom of the Well: The Permanence of Racism* (New York: Basic Books, 1992).

Bell, Derrick, "A Radical Double Agent," in Chrisman and Allen, pp. 36–37.

Bennett, William, *To Reclaim a Legacy: A Report on the Humanities in Higher Education* (Washington, D.C.: National Endowment for the Humanities, 1984).

Berman, Paul, ed, *Debating P.C.* (New York: Laurel Trade Paperback, 1992).

Bernal, Martin, *Black Athena, Volume I: The Afroasiatic Roots of Classical Civilization, and II: The Archaeological and Documentary Evidence* (Newark: Rutgers University Press, 1987–91).

Bernstein, Richard, "Guilty If Charged," *New York Review of Books* XLI, nos. 1, 2 (Jan. 13, 1994): 11–14.

Bestor, Arthur, *Backwoods Utopias* (Philadelphia: University of Pennsylvania Press, 1970).

Bloom, Allen, *The Closing of the American Mind: How Higher Education Has Failed Democracy and Impoverished the Souls of Today's Students* (New York: Simon and Schuster, 1987).

Bowles, Samuel, "Unequal Education and the Reproduction of the Social Division of Labor," in Elizabeth Steiner, Robert Arnove,

B. Edward McClellan, *Education and American Culture* (New York: Macmillan Publishing Co., 1980).

Boyer, Ernest L., *College: The Undergraduate Experience in America* (NY: Harper & Row, Publishers, 1987).

Boyer, Ernest L., *High School: A Report on Secondary Education in America* (New York: Harper & Row, 1983).

Branch, Taylor, *Parting the Waters* (New York: Simon and Schuster, 1988).

Bray, Rosemary L. "Taking Sides Against Ourselves," in Chrisman and Allen, pp. 48–49.

Brown, Dee, *Bury My Heart at Wounded Knee* (New York: Bantam Books, 1972).

Browne, Malcolm W., "A Look at Success of Young Asians," *New York Times* (March 26, 1986): A31.

Brownmiller, Susan, *Against Our Will* (New York: Random House, 1975).

Buckley, William F., Jr., *God and Man at Yale: The Superstitions of Academic Freedom* (Chicago: Regnery Gateway, 1977).

Burr, Chandler, "Homosexuality and Biology," *Atlantic Monthly* 271, no. 3 (March 1993): 47–65.

Butler, Johnnella, and Betty Schmitz, "Ethnic Studies, Women's Studies, and Multiculturalism," *Change* (January/February 1992): 37–41.

Cage, Mary Crystal, "Graduation Rates of American Indians and Blacks Improve, Lag Behind Others," *The Chronicle of Higher Education* (May 26, 1993): A29.

Cage, Mary Crystal, "On Campuses Across the Country. . .," *The Chronicle of Higher Education* (May 13, 1992): A33.

Carter, Don, "Ferries Act to Curb Race and Sex Harassment," *Seattle Post-Intelligencer* (May 9, 1991): B2.

Carter, Stephan L., *Reflections of an Affirmative Action Baby* (New York: Basic Books, 1991).

Chodorow, Nancy, *The Reproduction of Mothering* (Berkeley, CA: Stanford University Press, 1978).

Chrisman, Robert, and Robert L. Allen, *Court of Appeal: The Black Community Speaks Out on the Racial and Sexual Politics of Clarence Thomas vs. Anita Hill* (New York: Ballantine Books, 1992).

Collison, Michele N-K, "Young People Found Pessimistic About Relations Between the Races," *The Chronicle of Higher Education* (March 25, 1992): 1.

Cookson, Peter W., Jr., and Caroline Hodges Persell, *Preparing for Power: America's Elite Boarding Schools* (New York: Basic Books, Inc., Publishers, 1985).

Coon, Stacy, with Robert Dietz, *Presumed Guilty: The Tragedy of the Rodney King Affair* (Washington, D.C.: Regnery Gateway, 1992).

Counts, Connie, "Towards a Relational Managerial Model for Schools: A Study of Women and Men as Superintendents and Principals," doctoral dissertation, Harvard Graduate School of Education, 1987.

Crawford, James, *Hold Your Tongue: Bilingualism and the Politics of "English Only"* (Reading, MA: Addison-Wesley Publishing Company, 1992).

Cushman, John H., Jr., "Top Admiral Backs Full Combat Roles for Women in Navy," *New York Times* (April 5, 1993): 1.

DeMott, Benjamin, *The Imperial Middle: Why Americans Can't Think Straight About Class* (New York: Morrow, 1990).

Domhoff, William, *The Bohemian Grove and Other Retreats* (New York: Harper & Row, 1984).

D'Souza, Dinesh, *Illiberal Education: The Politics of Race and Sex on Campus* (New York: The Free Press, 1991).

Duster, Troy, "They're Taking Over! and Other Myths About Race on Campus," *Mother Jones* (September/October 1991): 30.

Dworkin, Andrea, *Pornography: Men Possessing Women* (New York: Perigree Books, 1981).

Dziech, Billie Wright, and Linda Weiner, *The Lecherous Professor: Sexual Harassment on Campus*, Second edition (Urbana: University of Illinois Press, 1990).

Eccles, Jacquelynne S., and Janis E. Jacobs, "Social Forces Shape Math Attitudes and Performance," in Mary Roth Walsh, ed., *The Psychology of Women: Ongoing Debates* (New Haven: Yale University Press, 1987), pp. 341–354.

Edsall, Thomas Byrne, and Mary D. Edsall, *Chain Reaction: The Impact of Race, Rights, and Taxes on American Politics* (New York: W. W. Norton and Company, 1992).

Ehlers, Henry, *Crucial Issues in Education*, Seventh edition (New York: CBS College Publishing, 1981).

Faderman, Lillian, *Odd Girls and Twilight Lovers: A History of Lesbian Life in Twentieth-Century America* (New York: Penguin Books, 1991).

Faludi, Susan, *Backlash: The Undeclared War Against American Women* (New York: Crown Publishers, 1991).

Fausto-Sterling, Anne, *Myths of Gender: Biological Theories About Women and Men* (New York: Basic Books, 1987).

Fausto-Sterling, Anne, "Why Do We Know So Little About Human Sex?" *Discover* 13, no. 6 (June 1992): 28–31.

Fox-Genovese, Elizabeth, *Feminism Without Illusions: A Critique of Individualism* (Chapel Hill and London: University of North Carolina Press, 1991).

Gates, Henry Louis, Jr., "Beware of the New Pharaohs," *Newsweek*, (September 23, 1991): 47.

Gates, Henry Louis, Jr., "Whose Canon Is It, Anyway," in Berman, pp. 190–191.

Geller, Thomas, ed., *Bisexuality: A Reader and Sourcebook* (Hadley, MA: Times Change Press, 1990), pp. 31 and 52.

Gelman, David, "Born or Bred?" *Newsweek* (February 24, 1992): 53.

Gilligan, Carol, *In a Different Voice* (Cambridge, MA: Harvard University Press, 1982).

Gilligan, Carol, Nona P. Lyons, and Trudy J. Hanmer, eds., *Making Connections: The Relational Worlds of Adolescent Girls at Emma Willard School* (Cambridge: Harvard University Press, 1990).

Glazer, Nathan, *Affirmative Discrimination: Ethnic Inequality and Public Policy* (Cambridge, MA: Harvard University Press, 1987).

Golding, William, *Lord of the Flies* (New York: Putnam, 1956).

Gonsiorek, John C., and James D. Weinrich, *Homosexuality: Research Implications for Public Policy* (Newbury Park: Sage Publications, 1992).

Goodlad, John I., *A Place Called School* (New York: McGraw-Hill, 1984).

Gordon, Ted, and Wahneema Lubiano, "The Statement of the Black Faculty Caucus," in Berman, p. 251.

Graubard, Stephan G., "Why Do Asians Win Those Prizes," *New York Times* (January 29, 1988): A35.

Greenhouse, Linda, "Court, 9–0, Makes Sexual Harassment Easier to Prove," *New York Times* (November 10, 1993): A1, A15.

Grendler, Paul F., "The University of Padua 1405–1600: A Success Story," in *History of Higher Education Annual* 10 (1990): 7.

Griggs v. Duke Power Company (401 U.S.424, 1971).

Groce, Nora Ellen, *Everybody Here Spoke Sign Language: Hereditary Deafness on Martha's Vineyard* (Cambridge, MA: Harvard University Press, 1985).

Hacker, Andrew, "Class Dismissed," *New York Review of Books* XXXVIII, no. 5 (March 7, 1991): 44–46.

Hacker, Andrew, *Two Nations: Black and White, Separate, Hostile, Unequal* (New York: Ballantine Books, 1992).

Hall, Roberta, "The Classroom Climate: A Chilly One for Women?" Project on the Status and Education of Women, Association of American Colleges, 1982.

Hamm, Cornell M., "Providing Content to Moral Education," reprinted in Ehlers.

Harrison, Lawrence, *Who Prospers? How Cultural Values Shape Economic and Political Success* (New York: Basic Books, 1992).

Hoachlander, E. Gareth, and Cynthia L. Brown, "Asians in Higher Education: Conflicts over Admissions," in *Thought and Action* pp. 5–20.

Hollingshead, A.B., Elmtown's Youth, (New York: John Wiley and Sons, 1949).

Horowitz, Helen Lefkowitz, *Campus Life: Undergraduate Cultures from the End of the Eighteenth Century to the Present* (New York: Alfred A. Knopf, 1987).

Howe, Irving, "The Value of the Canon," *New Republic* (February 18, 1991): 40–47.

Hummel, Ralph, *The Bureaucratic Experience*, Second edition (New York: St. Martin's Press, 1982).

Hutchins, Loraine, and Lani Kaahumanu, eds., *Bi Any Other Name: Bisexual People Speak Out* (Boston: Alyson Publications, Inc., 1991).

Isay, Richard A., *Being Homosexual: Gay Men and Their Development*, (New York: Avon Books, 1989).

Ivins, Molly, *Molly Ivins Can't Say That, Can She?* (New York: Random House, 1991).

Jackson-Leslie, Llenda, "Tom, Buck, and Sambo or How Clarence Thomas Got to the Supreme Court," in Chrisman and Allen, p. 107.

Jaschik, Scott, "Winthrop College to Alter Program for Black Students," *The Chronicle of Higher Education* (March 18, 1992): A26.

Jaynes, Gerald David, and Robin M. Williams, Jr., eds., *A Common Destiny: Blacks and American Society* (Washington, D.C.: National Academy Press, 1989).

Jencks, Christopher, and Paul E. Peterson, *The Urban Underclass* (Washington, D.C.: Brookings Institution, 1991).

Kanter, Rosabeth Moss, *Commitment and Community* (Cambridge, MA: Harvard University Press, 1972).

Kanter, Rosabeth Moss, *Men and Women of the Corporation* (New York: Basic Books, 1979).

Karen, David, "Access to Higher Education in the United States, 1900 to the Present," in Kevin J. Dougherty and Floyd M. Hammack, *Education & Society, A Reader* (San Diego, CA: Harcourt Brace Jovanovich, Publishers, 1990).

Kelley, Alfred H., and Winfred A. Harbison, *The American Constitution: Its Origins and Development*, Fourth edition (New York: W. W. Norton and Company, Inc., 1970).

Kimball, Roger, *Tenured Radicals: How Politics Has Corrupted Our Higher Education* (New York: Harper and Row, 1990).

Kimura, Doreen, "Sex Differences in the Brain," *Scientific American* 267, no. 3 (September 1992): 119–125.

King, Martin Luther, Jr., *Stride Toward Freedom: The Montgomery Story* (New York: Harper and Row, 1958).

King, Martin Luther, Jr., *Why We Can't Wait* (New York: Penguin Books, 1964).

Kozol, Jonathan, *The Night Is Dark and I Am Far from Home*, revised edition (New York: Touchstone Books, 1990).

Lapham, Lewis H., *Money and Class in America: Notes and Observations on Our Civil Religion* (New York: Weidenfeld & Nicolson, 1988).

Lasser, Carol, *Educating Men and Women Together* (Urbana: University of Illinois Press, 1987).

Lauter, Paul, *Canons and Contexts* (New York: Oxford University Press, 1991).

Legerman, Douglas, "Colleges Report 7,500 Violent Crimes on Their Campuses in First Annual Statements Required Under Federal Law," *The Chronicle of Higher Education* (January 20, 1993): A32.

Lemann, Nicholas, "Black Nationalism on Campus," *Atlantic* 271 no. 1 (January 1993): 31–47.

Lemon v. Kurtzman (403 U.S. 642, 1971).

LeVay, Simon, "A Difference in Hypothalamic Structure Between Heterosexual and Homosexual Men," *Science* 253 (August 1991): 1034–1037.

Mabry, Marcus, "The Ghetto Preppies," *Newsweek* (November 4, 1991): 44–48.

Magner, Denise K., "Faculty Members at Berkeley Offer Courses to Satisfy Controversial 'Diversity Requirement,'" *The Chronicle of Higher Education* (March 11, 1992): A1.

Mahowald, Mary Briody, ed., *Philosophy of Woman: An Anthology of Classic and Current Concepts*, Second edition (Indianapolis: Hackett Publishing Company, 1983).

Marion Lowe, "Social Bodies: The Interaction of Culture and Women's Biology," in Ruth Hubbard, Mary Sue Henifin, and Barbara Fried, eds., *Biolgical Women: The Conventional Myth* (Rochester, VT: Schenckman Books, 1982).

McClellan, B. Edward, "Moral Education and Public Schooling," in Elizabeth Steiner, Robert Arnove, and B. Edward McClellan, *Education and American Culture* (New York: Macmillan Publishing Co.).

McCurdy, Jack, "Colleges in Los Angeles Area Mobilize. . .," *The Chronicle of Higher Education* (May 13, 1992): A34.

McNeill, William H., *Plagues and Peoples* (Garden City, NY: Anchor Press/Doubleday, 1976).

Mercer, Joye, "Students in Atlanta Angered. . .," *The Chronicle of Higher Education* (May 13, 1992): A33.

Mezey, Susan Bluck, *In Pursuit of Equality: Women, Public Policy, and the Federal Courts* (New York: St. Martin's Press, 1992).

Miller, Perry, *Errand into the Wilderness* (New York: Harper Torchbooks, 1964).

Moffett, Michael, *Coming of Age in New Jersey: College and American Culture* (New Brunswick, NJ: Rutgers University Press, 1989).

Montellano, Bernard Ortiz de, "Avoiding Egyptocentric Pseudoscience: Colleges Must Help Set Standards for Schools," *The Chronicle of Higher Education* (March 25, 1992): B1.

Morrison, Toni, ed., *Race-ing Justice, En-gendering Power: Essays on Anita Hill, Clarence Thomas, and the Construction of Social Reality* (New York: Pantheon Books, 1992).

Mydans, Seth, "As Cultures Meet, Gang War Paralyzes a City in California," *New York Times* (May 6, 1991): A1.

National Institute Against Prejudice and Violence, *Ethnoviolence on Campus: The UMBC Study*, report no. 2 (Baltimore, MD: The Institute, 1987).

Nicolosi, Joseph, *Reparative Therapy of Male Homosexuality*, (Northvale, NJ: Jason Aronson, 1991).

Noyes, John Humphrey, *Strange Cults and Utopias of Nineteenth Century America* (New York: Dover Publishing, 1966).

Okin, Susan Moller, *Justice, Gender, and the Family* (New York: Basic Books, 1989).

Okin, Susan Moller, *Women in Western Political Thought* (Princeton, NJ: Princeton University Press, 1979).

Oxnam, Robert B., "Why Asians Succeed Here?" *New York Times Magazine* (November 30, 1986): 70.

Paglia, Camille, *Sex, Art, and American Culture: Essays* (New York: Vintage Books, 1992).

Parrillo, Vincent N., *Strangers to These Shores*, Fourth edition (New York: Macmillan Publishing Company, 1994).

Partridge, Eric, *Origins: A Short Etymological Dictionary of Modern English* (New York: Greenwich House, 1983).

Patterson, Orlando, *Freedom, Volume I: Freedom in the Making of Western Culture* (New York: Basic Books, 1991).

Penelope, Julia, Call Me Lesbian (Freedom, CA: The Crossing Press, 1992).

Phillips, Kevin, *Boiling Point: Democrats, Republicans, and the Decline of Middle-Class Prosperity* (New York: Random House, 1993).

Pollitt, Katha, "Why Do We Read?" *Nation* (September 23, 1991): 204–210.

Porter, Michael E., *The Competitive Advantage of Nations* (New York: Free Press, 1990).

Powell, Gary, *Women and Men in Management* (Newbury Park, CA: Sage Publications, 1988).

Reichley, James, *Religion in American Public Life* (Washington, D.C.: The Brookings Institution, 1984).

Rokeach, Milton, "Toward a Clarification of Our Values," in Ehlers, p. 249.

Rothenberg, Paula, "Critics of Attempts to Democratize the Curriculum Are Waging a Campaign to Misrepresent the Work of Responsible Professors," in Berman, pp. 265–266.

Rudolph, Frederick, *The American College and University: A History* (New York: Vintage Books, 1962).

Russell, Diana E. H., *Sexual Exploitation: Rape, Child Sexual Abuse, and Sexual Harassment* (Beverly Hills, CA: Sage, 1984).

Sacks, Oliver, *Seeing Voices: A Journey into the World of the Deaf,* (Berkeley: University of California Press, 1989).

Said, Edward W. "The Politics of Knowledge," *Raritan* (Summer, 1991), in Berman, p. 177.

Sawhill, Isabel V., "Poverty in the U.S.: Why Is It So Persistent?" *Journal of Economic Literature* XXVI (September 1988): 1073–1119.

Schlesinger, Arthur M., Jr., *The Disuniting of America: Reflections on a Multicultural Society* (New York: W. W. Norton and Company, 1992).

Schmalz, Jeffrey, "Poll Finds an Even Split on Homosexuality's Cause," *New York Times* (March 5, 1993): C19.

Schmitt, Eric, "Compromise on Military Gay Ban Gaining Support Among Senators," *New York Times* (May 12, 1993): A1, A8.

Schmitt, Eric, "Gay Shipmates? Senators Listen as Sailors Talk," *New York Times* (May 11, 1993): A1, A9.

Schmitt, Eric, "Pentagon Plans to Allow Combat Flights by Women," *New York Times* (April 28, 1993): 1.

Searle, John, "The Storm over the University," *New York Review of Books* (December 6, 1990): 36–44.

Shanley, Mary Lyndon, and Carole Pateman, eds., *Feminist Interpretations and Political Theory* (University Park: The Pennsylvania State University Press, 1991).

Simeone, Angela, *Academic Women: Working Towards Equality* (South Hadley, MA: Bergin & Garvey Publishers, Inc., 1986).

Simon, Julian L., *The Economic Consequences of Immigration* (Cambridge, MA: Basil Blackwell, 1989).

Sims, Calvin, "Late Bloomers Come to Campus," *New York Times Education Life* (August 4, 1991): 16–17.

Smith, Page, *Killing the Spirit: Higher Education in America* (New York: Penguin Books, 1990).

Smith, Steven G., *Gender Thinking* (Philadelphia: Temple University Press, 1992).

Sparks, Donald L., and December Green, *Namibia: The Nation After Independence* (Boulder, CO: Westview Press, 1992).

Spickard, Paul R., *Mixed Blood: Intermarriage and Ethnic Identity in Twentieth Century America* (Madison: University of Wisconsin Press, 1989).

Spring, Joel, *American Education: An Introduction to Social and Political Aspects*, Fifth edition (White Plains, NY: Longman, 1991).

Steele, Shelby, *The Content of Our Character: A New Vision of Race in America* (New York: St. Martin's Press, 1991).

Steinberg, Stephen, *The Ethnic Myth: Race, Ethnicity and Class in America* (Boston: Beacon Press, 1989).

Stetson, Dorothy McBride, *Women's Rights in the U.S.A.: Policy Debates and Gender Roles* (Pacific Grove, CA: Brooks/Cole Publishing Company, 1991).

Steward, Robbie J., Joyce A. Davidson, and Sherry A. Borgers, "Racial Majority vs. Minority Status: A Study of Interactional Styles of Successful White Students on a Predominantly White University Campus," *Journal of College Student Development* 34 (July 1993): 295–298.

Takaki, Ronald, ed., *From Different Shores: Perspectives on Race and Ethnicity in America* (New York: Oxford University Press, 1987).

Tannen, Deborah, *You Just Don't Understand: Men and Women in Conversation* (New York: Wm. Morrow and Company, 1990).

Thorne, Alan G., and Milford H. Wolpoff, "The Multiregional Evolution of Humans," *Scientific American* 266, no. 4 (April 1992): 76–83.

Tocqueville, Alexis de, *Democracy in America* (New York: Schocken Books, 1961), translated by Harry Reeve.

Tuana, Nancy, *Women and the History of Philosophy* (New York: Paragon House, 1992).

United Steelworkers of America v. Weber (443 U.S. 193, 1979).

Walsh, Mary Roth, ed., *The Psychology of Women: Ongoing Debates*, (New Haven, CT: Yale University Press, 1987).

Weber, Max, *The Protestant Ethic and the Spirit of Capitalism* (New York: Scribner, 1950).

West, Cornell, *Race Matters* (Boston: Beacon Press, 1993).

Wilson, Allan, and Rebecca L. Cann, "The Recent African Genesis of Humans," *Scientific American* 266, no. 4 (April 1992): 68–73.

Wolff, Robert Paul, *The Ideal of the University* (New York: Transaction Publications, 1992).

Wollstonecraft, Mary, *A Vindication of the Rights of Woman* (London, 1792).

X, Malcolm, *The Autobiography of Malcolm X* (New York: Grove Publishers, 1964).

Index